Susan Elliott ~~was married to~~ Denholm Elliott for over thirty years. Since Denholm's death in 1992, Susan has set up the Denholm Elliott Project in Ibiza (where they had their main home) – a centre to give support to people with HIV and AIDS and their loved ones.

Some reviews of the hardback edition:

'I worked with him only twice. Once, in 1971, when he played a chilling Judge Brack in my adaptation of *Hedda Gabler* and five years later when we both appeared in a rather prosaic television melodrama, which he graced with his presence. He was delightful company, convivial, courteous, yet shining with a disarmingly truthful nature. He was quite open about his double life and was relishing another sabbatical in London from the domestic pleasures of Ibiza. He suggested we meet for a drink at the Garrick. He snorted with enjoyment: "Trouble is – I can't take the *boys* in there." He had an infectious, unforced Puckish playfulness which matched his melancholy. Taken all in all, his life, professionally and personally, appears to have been as satisfying and successful as most of us can sensibly expect.

What a superb model he was to his profession, both on stage and film, an abiding rebuke to bombasts and phoneys, Harrises and Hoffmans. Forget the remittance men, abortionists, even all those boy heroes he played. He was a definer of the English character, neither rural nor urban, a miniaturist of grandeur, a star-stabbing princeling among players. This is a brave and honest book. He would approve.'

John Osborne, *The Spectator*

'I did not know Denholm well (did anyone?), but over the years we had a number of sharp, passionate conversations in which – as in his performances – he laid his life bare.

Susan knew when she married him that Denholm was bisexual; as the years went on he became increasingly interested only in sex with men, literally roaming the globe in search of ever more intense experiences with them. This was not the outcome of an excess of hormones, nor even a desire for more sensual indulgence. It was, in its own curious way, highly romantic, a quest, indeed, for love, but one doomed to failure because in the end Denholm could never believe that the love he got could be enough. He received a great deal of it – in every shape and form, from men, women and his own children – but, as Susan Elliott says in an acute perception, one of many: "Denholm's constant need for bolstering was ill-matched with his inability to give much in return."

It is a very common predicament of English men, which is why he was so wonderfully good at portraying us. Susan's compulsively readable book lovingly and forgivingly records the life and work of one of our most remarkable actors.'

Simon Callow, *Sunday Express*

'This revealing biography by his wife Susan captures Denholm exactly and is refreshingly free of the gush that commonly mars such intimate accounts. So often theatrical biographies consist of a series of rehashed press-cuttings, but *Quest for Love* is an apt and accurate title for a book that describes the story of a man who constantly fought his own private demons while pursuing a very public career. I found it intensely moving, for it is one of the great ironies – ignored by those who wish only to condemn – that the scourge of AIDS often stems from an act of love.

Susan Elliott's own dignity matches that of Denholm's both in life and on these pages. There is a tenderness about her recollections of their unusual, 30-year marriage, the way in which she understood and accepted Denholm's bisexuality, her courage during the last agonising months when they realised the final curtain-call was imminent.

The masks of tragedy and comedy are often interchangeable and Denholm wore both with panache. No reader could fail to be moved by the final chapters, written with no false sentiment or self-pity, and

I urge others to share this brave testament to the human spirit resolute in the face of unfair adversity.

Bryan Forbes, *Daily Telegraph*

Elliott never gave a bad performance, and never received a bad review. His velvet voice, twinkling eye, ravaged good looks and consummate technique adorned and rescued countless bad movies. On stage, he was the ideal interpreter of Strindberg and Ibsen.

Susan Elliott writes cheerfully of her open marriage, and explains that she tolerated Elliott's waywardness for the wit of his company and generosity of his spirit and their own sustained physical relationship.

Michael Coveney, *Observer*

DENHOLM ELLIOTT

Quest for Love

SUSAN ELLIOTT

with Barry Turner

HEADLINE

First published in 1994
by HEADLINE BOOK PUBLISHING

First published in paperback in 1995
by HEADLINE BOOK PUBLISHING

10 9 8 7 6 5 4 3 2 1

ISBN 0 7472 4378 6

Printed and bound in Great Britain by
Cox & Wyman Ltd, Reading, Berks

HEADLINE BOOK PUBLISHING
A division of Hodder Headline PLC
338 Euston Road
London NW1 3BH

To my children
Jennifer and Mark Elliott
and to Jean Diamond
with love

Contents

Acknowledgements

Denholm and I often discussed the possibility of writing a book about our lives together. When it became clear that we had run out of time for it to be a joint effort he urged me to go ahead on my own one day. He often said, 'It must be an honest book, Susan, or there's no point in doing it'. This cannot be the book that would have been written if Denholm were still alive but I have done my best to tell his story, and mine, as frankly and honestly as I can.

Wherever possible we have drawn upon accounts of various events in his life which he wrote himself – particularly those covering the war years. We've even taken the liberty of identifying Denholm with the book by using a facsimile of his distinctive signature on the front of the cover.

I am grateful, first of all, to those who helped me in the writing of the book: my co-author, Barry Turner; Roger Houghton my editor at Headline and Caroline North who most skilfully copy edited the manuscript; and to Schuyla

Van Dyke de Curtis for her help with research, for her knowledge of computers and for her sense of humour.

In addition I would like to thank: Bill and Ulla Allen's family kitchen for keeping me watered, fertilised and entertained in moments of sheer despair and panic; Nina van Pallandt for sharing endless bottles of champagne with me, Steve and Sinbad on the high seas; Stephen Burnett and Terry Pettigrew who organised my life for six months after Denholm died; Dr Stuart Ungar, Brian Gazzard (the off-the-wall eccentric genius who Denholm trusted completely '. . . it takes one to know one', he would say); Red Ribbon International especially the founder Andrew Butterfield, John Campbell and Terry White of UK Coalition of People Living with HIV and AIDS; the Ibiza Cares contingent in Ibiza: Mercedes Trafford Roig, Keith Snellin, Lem Lubin, Hazel Howath, Jan Ingram, Ron and Felicity; Mel and Phil at Monroe's for their amazing efforts to raise funds for the Denholm Elliott Project.

To all the Robinsons, Ropers, Darbys, Elliotts and Keatings who contributed photos and stories to complete this book, I offer profound thanks.

Susan Elliott
London and Ibiza
June 1994

Prologue

My song was *Daddy Wouldn't Buy Me a Bow-Wow*. I wore a long black dress down to the ankles, a high white collar and a frilly apron – the model of a Victorian parlourmaid. While singing I also had to serve drinks.

Performing as a singing waitress is like the party trick of stroking your stomach and patting your head at the same time. It looks easy but few can do it well. I was one of the many.

The year was 1961, the place, the Strollers' Club on Fifty-third Street in mid-town Manhattan. I was just nineteen, a drama student trying to make some pocket money. The Strollers was a spin-off of the Players' Theatre in London, an old-style music hall tucked away under the railway arches at Charing Cross. And still going strong, incidentally, unlike the Strollers, which has long since disappeared under an office block. Both places were popular with actors who came in after their own shows for cheerful cabaret and a late supper. Our second house didn't start until 11 p.m.

After we closed, I went backstage to clean up and change into student gear. Then I had to walk through the auditorium – thick velvet curtains and plush seats – to get to the street. By the box office stood a man, slim with straight dark hair which flopped over his forehead. He wore a camel-hair coat with a black fake-fur collar. I can still remember the powerful whiff of aftershave – Aqua de Silva. He looked lost and vaguely distressed. With no way of knowing that that was how Denholm Elliott usually looked, I asked if I could help.

He said he was meeting a girl from the cast; he wasn't too sure of her name or where precisely the meeting was to take place. He did know they were going for late-night drinks. I made my way back to the dressing room where there was still a crowd of reluctant homegoers.

'Anyone here waiting to see Denholm Elliott?'

Nobody was but the girls looked disappointed they weren't on his party list. All innocence, I asked the obvious question. 'Who is he?'

Although Denholm, big on Broadway, had made a few films, at thirty-nine, he was no longer the young romantic lead. Yet he could still ride on the image created in movies like *The Cruel Sea*, *The Night My Number Came Up* and *Pacific Destiny*.

I went back to the front of house with my mission-failed expression fixed. Denholm was not put out. Instead I was rewarded by a huge grin. Suddenly, he looked much younger.

'I don't suppose . . .' he started hesitantly. I was caught on the very English accent. 'Would you happen to be free?'

We walked across to P. J. Clark's, a late-night restaurant which, alone among our favourite haunts in the district, has survived the mania for high-rise apartments and offices. It

2

looks lonely, caged by skyscrapers, but it is still a fun place to go.

I recall little of that first conversation. I know I made Denholm laugh, which was a good start except that I was not thinking of it being the start of anything – not then, anyway. But I must have been intrigued because when Denholm asked me out for the following night, I said yes immediately, quite forgetting an earlier promise. I did not know where Denholm was staying or how to get in touch with him so I had to wait until he turned up again at the Strollers, expecting me to be ready and waiting, to give him my confession. He took it well, considering. He suggested we made it a day later.

My relief was tempered by a niggling worry I couldn't quite identify until, once more, Denholm had disappeared into the anonymity of New York. Then it came to me. I had done it again; double-booked. I was pulled between the awful embarrassment of standing up Denholm a second time and the fear of wounding a close friend I knew I wouldn't see again for some time. At the second confrontation, Denholm was not quite so accommodating.

'Look,' he said, 'I'm not desperate for company. You're very attractive and I'd like to take you out but there are plenty of other women in New York.'

He took a piece of paper out of his wallet and scribbled down a number. 'This is where you can reach me. Give me a ring around midday tomorrow. If you want to, that is. If I don't hear from you, I'll understand.'

Then I was alone on the sidewalk, feeling guilty.

The next day, I waited until twelve noon precisely before ringing Denholm. I got the engaged tone. I called again. I tried again and again and again. No luck. It was now past one o'clock. Nobody could be that long-winded. With my poor brain in a jumble, the likeliest explanation took time to filter through. Of course, there was a fault on the line. I dialled the operator, who came back with the information that it wasn't exactly a fault; Denholm had taken the receiver off the hook. The story, told to me later by a contrite actor, was that he had wanted to save himself from interruptions for a morning's session on the piano. Pat van Allen, herself a superb pianist, had come over to Denholm's apartment to help him extend his range to classical jazz. The lesson over, Denholm, being Denholm, had forgotten to replace the receiver.

If I had known the man better I would have made some such assumption. As it was, growing panic gave me the courage to tell the operator why I was so desperate to get in touch. My teachers at the Academy for Dramatic Art would have been proud of me. My best performance to date brought me loads of sympathy and a practical suggestion. The operator would send a warning screech down the line. Romance was still alive at the Bell Telephone Company.

Within seconds, Denholm was mumbling sheepish apologies. He had almost given me up. Instead, I sent vibes of utter relief all the way across town. We fixed a date, a firm one this time. I put down the telephone. The affair had started.

I must try to describe Denholm as he was then, not as he became. As young as I was, I did come from a family of writers and it didn't take me long to realise that he was having to cope with nightmares of insecurity. He could be moody and brittle, more so after working his way through a vodka bottle. In our first weeks together, he kept his problems to himself – out of a sense of delicacy, I think. He later told me that he had a failed marriage behind him. He had adored Virginia McKenna and made no secret of the pain caused by the break-up. But he would not then talk about why it all went wrong.

He had troubles with his career. After a succession of starring appearances on Broadway, not to mention two prestigious awards, he was now below the title in a potboiler mystery called *Write Me a Murder* at the Belasco Theater. Frederick Knott, famously associated with *Dial M for Murder*, had come up with an English country-house setting for his latest whodunit. Hence there were two English imports to play rival brothers: Denholm, and, above him in the credits, James Donald, now best remembered as the Army doctor in *Bridge on the River Kwai*. James and Denholm were often cast for the same roles, but they did not get on. The bone of contention was working methods. Denholm was a planner. He calculated every line and move in relation to the direction and having established his role, stuck to it. James was more of an improviser, changing dialogue where he thought his own words improved on the author's and altering stage directions as the mood took him.

The war of the irreconcilables went on for weeks, and on one occasion, Denholm brought the conflict home to his apartment by taking it out on an inoffensive room-divider. It collapsed, a splintered wreck, before the force of his anger.

The remedy came by inspiration. During a matinee when James Donald threw the action off balance by moving stage right instead of stage left, Denholm slotted into the script a rebuke he remembered from his nursery. 'If you don't stop behaving like this, you know what will happen, don't you? I'll have to smack your hands.'

I wonder what the maiden aunts in the front stalls made of it? Denholm stayed in character throughout so it was not clear that he had ventured from the script. In any event, Denholm's retaliation had the desired effect. The wayward James Donald sharpened up and stuck to the script.

But Denholm's unhappiness with *Write Me a Murder* was a symptom of deeper troubles. He talked a lot about the risks of being typecast as an 'Anyone for tennis?' actor at a time when kitchen sink plays were becoming fashionable. In darker moments, he portrayed a career on the skids. After ten or more years as a much-favoured up-and-coming actor rarely out of work, he now had to look for jobs and be ready to take anything that came along.

The days of promise, it seemed, were over. In fact, they were only just beginning.

Part One

Part One

1

A Precarious Youth

Why should anyone want to be an actor? Denholm had an answer which could stop a dinner conversation dead in its tracks. He took up acting, he said, as a cure for kleptomania.

No, I didn't believe it either on first telling. But like most of Denholm's stories, it was founded on truth. It started when he was at Malvern College, a thoroughly confused teenager who made petty larceny his special subject. This being a respectable private school, fearful of scandal, his inevitable unmasking led not to a police court but to a friendly psychiatrist. Dr Sylvia Paine, a disciple of Freud and a friend of Anna Freud, reasoned that stealing was Denholm's cry to be noticed and that if he was so keen on self-expression he should do it properly with a course at the Royal Academy of Dramatic Art. The idea was not entirely simplistic. Denholm had already shown a talent for acting and in trying to explain to himself his need to steal he revealed an actor's mind, that ability to split off from himself as a different and not necessarily sympathetic person.

'It's a strange process once you start,' he said later. 'Sort of half of you does it while the other half looks on, not accepting it.'

The RADA prescription had mixed results. Denholm stopped taking things but he failed to measure up to the standards of the senior drama school. After a year, it was politely suggested that his departure would come as a welcome release to the family budget and allow his teachers to redirect their efforts to a more deserving case. At seventeen, Denholm was out on his own without much idea of what he could do or what he wanted to do.

I never cease to wonder how a resolutely conventional, middle-class family could have produced such an exceptional son. By his own account, Denholm's early years were idyllic. Born in May 1922 in what is now the London suburb of Ealing but what was then open countryside, a world away from the scrambling capital, Denholm wrote of a childhood spent in a 'cocoon of warmth and security'. To the end of his life, the smell of a farmyard conjured up 'misty golden days' of total contentment. 'It is the most beautiful smell in the world. If it could be bottled, I would buy the factory.'

The Elliotts were part of the national backbone. Denholm's father, Myles Elliott, was the latest in a line of eminent barristers, the performers of the criminal courts. His grandfather, George, was said to be capable of moving the jury – and the judge – to tears. His impassioned plea for justice tempered with mercy was once so effective that an accused man standing at the back of the court waiting for his case to be heard promptly changed his plea to guilty. In later years, Denholm compared his acting to 'a sort of desperate advocacy'. On his mother's side, he was descended from Scottish colonials who made their money chiefly in India and had an estate in Ayrshire. Brought up in India, Nina Mitchell was a proper young lady with a passion for antiques and bridge. She was to be a strong force in Denholm's life.

The marriage of Myles Elliott and Nina Mitchell produced two children: Denholm and Neil, his elder brother by two years. They lived in a spacious apartment, bigger than most houses, in a four-storey mansion block, the sort of building that is now part of the urban landscape but was originally built to combine the conveniences of the town house with healthy rural living. Surrounded by fields, living in by far the grandest and largest construction in the neighbourhood was a bit like setting up home on a passenger liner. Denholm was always convinced that his father was a reluctant lawyer, that he would much rather have been a gardener. 'He worked out his frustration by creating a perfect allotment in a field at the back of the house.' It became Denholm's 'Garden of Eden'. He would sit there for hours, hypnotised by the insect world.

The brothers were cared for by Ethel Louisa Nightingale, otherwise known as Nursie. Denholm loved her as a mother.

She came to work for us as a general help at the age of sixteen and stayed for forty years to become our mother's dearest friend. She was, without doubt, among the kindest persons I have ever known. Every penny she earned, which couldn't have been much, she spent on others, usually children. When she arrived at our house as a young girl she brought with her her toothbrush, her nightdress and her pride and joy, her mando-

11

lin, a beautiful black and pearl mandolin. She never played it. It sat in her room for forty years – the centre of her private life. She had black hair and clear translucent skin that made you feel as if it might melt into thin air.

Denholm was in awe of his brother. It was partly the age difference but springing from that was a divergence of personalities. While Denholm was shy, sensitive and easily discouraged, Neil was outgoing, sports-loving and self-possessed. The contrast took some time to show itself. If Denholm suffered from bullying at school, Neil experienced his full measure of ill-treatment at the hands of a sadistic governess called, menacingly, Miss de Prey.

> When my parents were out of the way, she would batter me with her heavy handled brush and with a leg of a chair and I was reduced to a state where I was frightened to death of her. Whenever I learned that my mother was going out I used to burst into tears. Eventually, after my parents had been away for a few days, they returned to find me black and blue and this led to a showdown. Miss de Prey left immediately. I had to be taken to Scotland to stay with my grandmother to recover.

But Neil soon toughened up. He actually enjoyed school and went on to Cambridge, where he took a respectable degree before going into estate management. In later years when I experienced with Denholm the often lunatic world of filmmaking, I was able, occasionally, to rein him in with the reminder that his sibling was resident agent for the Duke of Portland.

When they were both in short trousers it was always Neil who took the lead, inspiring in Denholm a faith that survived the most diabolical of childhood treacheries. Who but a trusting disciple would have allowed Neil to equip him with brown paper wings tied on with string before leading him out on to the balcony for his first flying lesson? Recalls Neil:

We practised a bit by jumping up and down on some spring beds before our first real flight. Of course, we had to wait until our mother was out. By some divine providence she returned early. As her car pulled into the drive she saw Denholm balancing on the outer lip of the balcony, his arms outstretched. He was calling out to me, 'Shall I jump, Neil, shall I?' and I was encouraging him for all I was worth. 'Yes, go on, Denholm – jump.'

Nina kept her nerve. 'She wooed me to safety with a sweet,' said Denholm.

Within weeks, he was once more the victim; this time with more serious consequences. They were on holiday on the Isle of Wight. Left to play on a green tennis court, Neil discovered the hypnotic pleasure of lawn-mowing. The whirling blades throwing off a cloud of grass cuttings naturally attracted Denholm, who stretched out an investigative hand. A few seconds later he was minus the top of his right thumb. The accident made him self-conscious. In later years he had a tendency to tuck his thumb into his palm in a sort of clenched fist. And he took to writing with his left hand.

Whatever the anguish he suffered as a small boy, Denholm always had a remedy. He could run to Nursie, who would soothe away his troubles. It made the eventual parting, when

Denholm was packed off to boarding school, that inevitability in every young gentleman's upbringing, all the harder to bear. Neil took it in his stride, adapting to a muscular regime with a determination to succeed. For him, the rugger and the boxing, the cold baths (summer and winter) and running wild over the hills came as an exhilarating release for compressed energy. He learned to ride, was appointed main bowler in the school cricket team and won a cup for target shooting.

Denholm was quite the opposite. When at the age of nine, he was dispatched to Ripley Court in furthest Surrey, he made his displeasure known by turning in on himself, creating a world that was beyond intrusion. 'My life, like that of most children, was heavily laden with fantasy and make-believe. But unlike most children, as time passed, I saw no reason to correct this imbalance and whenever I met a difficult situation I would prefer, like Scarlett O'Hara, to think about it tomorrow.'

Peter Newbolt, a prep school contemporary of Denholm's who was with him in the same (bottom) class, remembers having to form a queue after morning prayers to be led in single file to a classroom in a building fifty yards away. 'I have a vivid picture of him, during his last term, of queuing – at the tailend, like Dopey with the other dwarfs. He was an insecure, waif-like child, in perpetual movement with angular elbows and hunted, flickering eyes.' But if Denholm was not very bright at lessons, there were moments when he could outshine the entire school, as Peter Newbolt recalls.

The school concert was a grand affair for such a school, given on two consecutive nights, and including a short play produced by the classics master, R. N. Bloxam, who directed Denholm's first three or four stage appearances. They were all outstanding successes, cheered to the echo. One was called *In the Cellar*, in which a gentlemanly household assembles with members of staff during the course of a zeppelin raid. In this 'upstairs, downstairs' comedy Denholm played the 'tweeny' whose sharp remarks innocently point out the errors of all her superiors' ways. He brought the house down – a house of enthralled boys, parents and local dignitaries. It was, I think, from this performance that his talent was recognised: in following years he played leading parts, and his self-confidence in other fields began to grow.

He also played Catherine Parr, with Mr Bloxam as Henry VIII, in Clifford Bax's *Alexander's Horse*, a two-character sketch based on a royal argument as to whether Bucephalus was black or white. Although he was again playing a female part, Denholm's skill and presence had grown sufficiently to give real pleasure, and he acted his producer off the stage. He was then thirteen years old.

When he read a book, Denholm would always find a character he wanted to be and imagine himself into the part. 'I found myself constantly identifying with the weirdos in *Alice in Wonderland* and *Through The Looking Glass*. As I later found out, the Reverend Dodgson was always accompanied on his outings by his close friend, the Reverend Robinson Duckworth, who was a distant relative of mine.' It was the White Knight who had a particular appeal for him, 'because he was the white knight in the dark wood. It was how I saw myself'.

The Elliott family, turning up to Denholm's school performances more out of loyalty than any expectation of achievement, led the applause for his triumphs. It should not have come as a total surprise. There were many stories of Denholm's formidable powers of mimicry and Neil can still remember when his brother, aged three, came home to give a perfect rendition of a busker's song-and-dance act he had seen in the street.

For Denholm, the excitement of acting was heightened by knowing that it would soon be the end of term. At home, he recovered his spirit, ever willing to throw himself into Neil's adventures, still with a naive disregard for his own safety. When Neil was given a chemistry set for Christmas, Denholm didn't think twice before accepting the role of laboratory assistant. As Neil tells it:

I discovered that if I put magnesium ribbon into hydrochloric acid it frothed in a very pleasing way to give off pure hydrogen. Hydrogen I knew would burn, so I set up some apparatus to demonstrate this to Denholm. I filled a glass bottle-necked flask with the ingredients and, when it was frothing merrily, closed the flask with a rubber stopper with a delivery tube through its centre. The tube was to allow the gas to escape so that we could light it and watch it burn. Some sixth sense warned me that the experiment had its dangers, so I gave the matches to Denholm. He was cagey at first, knowing that his brother's advice was not always altruistic. But by totally unjustified taunts of cowardice and a reminder that if the gas was not lit quickly it would cease to be there at all, I got Denholm to strike his match.

Denholm escaped with minor shock.

His luck held when Neil demonstrated his skill at driving by starting up his mother's new Austin 7, a lightweight runabout with the power equivalent, by today's standards, of a Reliant Robin. An admiring Denholm was too close to the front of the vehicle when it lurched forward across the lawn. On contact, Denholm was running over a flowerbed where he fell face first into the rhododendrons. The car went over him and stalled to a halt. This time Denholm suffered shock *and* bruises.

His loss of innocence started when he heard his parents talking about money problems. This was in the early thirties when recession and unemployment were hitting every occupation, the law included. The Elliotts were not exactly on the breadline (an older Denholm interpreted their hard times as eating pheasant only on Tuesdays and Thursdays), and while briefs were slow to come Myles' way, there was a remedy to hand in the offer of an overseas job. But the eavesdropping schoolboy understood no more than the first half of the story. The family fortune was spent. The bailiffs were at the door.

I determined to do my bit to save the family from ruin, waited until my father had gone to work and then, entering the garden, proceeded to cut every one of his flowers. I tied them into small bunches with cotton and made off to Ealing Broadway, where, half an hour later, my piping treble voice could be heard shouting, 'Lovely flowers, halfpenny a bunch!' I sold the lot in minutes, and started off home with the money. On entering the flat, I found my family, ashen-faced, having discovered what I had done, and predicting some terrible vengeance my father would inevitably exact in retribution. I waited alone in my room for his return. Finally the door opened and he came in and stood in front of me looking at me. And then slowly a gentle smile spread from his eyes to his face, and I felt he was looking at me for the first time.

The opportunity to work abroad for a period was attractive. It offered a regular income and security for the future. The post of crown prosecutor in Palestine was not without its risks. After the violence of recent years, the country was relatively calm. But with Jews and Arabs ready to fight for territory to which they both claimed exclusive right, no one doubted that the storm would come. Trapped in a League of Nations mandate, the British had the unenviable task of overseeing a political bedlam. With a degree in Arabic and wartime experience of the Middle East, Myles was clearly well qualified to join the legal administration. He only had to watch that his fondness for Arab culture did not lead to accusations of bias.

Although Nina was able to visit her husband several times in Palestine, the boys, away at school, missed Myles a great deal. Compensation came with the promise of an extended holiday in Jerusalem over the long summer break. In July 1933, Nina and her sons were on the P & O liner *Naldera*, bound for Port Said. From there, they took the train to Jerusalem. Myles was waiting for them. It was a joyful reunion, and the boys were enchanted by their father's Talbot Tourer, several steps up from Nina's Austin 7 runabout at home.

It was a strange country, full of exotic promise. The open

Talbot Tourer took them, in splendid style, over the dusty roads to the old city of Jerusalem. The view was quite unlike anything they had ever experienced. The old still dominated the new – a traffic jam was less likely to be caused by motors than by a tangle of oxen, and the brightly robed citizens looked like players in a biblical pageant.

In the days that followed, Denholm and Neil took a donkey ride round the walls of Jerusalem and threw stones at Absalom's Tomb. They visited the *souk* in the cramped streets of the old city. They went to the Church of the Holy Nativity in Bethlehem and to the Mount of Olives. They bathed in the Dead Sea and washed off the residue of salt by lying in the tepid volcanic waters at Wadi Zurka. In between times, the boys were entertained at the Jerusalem Club, where they played tennis against an Arab boy who used a wooden bat for a racket. Neil won the under-fifteen tennis singles championship. It was the pinnacle of excitement in the holiday of a lifetime.

Their father waved them off at the port. It was the last they ever saw of him.

Back at school, Denholm was told nothing of the hit-and-run driver who left Myles Elliott in the gutter, unconscious and bleeding. Neil, who had moved on to Repton, was woken one night by his housemaster to be told that his father had met with an unspecified accident but not to worry too much as 'no news is good news'. It was not until Neil came home for the Christmas holidays, to be met at the railway station by Nina's sister, that he was told his father had died. It then fell to Neil to break the news to Denholm a few days later.

Immediately the first news had come through, Nina had left for Palestine. The leisurely, old-fashioned journey

19

enjoyed a few weeks earlier was now a torment of frustration. She had gone straight to the hospital to be told that Myles was fighting a losing battle with septicaemia. In a few hours, he was dead.

For the boys, there was no funeral and so no signing off – they were in limbo. Of course, it was a devastating blow.

It was twenty years before the brothers sought an explanation for their father's death that went beyond the pious tributes and official regrets. The hit-and-run vehicle was a taxi. It is not facetious to say that anyone who has experienced Jerusalem taxis will acknowledge their disregard for pedestrians. Throughout living memory, speed has been much favoured over safety. In court, the driver relied for his defence on the absence of street lights. It was late evening. Myles was walking on the roadway. How could it not have been an accident? The small fine handed down from the bench endorsed the plea of mitigation.

But that was not all of it. Witnesses, friends of Myles who were walking home with him after a supper party, reported that the taxi had darted out of a side road, then veered in towards the pavement as if to make a deliberate strike. There was a strong suspicion that he might have been murdered. But why should anyone want to murder Myles Elliott? In his last weeks, Myles had prosecuted a businessman who was accused of setting fire to his warehouse to claim the insurance. There were whispers that his death might have been an act of revenge connected to the case. Who knows? Whatever the truth, nobody was ever brought to trial.

Myles' bequest to his younger son was not much appreciated. It was to send the thirteen-year-old Denholm to his old school, Malvern College in Worcestershire. The unhappiness he had known at Ripley Court was compounded many times at Malvern. A quiet, sensitive boy who had no capacity for games was suspect to the robust type of teacher then favoured by most private schools. The first duty of any master was to beat the nonsense out of his pupils and Denholm had a lot of what passed for nonsense in him. He was terrorised by his form teacher, who took pleasure in standing him up before the class. Forty years on, Denholm could launch into a deadly imitation, taking off the top of an imaginary fountain pen, peering over his imaginary spectacles, jabbing a piece of paper and sniffing, 'Well, well, well, Mr Elliott, we haven't been working very hard, have we?' When his fear of being caught out on some silly error and of the humiliation that would follow caused him to break down, he was derided for his weakness.

Though Malvern was resolutely macho (Lord Weatherill, former speaker of the House of Commons and a contemporary of Denholm's at the college, recalls a vicious thrashing for merely suggesting an annual dance with the local girls' school), beyond the usual adolescent crushes, there were no close attachments or even lasting friendships. Looking back, Denholm insisted that he was unpopular with the other boys. 'I must have given out something that was unattractive. There are people who invite trouble. I was one.' His only expression of individuality was in the way he dressed. Whenever he was out of school uniform, he sported a pinstriped suit, pigskin gloves and a Homburg that was just a little too large for him. He was the very model of a teenager trying desperately to be grown up. He so wanted to be taken seriously.

When he went back as an Old Boy to give away some

prizes, the headmaster asked if he had been happy at the college. 'I had to tell him that when my psychiatrist's bills were as high as my school fees had been I might begin to recover from the damage done to me there.'

RADA was an improvement on Malvern, but not by much. It wasn't simply that Denholm was misjudged by those who were supposed to be able to spot talent – given his state of mind, the mistake is easy to forgive. His aversion to the place had more to do with his feeling of being ostracised by the society types who were there in force. With names like Vicki Henderson-Chimas, Gertrude St John Jones and Brian Hanbury-Sparrow gracing the student list, RADA was like an exclusive finishing school for youngsters whose parents couldn't think what else to do with them. Of course, Denholm himself was of this group, which made the feeling of rejection all the harder to bear. His soft spot was for a student called Robin Hood. Maybe it was his real name, but Denholm held to the belief that here was an actor who was determined to be noticed. When I asked what had happened to him, Denholm shrugged. 'No idea. Too much typecasting, I imagine.'

Denholm was attracted to the idea of acting but he didn't really know if he could act. He needed a push to get him started. Instead, he had to make out as best he could, which meant that he was always last in line for the meaty roles. One who sympathised and tried to help was his fellow student Douglas Wilmer.

I have to say that he was not at all a promising student, awkward and very young for his age and lacking in confidence, but gentle and pleasant in a rather tongue-tied way. I liked him and felt very sorry for him, as he appeared unhappily out of his element. When John Wyse directed *Love's Labour's Lost*, he rather cruelly cast Denholm as Costard, one of Shakespeare's more ghastly clowns. That, I would think, was probably the nadir of Denholm's career and certainly a contributory, if not the final, cause of his departure from RADA.

Denholm lasted two terms (at 15 guineas a term). To his credit, 1940 was not the easiest year for theatrical or any other sort of artistic training. When Denholm enrolled there was supposed to be an intake of 246 students; in the event only 95 turned up. Of these, 50, including Douglas Wilmer, left early to join the armed forces.

There were opportunities at RADA for those ambitious enough to take them. For an actor in the making, Denholm was short on strength of purpose, a problem that would recur at intervals throughout his life. Not that he ever saw it this way. He remained unforgiving. He was not at all sympathetic when, in April 1941, the school's Big Theatre in Malet Street was destroyed by a landmine. After we married, whenever we were driving through the West End and happened to pass RADA, Denholm would exercise two fingers through the open window. His dislike of the place was only marginally less than his dislike for Malvern.

After RADA Denholm had little choice but to wait for the inevitable call-up papers. His mother had moved out of London to escape the blitz and Denholm went to join her at the Berkshire home of his uncle, Sir Gerald Canny, a high-court judge. There he spent the six months to his eighteenth birthday working hard on his golf handicap. Neil was already in the Royal Artillery, a suitably gallant outfit, one might have thought. But Denholm was drawn to the RAF. He had never before been up in a plane and, so far as anyone can recall, had not previously shown any great desire to fly. His own explanation for his unexpected choice was the sexiness of the leather and wool bomber jacket sported by young RAF types. For Denholm, there was nothing in the Army or Navy wardrobe to match it.

But there was, I believe, a more serious underlying motive. Denholm was a great one for playing his chances. This may seem to conflict with the withdrawn side of his character but the two are compatible. He never saw himself as the great heroic figure, nor would he submit himself to the hype that was necessary to become a major star. He achieved fame as a second or third lead, the ever-reliable supporting actor. But he was prepared to take risks, not least in accepting roles that many other actors wouldn't touch with a bargepole, and making them into something substantial. It was the same with all parts of his life; the risks were essential to the fun. This went all the way from his dotty affection for powerful motorcycles to his hot pursuit of casual sex.

He had some way to go before motorcycles – or sex, for that matter – began to occupy him. But at eighteen, the thrill of taking off into the clear blue sky appealed to his romantic nature. A few days after his eighteenth birthday, Denholm went to the recruiting office at Uxbridge to sign on for the Royal Air Force Volunteer Reserve. 'We recruits were sent to an enormous very bare sort of barracks to be kitted out. The uniforms were primitive – like sandpaper – and the shirts were made of tough, hardwearing material, I remember, and there were military boots and all the other issue stuff that made up our kit.'

The luck of the draw made Denholm a trainee wireless operator which, in his case, meant starting from the most basic of basic knowledge. He was packed off to Blackpool to learn the rudiments of his craft and to be introduced to the tedium of military routine – 'hour after hour after hour of parade-ground drill'. In periods between marching up and down, he learned Morse code. His classroom was one of the big dance halls – the Palace or the Royal Opera House – where he and hundreds of other recruits sat at trestle tables tapping out messages to each other.

Sitting opposite me was a chap called Davey with a great walrus moustache who looked just like my idea of Mr Chips. Normally he was a schoolmaster, so it was only natural that I should call him Chips. Later during the war he was commissioned and became an intelligence officer. He became a lifelong friend of mine. One of the letters I could never remember was 'V' and he said, 'Well, it's like Beethoven's Fifth Symphony – it's di di di da,' and that's how I learned to remember it.

Despite coaching by Chips, the course was too much for Denholm. The RAF was not sure what to do with him. He became, in his own words, 'the forgotten man'.

I wandered round Blackpool for weeks, just turning up to be paid, and having an absolutely marvellous time. Finally, my uncle, Sir Gerald Canny, intervened on my behalf and before long I was back on the training course.

I worked very hard this time and passed. I was sent to Yatesbury and then to Calne to learn about the theory of radio, which was incredibly complex, and to continue Morse training.

In the evenings there were pubs to go to, a new experience for Denholm, who took easily to the boisterous camaraderie of young men out on the booze. For the first time in his life he felt the warmth of companionship of friends from all backgrounds, who accepted him for what he was. In the least hidebound branch of the military, no one tried to make him be what he did not want to be. Free at last from the monastic uniformity of school, he showed more of the spark, the sense of fun, that so far only his family, and Neil in particular, had seen.

He met a girl called Penny Patenham Walsh, whose family in Guildford adopted Aircraftman Elliott for country weekends. Denholm felt a close affinity with Penny's father, a learned man who, among other talents, spoke Sanskrit, the ancient language of Hindustan. The two youngsters showed an interest in the theatre and, post-war, when Penny was an assistant to Peter Ustinov, she was able to give Denholm a helping hand when he most needed it.

Denholm was also able to visit his mother, who was still lodging in the spacious house of Sir Gerald Canny. An attractive woman of some style, Nina was also strongly maternal, adoring both her children but having a soft spot for Denholm. For his part, Denholm was eager, if not always able, to please. He revered his mother and suffered anguish if he thought that any of his misdemeanours were liable to get back to her.

At the time he most certainly would not have wanted Nina to find out about the night out in Reading which landed him in jail, although in later years they had a good laugh about it. He and a friend, Tony Kelly, a bagpipe player of some notoriety, had gone beyond the time limit on their passes and so, technically, were absent without leave. The Air Force Police spotted them at the railway station. They made a run for it but Denholm was caught. When the excitement was over it gave him some amusement to spend a few hours in Reading jail where, in memoriam, he was able to pencil on the wall a few verses of Oscar Wilde's ballad.

Several notches higher on the confessional scale was his sexual initiation. Denholm lost his virginity to a bar girl called Rosie who, towards closing time, asked him if he wanted to go upstairs for a good time. The lack of subtlety should have warned him that this would not rank as one of his more romantic experiences but, true to his nature, he was incapable of resisting when someone else took the initiative. Rosie had two passions, sex and whisky, and it was said that when the balance was right, she was unbeatable. But on this particular night, the whisky was in the ascendant. A botched performance ended quickly with both erupting but, in Rosie's case, at the wrong end. After she was sick on the carpet the room stank of cheap spirits. It put Denholm off whisky for the rest of his life. It's a wonder that it didn't put him off sex.

Denholm's first contribution to the war effort was as a beacon flasher. He and three other servicemen did night duty at West Malling Airfield, flashing at incoming aircraft to show the pilots where they were supposed to land.

We more or less ran our own show. We cooked up

marvellous meals of bacon and eggs and bangers on a big fire and all the local birds from the village would come round and misbehave outrageously. Occasionally, I would hitch-hike into Maidstone and go to the inn there which was halfway up on the left hand side – a marvellous old coaching inn – and treat myself to crayfish or something.

At the local he saw *Pride and Prejudice* with Martita Hunt. 'Thirty years later, when I was playing with the National Repertory Company in Los Angeles, she came round to my dressing room. I was so surprised I was lost for words and never did get round to telling her how she had made a young aircraftman happy.'

After six months in uniform, Denholm was promoted to sergeant wireless operator air gunner and posted to No. 16 OTU Upper Heyford. It was his proudest achievement to date, the very first acknowledgement that he was capable of being his own person. The transformation was confirmed a few days later when Denholm was sent on his first bombing raid. The target was Düsseldorf. He was just twenty.

You were not permitted to transmit when you were flying, because you could get picked up – they could radio locate you – but you had to listen out and we listened out for the various recall signals which were sent out on a tiny little transmitter from our home station. We were halfway to Düsseldorf and I picked up this recall signal. I listened for quite a while, thinking it couldn't be a recall signal. My Morse was pretty good and I realised that it definitely was. I said to the skipper,

'I think we've been recalled,' and he said, 'Oh no, dammit.' A 'phew' went through the whole crew, thanking their lucky stars. Anyway, I was right and ours was one of the few planes that had picked up the signal. A lot of the other bombers never came back. A lot went on to the target where the Germans were waiting with a very heavy anti-aircraft cover and night fighters and everything else. And so that was quite good – I felt as if I'd earned my keep for once.

Shortly afterwards, he joined Leonard Cheshire's squadron at Linton-on-Ouse near York. The feeling of interdependence and mutual trust for which Cheshire's outfit was famed appealed strongly to Denholm. Here was the team spirit he had failed to detect at Malvern College – if indeed it was there at all. At Linton, each crew came together by a process of self-selection. As they were encouraged to spend time in each other's company – the beer flowed cheaply for those who socialised in the mess – there was every chance to discover likes and dislikes. Those who got on well together were liable to end up in the same crew. Denholm was flattered when one of the top pilots of the squadron, Flight Commander Barnard, said he was looking for a radio operator. If Denholm would like to think about it? Denholm said yes immediately.

The Air Force was Denholm's first opportunity to enjoy real friendship. Though not as boisterous or back-slapping as some – he was known as the quiet one – he had a good line in tall tales and was able to deliver a punchline with the perfection of timing that belies the weakness of the joke. He found himself popular – an entirely new sensation – and made a lot of friends. One in particular was an extrovert Canadian, Dougie Mann. Of all that Denholm had to endure in his near future, the hardest was the news that Dougie had been killed when his plane hit a cliff on the Norwegian coast.

Denholm flew on three missions. The third was over Denmark to hit the submarine base at Silt while dropping propaganda leaflets urging resistance to the occupying Germans. It did not start promisingly. The night before the raid Denholm dreamed that their aircraft, *K for King*, was shot down over the North Sea. Unwisely, he told the rest of the crew. 'Thanks a lot,' they said. As Denholm was walking out to the plane, he chatted with an engineer who had just finished working on the nuts and bolts.

'What do you do?'

Denholm said he was wireless op. for *K for King*.

'Oh, Christ.'

'Why, what's wrong?'

'Well, the last one got a cannon shell up his arse.'

The omens were distinctly forbidding.

They made it as far as the target before they were caught in a criss-cross of search lights. It felt as if every one of them held the plane in its glare. The crew knew very well that reflection off the clouds gave only the illusion that the enemy on the ground was all-seeing, but that was no great comfort when the guns started firing. It was a first time for Denholm.

The shells bursting below us threw the machine about like a toy. Suddenly, there was the most enormous explosion and we realised that we had been hit. The port outer engine was on fire. All the lights went out. I was fumbling desperately to try and find the wire clippers to send a distress signal on the automatic SOS but the plane was going down and there just wasn't time. I rushed – I just jumped out of my seat, which was at the very front of the plane, tore to the middle of the aircraft as it was going down, and got into what they call a ditching position, feet up against the central spar and hands behind the neck to take the shock. As I passed the observer, who was also trying to find a place, he sort of grinned in a sickly way. That was the last time I saw him. He was killed. Water was pouring into the plane and someone managed to get the hatch open. I'm afraid I was very ungentlemanly, I was scrambling over everybody else to get out. There we were, on top of the plane, floating silently on the North Sea with the moon above. The thing that hit me most was the thought that I would never see my friends again, particularly Dougie Mann, and the squadron. I thought, 'This is it, you know, it's all over.' The plane was sinking slowly and the dinghy hadn't come out.

Denholm escaped with, as he put it, 'a tiny bruise on the back of the head'. The only other survivors were the pilot and the mid-upper gunner. He had no memory of who it was who climbed back into the aircraft to release the dinghy. But out it came and the three of them clambered aboard. He heard someone say, 'The next time you have a dream, keep it to yourself.' They reckoned they were about a mile off land that was now part of the Third Reich. Their only chance of escape was to paddle towards neutral Sweden, a long way indeed. At the end of September in the North Sea, an open boat was not likely to stay afloat for very long.

Denholm it was who suggested, 'Why don't we just send up a distress signal and head for the shore?'

The vote was unanimous and at the pull of a cord, twenty-one silver stars lit up the sky. Before long they were picked up by a tugboat. As they were escorted on to dry land, they were met by a ramrod German officer who looked like a parody of Erich Von Stroheim. He wore a monocle and smoked a cigarette from a long holder. His opening words were – and Denholm swore this was true – 'For you ze vor iss ofer.'

Denholm was filled with the urge to reply with a theatrical cliché, the stock response from cynical producers and agents down the years: 'Don't ring us, we'll ring you.'

2

Stalag VIII B

The first days of captivity were more than tolerable. The three survivors of *K for King* shared a huge sense of relief at still being alive. However hard the conditions, they would have found something to laugh about, but as it happened they were treated very well. When they landed, there was an army truck on the quayside waiting to take them to a hospital, where they were given warm beds for the night.

The next day, they were put on a train to Dulagluft, the interrogation centre for air crews near Frankfurt. So far, the most they had to complain about was the state of their uniforms, still damp after their dip in the North Sea. They changed trains at Hamburg, where their guards sat them down at the station restaurant for the best meal they had had in days. It was a curious experience, tucking away surrounded by German travellers and German servicemen, there at the heart of one of the prime targets for British bombers. Denholm thought about his own part in raids over Germany. He knew that it counted both ways but he couldn't help feeling grateful that he had been spared a bigger contribution to mass destruction.

At Dulagluft the *K for King* crew was split up. In a cell by himself, Denholm filled a waiting hour looking out of his window on to a clearing in the pine forest. Prisoners who had been brought in earlier were playing football.

Suddenly a young German officer of about my own age came in and shut the door. He wandered over slowly and looked out of the window and offered me a cigarette, which was an English one – a Player's – and he said: 'What is your squadron?' I told him that under the Geneva Convention I was only allowed to give him my name, rank and number and he said, 'Oh yes, indeed.' He spoke perfect English. 'Well,' – after a long pause during which he looked out of the window rather dreamily – 'you are from 76 Squadron, Linton-on-Ouse, your commanding officer is Wing Commander Cheshire, he has got three children, they go to school at . . .' etc. etc. He knew more about my squadron than I did. Finally he said, 'It has been a pleasure. Goodbye,' threw me the packet of cigarettes and left.

Then it was another long train journey, going east across what is now the Polish border into Upper Silesia. The carriage had wooden slatted seats, bearable for short journeys but agony over hundreds of miles. When Denholm and his friends were put off at Breslau it was after midnight. They were marched along sandy tracks through clumps of pine trees, silhouetted against a full moon, until they came to the gates of Lamsdorf, better known by its inmates as Stalag VIII B. An uninspired name for an uninspiring place, thought Denholm. Originally built for British prisoners in the First World War, Lamsdorf was Germany's largest *stalag*. By early 1943 it held upwards of 21,000 men, split up into compounds by nationality or service. Peter Skinner, who had been in training with Denholm and was now to meet him again in less amusing circumstances, remembers Lamsdorf as a vast labour camp:

As many as 17,000 prisoners were employed on working parties. They were used for work in factories, construction, railway yards, mines and a few lucky ones worked on large farms or in the forest. All were housed at or close to their work in buildings akin to prisons or *laagers* akin to mini *stalags*. Meanwhile in the *stalag* proper were twelve medium-sized compounds, with a hospital, which was virtually another large compound, placed outside the camp perimeter. Smack dab in the middle of this camp was the RAF compound. Like the others, it had four breeze-block huts to house its inmates. They had bunks on three tiers, the highest just a few inches from the ceiling.

The newcomers were left in no doubt that the good times were over. Denholm was made to hand over his flying boots and bomber jacket, the jacket that had persuaded him to sign on for air crew. In return he was given a pair of ill-fitting clogs and a tattered army greatcoat. 'Immediately', he said, 'you *felt* like a prisoner.' He was led off to one of the huts. It was in pitch darkness; the only sound was the sleepers' chorus. A voice from out of the black said, 'Find yourself somewhere to kip, I'll talk to you in the morning.' Denholm stumbled over a mattress, sacking filled with straw, shook off his clogs, stretched out and, using the greatcoat as a blanket, tried, not very successfully, to sleep.

The first few days were taken up with learning the rules of survival. The big talking point was food and how to make very little go a long way. What passed for lunch was a watery vegetable soup – mostly swedes – served out of a large metal bin. Everybody stood in line holding out their billy cans for a ladle (in this case a tin can wired to a stick) of this murky fluid. A loaf of bread – *Landsbrot* or black bread – had to be divided between up to seven prisoners. Enormous efforts went into ensuring fair shares for all. A favoured technique was 'yours or mine'. One prisoner would turn his back while another pointed to a slice of bread. The choice was then with the one who could not see what was on offer. He could take a chance on it being a thick slice ('mine') or thin ('yours'). Denholm found all this highly contemptible to start with. 'They were so eager to get their hands on such wretched food and I thought, "Oh, *really*. They've no self control." ' But he was soon in amongst them. For the first time in his life he found out what it was like to be truly hungry.

If, at Stalag VIII B, advanced cuisine was not much in demand, it was amazing what could be done with a little imagination. They concentrated on whatever was handed out in the evening – maybe a chunk of ersatz cheese made from fish mince accompanied by turnip jam with coloured flavouring. The idea was to make this gunge palatable enough for stomach lining. On an empty stomach it was almost impossible to sleep. Denholm would crush the cheese or some bread in his billy can, add a dollop of jam and simmer the mixture over hot coals. The only place this could be done was at the centre of the hut where a pot-bellied cast-iron stove threw out enormous heat across a short radius. The stove had small grills which opened far enough to place a billy can on top of the coals. The finished meal, eaten very slowly and with great relish, was thought to be worth the risk of burns. It was moments like this that gave Denholm a sensation of pure joy.

I was pleased with so little, because I had so little. For a long time after the war I got terribly irritated with people who complained about food. You know: 'The steak at the Savoy has gone off,' or 'I didn't think the Beef Wellington at the Caprice was very good.' My inclination was to smash a plate over their stupid heads. When you have been extremely hungry you get down to basics and learn the real value of a humble piece of bread.

The Lamsdorf diet was supplemented by a portion of ersatz margarine and sugar and a daily cup of what was said to be coffee. Once a month, each prisoner was given a cup of porridge oats. Meat was unknown and there was a scarcity of water.

Learning to sleep was as hard as learning to eat without feeling sick. Straw mattresses could be shaped to the body to make acceptable beds but then the fleas kept you awake. Once a week the mattresses were taken out to hang in the sun. This brought the fleas to the surface and a rare sport began with much-bitten *stalag* residents wetting fingers to catch the little blood-suckers. They were then disposed of by cracking them between two thumbnails.

Coping with fleas was one thing but even with a clean mattress Denholm found it hard to close his eyes. Like so many others, he was a victim of delayed shock. After the relief of survival came the awful realisation of what might have been. At night, when he eventually nodded off, it was with images of horror in his mind. Before long, his nightmare screams roused him and anyone near him from their slumbers. It got so bad that a senior officer who slept in the bunk below Denholm ordered him on to the floor where he was susceptible to a sharp kick.

Prison-camp life had its rare compensations. Shortly after arriving, Denholm risked a share of his cigarette ration in a camp lottery and won. Suddenly he was a wealthy man, the enviable possessor of several hundred cigarettes which could be used as exchange for chocolate, coffee or tea. Such reckless living would not recur until, a year to eighteen months after his capture, Red Cross food parcels started coming through. Those from Canada were the most eagerly awaited. They were packed with half-remembered goodies like dried milk and bully beef. It was the equivalent of dining at the Ritz. Exotic foods came from India. Many of the prisoners had never before tasted curry.

There was much talk of how long the war would last. Optimistic prophecies that the gates would open any day gave way to more realistic expectations. Weighing up the chances of an escape, Denholm reckoned, along with a lot of other prisoners, that nothing short of a miracle would see them through. The choice of route was to make for either a Baltic port – a long, hard slog – or the Swiss border, which was alive with patrol dogs. Denholm settled for the belief that Stalag VIII B was to be home for a long time to come.

This prompted another consideration: how best to spend the waking hours that were not set aside for domestic tasks like flea-crushing. Sport was not much of a diversion for Denholm. More of a prospect was a half-decent library, stocked with books from the Red Cross. Denholm toyed with the idea of studying for a law degree but however much this would have pleased his family, his resolve soon faded. 'I wasn't clever enough,' he speculated modestly, 'or I was destined for other things.'

He went to see Stanley Platts.

Stanley Platts ran the drama group. An amateur before the war, he was proud of his magisterial delivery. He had the booming, sepulchral voice of an actor who scorned the use of microphones. Since microphones were not to be had at any price, he was much appreciated for his powers of voice projection. Denholm was not exactly welcomed with open arms. The camp boasted an excess of aspiring actors and casting was well advanced for weeks ahead. But he soon revealed a quality that was in demand. With his slim body and delicacy of hands and face, Denholm could be made up to look like a very attractive girl. Stanley put him in as understudy to the role of Leila in an immediately forthcoming production of *Rope*.

The fervently hoped-for indisposition of the first choice for Leila (nothing serious, just enough to keep him offstage for a couple of nights) did not materialise. But rehearsals gave Denholm a chance to show what he could do. Here was an actor who was presentable, versatile and capable of learning his lines at short notice. As he put it, 'I found a talent emerging that I hadn't really felt when I was at RADA.'

Another of Denholm's friends, a Canadian, Bill Jackson,

saw him give his all to amateur dramatics. 'Denny was totally engrossed in the theatre and did everything to ensure each show was a success. To make our way down to the theatre to see the latest show was the highlight of our miserable day-to-day existence and I saw some prisoners actually trembling with excitement at the thought of a couple of hours' return to a happier life.'

Denholm went on to play a wild medley of parts from Sergius Seranoff in *Arms and the Man* to Eliza Dolittle in *Pygmalion*; from Stanhope in *Journey's End* to Leonard Merrill in *Yeoman of the Guard*. As Macbeth, 'I was so thin that by the time I got the beard on all you could see were a couple of eyes like currants among all this hair, and the voice of a twenty-year-old boy coming out.' Not only a popular draw with the other prisoners, he even attracted a following amongst the guards, who were every bit as deprived of entertainment and culture as their captives.

The German military who ran Lamsdorf were a curious mismatch. A hard core of jackbooted heel-clippers was supported by an assortment of fresh recruits destined for the Russian front, battle invalids who had done their time and were grateful to be alive, middle-aged veterans and press-ganged Poles. By the dismal standards of a PoW camp, they at least treated the British like fellow humans, extending small privileges that never would have been granted to, say, the Russians. The fact that there was a theatre in which Denholm could act – a makeshift job with a stage made of Red Cross packing cases, but a theatre nonetheless – was thanks to German connivance at the bending of regulations.

After the war, Denholm put himself out to help a guard who had offered friendship when it would have been safer for him to take a harder line. Zander Führer Jansen had been part of German intelligence. Wounded at Stalingrad, he had lost the sight of one eye, an injury which put him out of active service and into Stalag VIII B. His special favour to Denholm and his friends was to apply a liberal interpretation to the tasks of work parties. The official idea, unsurprisingly, was to do some work – hedging and ditching, log-cutting, road-mending – any one of the mundane tasks that the Germans were eager to delegate. Jansen would have none of this. He preferred a leisurely stroll along country tracks, stopping off at a wayside inn for a beer and a chunk of bread or, when the going was really good, a slice of apple pie.

When Denholm told this story he could make you feel hungry, almost in anticipation of some huge treat. His respect for Jansen was all the greater because he was putting himself at risk. Not rashly so, though: with his one good eye he could spot an officer a mile off. Since binoculars were an unnecessary luxury he used a monocular which closed with a sharp snap. That sound, as distinctive as a word of command, was the signal to his wards to show a semblance of discipline until the killjoy – an officer on the prowl or a gossipy local – was out of sight.

Nearly ten years on, after Denholm had appeared in the film version of *The Cruel Sea*, the promotional people at Rank had the bright idea of centring the German premiere on a reunion between Denholm and Zander Führer Jansen. They tracked him down to his house in Westphalia but when it came to it Denholm had signed on for a play and was unable to make the trip to Hamburg. Instead, the two reluctant adversaries had a long telephone conversation. For Denholm, it was like trying to recapture images of another life. Jansen was more down to earth. 'It was war. We had to fight our own worst instincts.'

Another legacy of his time in uniform was that in the Air Force some of the inhibitions fell away. He was happy with women and enjoyed equally the companionship of men. Trouble was, for all the years of Denholm's war, only men were on offer. In the prison camp, Denholm had a more special friendship with another German guard. I don't know his name and I can't remember Denholm mentioning one, but he did say that he had a gentle voice and shy manner – a boy in uniform, an innocent, not unlike Denholm. What they shared was a warmth, a compassion. It certainly was not sexual. In any case, the low calorie count at Lamsdorf ruled out any possibility of sex for almost all prisoners. Food, the prospect of it or the acquiring of it, came before all.

Denholm was barely halfway to terms with his own sexuality. He knew – he could hardly fail to have known – that there was a fierce horror of emotional display, let alone sexual contact, between men. Bill Jackson insists that 'for a prisoner to become gay was virtually impossible. Life was far too unprivate'. He admits to 'isolated cases' and Peter Skinner knew of a couple who tried to escape together, but 'one must look at such a thing from a 1940s perspective, when the military dealt severely with such behaviour'. The military code was reinforced by social convention and the law. Making love was a criminal offence if both partners happened to be men. With Denholm's background the pressure to conform was massive.

At Lamsdorf, what counted was the opinion of friends and seniors, most of whom were assertively straight. At this early period of his life, Denholm had no desire to be seen fighting against the crowd. Nor did he want to be accused of consorting with the enemy. Furthermore, the German military did not look kindly on homosexuality and in Nazi eyes it ranked with communism and Judaism as one of the deadly sins. In the concentration camps those wearing the pink triangle were among the most abominably treated.

So Denholm's friendship with the German was expressed through small gifts of chocolate or cigarettes. It ended sadly. Denholm was standing by the wire, close to one of the gates, as a truck pulled up at the barrier. When the gates opened and the truck moved out, Denholm saw his friend sitting by the tailboard. There was no signal of recognition, not so much as a wave. But Denholm knew beyond doubt that this was the last time he would see him. He never did find out if he had been transferred by his own request.

At the height of its popularity, the Lamsdorf theatre went on tour. It was a German inspiration. Upper Silesia was smothered with PoW labour camps whose occupants were trying hard not to do too much to help the enemy war effort. A little cultural relaxation might act as an incentive. So convinced were those in charge of the virtue of their cause that they raided the Breslau Opera on behalf of their British actors, kitting them out in the finest costumes for their most ambitious production to date. The selected play was *Twelfth Night*, and Denholm was cast as Viola. The enterprise was not without its risks. When they performed at the Farben oil refineries, there was the constant threat of attack from US bombers mounting raids from their bases in northern Italy. Among the audience for the opening night at the Farben works was Andrew Macdonald-Bell.

They were few in number, perhaps eight or ten actors, but they were so different from the rest of us hunger-hardened, predatory PoWs that they could well have come from the other side of the cosmos. They had beautifully modulated voices, and elegant movements such as to embarrass us with our own uncomeliness and set us to wriggling on our bare benches and emitting oafish noises like the mindless work slaves we had become. But as the wonderful language began first to make sense to us, then became riveting entertainment, we were won over – especially by the lad who played Viola. Spellbound, we watched and listened as first he presented as a girl, then as a girl pretending to be a youth, then again as a girl.

Such was the reception that on the following night 'there was a near riot as the Kriegies fought to jump the queue for the second performance'.

And that was almost it. On the third day, as Andrew Macdonald-Bell remembers, the American air force appeared in strength. 'The *Angriff* wailed its urgent warning, the camouflage fog billowed out over the Farben complex, and the sinister throb and drone of mighty engines grew to terror proportions in the south-west.' But the danger passed – Farben was not targeted that day – and the shout went up that the final performance would go ahead after all. 'In the resultant rush, the small prefabricated theatre suffered a list from which it would not recover. The American liberators would blow it and a goodly number of us to Kingdom Come in the very near future.'

After it was all over, Denholm's abiding memory was of

the unfamiliar taste of strong drink. 'They made their own booze and we all got drunk on this illicit, terribly crude home-made alcohol.'

Andrew Macdonald-Bell remembered Denholm:

On the morning of the fourth day I watched as the actors prepared to take their leave of us. Quite on impulse, I walked over to the slim lad who had been Viola, and I thanked him for his marvellous performance. Denholm smiled, a long-lipped Irish sort of smile. 'Glad you liked it,' he said, while his quiet eyes drifted shyly away from mine and his hand went up to finger back a flopping wing of dark hair.

The triumph of *Twelfth Night* marked the end of German enthusiasm for amateur theatricals. They were turned off by fear – not of the live arts but of what was happening on the Russian front. For the first time the ruling force began to doubt its invincibility. With orders from Berlin to strain every sinew for victory, frivolous pastimes were a personal insult to the Führer. Denholm argued for the theatre as a serious activity, an exercise of the mind, though given the physical state of the Lamsdorf inmates, talk of any sort of exercise stretched the bounds of credulity. But there was a little room for compromise. Denholm founded an underground theatre and the guards turned a blind eye. 'We made our own scenery and our own costumes, our own lighting and water dimmers and that sort of thing and under cover of darkness we used to carry all this stuff to the various huts in Lamsdorf which were our base camp, and we would set it up on tabletops and, with a blanket for a curtain, we would put on our show.'

But the guards were less inclined to fudge another order from Berlin. It followed a widely publicised report that Canadian Commandos on the Dieppe raid had bound their German captives, tying the cord round their necks and down to their hands behind their backs. Retaliation was swift. Canadian and Commonwealth PoWs had to suffer the same indignity. 'They started by tying our hands in front of us with Red Cross string, which made life extremely difficult,' Denholm remembered. 'If you wanted to go to the lavatory it was very awkward. You had to get someone to undo your back buttons and it was altogether very unpleasant. They would tie us up first thing in the morning, about seven o'clock, and we would remain tied up until the mid-evening.'

After a few weeks the cord was replaced by iron chains, which made daily life yet more restricted and unpleasant until someone learned how to pick the locks with a sardine-tin opener. Whenever the guards were not around, the chains came off. But for the theatre evenings the formalities had to be obeyed. Denholm would stand in what he insisted on calling 'the wings' – just to one side and below the set of tables pushed together to make the stage – waiting for his cue. 'About a minute before I had to go on I held out my chained wrists to the Polish guard. "I say, would you mind, old boy?" Then he'd unlock my wrist bands and I'd go on to do my scene. When I came off, he chained me up again. It was a rather bizarre state of affairs.'

It now seemed that every setback the Germans suffered had to be taken out on their prisoners. When news of the Russian victory at Stalingrad came through – they heard about it on a home-made radio one of their number had managed to put together – they knew they were in for more hardship. But nothing prepared them for the sudden order to evacuate Lamsdorf. The order was to march west, towards the German border. It was the middle of winter. As Denholm's friend John Banfield remembers it: 'The weather was freezing. We were given very little food and on some days none at all. At times we ate snow just to relieve our parched throats. Some of our comrades died of exhaustion and those of us who survived lost up to a third of our weight.' Denholm takes up the story:

When we marched out of Stalag VIII B there was heavy snow on the ground and an endless road ahead. It was rather like Napoleon's retreat from Moscow. Prisoners shuffled along with guards on either side. On and on they went, and after some hours people began to jettison their cherished little possessions, scattering them on the snow as they went along. They were too heavy to carry. None of us was strong and the walking seemed endless.

At the end of the first day we were put into an enormous barn for the night. I had clung on to the rear of a horse-drawn cart for the last few miles because I was so very, very weak. When we got to this barn I just threw myself down in the snow and burst into tears. A young German officer, who couldn't have been any older than me, nineteen or twenty, came up (I just saw his jackboots and his uniform) and looked down at me. I looked up and saw his face in the moonlight. His look was one of such pathos, as if he would do anything he could to stop all this horror but there was nothing he could do. He was locked into it every bit as much as we were and it was horrible.

One day on, Denholm took part in a small mutiny. 'There were about fifty of us who said, "We can't go any further. Do what you like, but we can't go on."' They were in no doubt that they were risking their lives. But something of the stupid hopelessness of the enterprise must have got through to their commanders, because instead of being lined up for final dispatch, they were dumped off at another farm where they shared the outbuildings with the cattle. With one blanket between six, they slept together, said Denholm, 'like spoons'. At daybreak, he left his barn and wandered towards the tiny farmhouse. It was almost like sleepwalking. He had no idea what he was doing until he found himself in the kitchen.

It had a paved floor, rather like a Georgian house, and there, standing by the stove, a sort of hotplate stove, was a Polish girl, or she may have been German. She never looked round when I walked in. She was making some sort of muffins, four or five big muffins, and then she made a small one. She never looked at me. I just stood behind her and she turned them over and cooked them and finally she put a spatula under the smallest muffin and handed it over her shoulder to me and I took it and said thank you. She never looked round and I walked out.

A German officer came to shout at them. They were all criminals and deserved to be shot. On the other hand, since they were close to a mainline station, he, being a generous man, was ready to let a few of the prisoners travel on by goods train.

They drew straws to decide who would go. Denholm was in luck although, as he soon found out, fate was not handing him an easy option. The train was carrying cement. Denholm and his friends rode on top of and between the sacks, their knees wedged under their chins. For two days they concentrated on keeping their balance, choking on cement dust, and worrying about how they could relieve themselves without causing their companions more anguish. To make matters worse, they were attacked by Allied aircraft. 'The planes ripped along the line of the train with their machine-guns and six prisoners were killed. It was very frightening. I jumped off the cement truck and ran as fast as I could into a ploughed field and just threw myself flat.'

Their destination was a place called Thalangbostel, near Hanover.

This camp was occupied by Russians, French and Serbians and every hut had a different smell, a national smell somehow – even with very little to eat they somehow managed to create an odour that attached to each nation. The French compound smelled of French cuisine. I don't know how they contrived to do that.

The Serbians had these extraordinary waxed moustaches, standing straight up and bent at the ends – they looked like something out of the First World War – and gaiters. They were a quite extraordinary lot. The Russians were all sorts of girths and they were either three feet high or seven-foot-high Mongolian giants. I went into their compound once and they all surrounded me and all I felt was all these bodies pressing in round me, but by the time they walked away from me everything I had was gone, every little thing, my cigarettes and matches, my pen – everything. I never felt my pockets being picked but they simply took everything.

For the first few days, Denholm was in hospital where, at night, he heard the planes overhead, on their way to bomb Hanover. 'I became very nervous about that and to calm my nerves I searched round in the darkness for a cigarette. As I lit it I saw this guy who was in the next bunk to me sitting bolt upright in bed, staring at me with his face barely six inches from mine. He gave me the fright of my life. Anyway, poor man, the next night he died. The orderlies came in and took him out.'

Other prisoners who had marched for as long as three or four months were barely recognisable. Having lived off raw grain or anything else they could scavenge, their skin was wafer-tight against their bones. And their ordeal was not over. After a month in which the Allied invasion of France rolled in towards Germany, their minders decided, almost in panic, to march again, back towards the east. For the second time, Denholm resisted, this time mixing stubbornness with guile.

I thought, 'If they march us out of here I'm a goner. There's no way I'm going to walk any more. I can't handle this.' So there was a German medical officer standing there examining prisoners and I tapped a friend of mine on the shoulder and I said, 'Come with me,' and we both went up to him. I said, 'I can't walk, I've got frostbite,' and he didn't bother to look, thank God. My friend said the same and we were lucky enough to be left behind once again.

It was just as well, because a few days later the British arrived.

> Suddenly, there at the entrance to the camp was a small tank with Grenadier Guards in it. About five yards from the main gate there was an old German sentry standing there. The Grenadier officer took out an enormous pair of binoculars and focused them on the guard, then he leaned forward and beckoned the man towards him. He was only about twenty feet away. The old man came forward, the officer put out his hands and the guard handed over his rifle, and with that the officer jerked his thumb as if to say, 'Get out.' The old man rolled up his cap and stuffed it into his pocket, opened his jacket, put his hands in his trouser pockets and wandered off over a ploughed field into the forests back into civilian life.

Freedom took some getting used to. For days the released prisoners just wandered about the forest. Denholm found himself comforting a group of women, farmers' wives who had gathered together in one of their houses and barricaded themselves in. They were terrified of what might happen to them. 'I tried to reassure them that everything was all right and that the war would soon be over.'

But nothing was certain. When Denholm was flown back home, the plane ahead of his, carrying a group of Indian PoWs, crash-landed. There were no survivors. 'It was a bit rough,' said Denholm, 'after four years in the bag.'

3

Getting Started

The war ended for the Elliott brothers in March 1945. Neil was home first. After five years in the Royal Artillery, blazing a trail across India and the Middle East, he turned up at South Kensington tube station to walk to his mother's flat in Drayton Gardens. Two days later he answered the telephone to hear Denholm speaking from Reading.

His arrival was not entirely a surprise. Nina had been told that he was safe and as well as could be expected, though she had no idea when he might appear. She was not greatly worried. She had passed through the tension barrier four years earlier when, not knowing that Denholm had been captured, she had opened an official-looking letter from Group Captain Leonard Cheshire. He wrote that her son was missing, that the squadron could only guess what had happened to him but in celebrating the memory of 'one of the keenest and best' crews, they had to assume the worst. A few days later another letter arrived. It was picked up from the doormat by Nursie, who was now Nina's companion.

Recognising Denholm's handwriting she assumed the letter had been posted before Denholm had gone missing. She decided to open it, fearing that if it was left to Nina, the pain would be too much to bear. Denholm had signed off '*In vinculis*' (in chains), which did not mean anything to Nursie, but she did gather enough to realise that Denholm's luck had held out. The use of the Latin tag remained something of a mystery. What was its purpose? As Denholm later confessed: 'It would have been quite apparent that my letter had come from a prison camp so I don't know what this great message I was trying to transmit was worth, but anyway that was what I wrote.'

Nina was in the bath when Nursie brought her the news. 'She practically drowned with surprise and joy,' Denholm was told. She was a little calmer when Neil, having taken the call from Reading, shouted out that in a few hours both her sons would be back home.

On the surface, nothing much had changed. Nina was still the revered matriarch but she was in closer contact with Denholm than with Neil. Her elder son, always the assertive one, was now bolstered by an Army commission and five years of independent responsibility. Having made up his mind about what he wanted to do, he pushed ahead with his plan to go to Cambridge to read for a degree in estate management. Denholm was much slower off the mark. Clearly he needed time to recover from life behind the wire but there was more to it than that. The war had taught him that he was a survivor. He knew as well that he had a talent to entertain. But back in civilian life, many of the old doubts and insecurities resurfaced. Who would believe him as an actor? He had a dread of encountering the superior types he had met at RADA and who were now, for all he knew, in positions of power. He daydreamed of escape. In Lamsdorf he had talked of emigrating to South Africa, or Australia, or anywhere. No one took him seriously, but there was always in him the desire to cut loose. It was reinforced by his abiding hatred of authority. The aversion had started at school but the experience of Stalag VIII B had confirmed him as the natural enemy of bossy and pushy types. He was always on the side of the underdog, which is probably why he came to play the underdog so well.

It was Nina who gave him the courage to put his acting abilities to the test. She understood Denholm more thoroughly than he ever realised. He would only move if someone gave him a firm push and by voicing her faith in his ability to succeed, Nina was the force that set him off.

For those without the highest drama school awards the only way into acting was via walk-on parts in one of the many provincial repertory companies. In the era before mass tele-vision every town worth the name had its own rep. like every town had its own cinema, the two invariably competing for the same audience. But for those who cared about the live arts, the local rep. was also an essential feed for mainstream theatre, the source of aspiring actors and dramatists. Con-ditions were tough but whoever said that acting was for the faint-hearted?

Denholm worked his way through the list of prospects, setting out his justification for a chance to prove his worth before a non-captive audience. The first offer to try him out came from Amersham, very much a hand-to-mouth rep., 'the sort of place,' recalled Denholm, 'where you said hello to the director and were cast in a play the same day.' He had to read his first part onstage because there was no time to learn it. The pay hovered on the poverty line and there was no guarantee of work after the first month, but Denholm was not exactly flush with opportunities. He consoled himself with the thought that Amersham was close enough to London to enable him to top up his subsistence with an occasional home-cooked meal. Ten years on, when Denholm was packing away the booze with more than average enthusiasm, he liked to boast that his debut at Amersham was in the role of Arden Renselaw in *The Drunkard*.

He was not at Amersham for long. After a few weeks he moved to Windsor. The money was much the same but he was promised more substantial roles. By now his confidence was building up fast. He knew that he was as good as many and better than most. After four years as a PoW and at the age of twenty-three his patience with the small time was running out. Later in life he was never one to wallow in nostalgia for the golden age of repertory. 'Dressing rooms smelling of last night's beer, messages scrawled in greasepaint all over the mirrors, lunch in a greasy spoon café before a half-dead matinee. Who misses all that?'

The late forties were not the easiest time for young actors to make their names in the West End. The rush of talent out of the armed services, where the much-derided ENSA (Entertainment National Service Association or Each Night Something Awful) had helped to sort out the really talented from the merely stage-struck, came up against the serried ranks of established actors supported by conservative producers. Olivier, Gielgud and Richardson were doing their stuff but beyond classical revivals, mainstream theatre offered a modest diet of light musicals and even lighter comedies. Not unlike today, you might say. Except that post-war Britain was in political and social turmoil. There were issues and arguments in plenty for young playwrights to bite on. Instead, what serious new drama there was dwelled on the emotions of war 'to conjure up laughter and tears', like *The Hasty Heart*, which gave Emrys Jones his big chance as a temperamental outcast facing love and death in an Army hospital. Or set very firmly in the past, like Rattigan's *The Winslow Boy* and Priestley's *An Inspector Calls*.

Denholm joined the queue of young hopefuls at the door of H. M. Tennent, then and for twelve years to follow, the leading, or, as some would say, the dominant production company. In 1946 no fewer than eight West End theatres housed Tennent productions. At the head of the business was Hugh Beaumont, or as he was universally known, Binkie. Then in his late thirties, he was a master of manipulation and intrigue, both essential qualities for a successful career in the theatre. He also had the knack of reflecting popular taste. Few of his plays could be said to be intellectually demanding but they did make money.

Beaumont fancied himself as a great talent-spotter and promoter. He or his casting director, the tireless Daphne Rye, prowled the drama schools, signing up the best prospects. No matter that the pay was only £4 a week (the Equity minimum), a Tennent contract was sought after with a passion and ruthlessness normally reserved for love and war. The maestro's biographer, Richard Huggett, recycles a popular story of the time about an eager beginner who leaps all the obstacles to secure a minor role in a new Tennent play. He can hardly believe his luck and, dreading a last-minute hitch, he spends the week before rehearsals at a fever pitch of tension.

On the Monday morning, just as he is about to leave for the theatre, the postman arrives with a telegram. The actor almost faints with horror; obviously Binkie has had second thoughts and this is to break the news that he has been replaced by somebody better known. With trembling fingers he opens it, reads it and then bursts into tears of happy relief. 'What's the matter?' asks his wife anxiously. 'Nothing, darling, nothing at all. It's just that Mother's dead.'

Once in, a Binkie Beaumont protégé could hope to progress through a succession of West End plays, gaining popularity and earning power all the way. And indeed this is precisely what Beaumont intended. He wanted a kindergarten of acting talents raised in obedience and loyalty, beholden to him for the next pay cheque.

Denholm pushed himself as the romantic lead. With his matinee idol looks – the finely tuned boyish features, the floppy hair, the concerned expression implying emotional vulnerability – Denholm would have slotted easily into the upper-class mould favoured by the boulevard dramatists for their young heroes. But someone at Tennent's, maybe Beaumont himself, saw in him a capacity for deviousness and duplicity, a natural for the upper-class cad in a new play called *The Guinea Pig* at the Criterion. It helped that Jack Minster, the director of the play, had worked briefly with Denholm at Amersham Rep. *The Guinea Pig* was a somewhat overheated drama about a slum boy who wins a scholarship to a famous public school. It struck a chord with middle-class theatregoers, who were just beginning to realise the implications of the 1944 Education Act and what it would mean to have their small privileged world opened up to the masses. The play promoted the mildly radical thought that the sons of the working class might conceivably have brains but the message was wrapped in a traditional story that might have been lifted straight from the pages of a pre-war edition of *Boy's Own*.

The playwright, Warren Chetham Strode, was a dramatist of twenty years' standing with five other plays to his credit. By the tepid standards of his time, he appreciated the market value of a little controversy. In *The Guinea Pig* it comes when young Read rebels against the initiation rituals endured by new boys. His housemaster demands to know his objection to bowing before the statue of Henry VIII, to which Read replies: 'They just want you to bend down so they can kick you up the arse.'

Oh, my God. Nothing like it had been heard since the first night of *Pygmalion* when Eliza Dolittle had famously retorted 'Not bloody likely.' The theatre censor, parading under the ancient catch-all title of Lord Chamberlain, had taken his time over *The Guinea Pig*. In the end he had demanded two cuts, 'effs and bees' in Act I and 'Did he have one on you? No, sir, I wasn't his type' in Act II, both of which 'touched upon a delicate subject'. But in allowing a 'robust' colloquialism as appropriate to the context of *The Guinea Pig*, the censor may not have anticipated the collective gasp of disbelief when audiences heard the offensive word.

In *The Guinea Pig*, Denholm appeared as Grimmett, a

smarmy product of wealthy parents who has it in for the Cockney boy and who catches him when he tries to run away. Retribution comes when Read is accused of getting a local girl pregnant and it turns out – surprise, surprise – that Grimmett did it. Denholm drew encouraging notices for his portrayal of sneering superiority but the main interest was Derek Blomfield as Read and Robert Flemyng as the new teacher, just back from the war, who protects Read and sees him through his ordeal.

On the face of it, Denholm had no reason to complain. It was still only six months since he had turned professional and now he had a steady West End job (the play ran for a year and a half) which give him time to look about for other opportunities. Yet his situation contrasted with that of Derek Blomfield, his elder by two years, who, fêted by the critics, had a great future foretold. Denholm could hardly have known then that before very long their fortunes would be reversed. The big setback for Derek Blomfield was his failure to recapture the lead role for the Boulting Brothers' film of *The Guinea Pig*. He lost out to twenty-six-year-old Richard Attenborough, who was already under contract to the Boultings. Though he was somewhat old for the part, his persuasive imitation of a gauche schoolboy overran memories of Derek Blomfield's stage performance.

Denholm's chief pleasure from *The Guinea Pig* was meeting and falling for one of the understudies. Her name was Honor Blackman. Theirs was a platonic friendship – they were more like brother and sister than lovers. The relationship was sealed by Nina, who came to Honor's rescue with the offer of the spare room in her London flat. She stayed for ten months. Lodging with Nina and Denholm was an education in itself. From an ordinary working family, Honor was grateful for Nina's help and advice. 'Nina talked as no other adult had ever talked to me. She didn't lecture. It was all very casual, but I learned so much from her.'

It was the pre-London tour of *The Guinea Pig* that brought Denholm and Honor together. Robert Flemyng remembers them together on a long train journey south. 'We had to change at Preston and there we all were huddled together in the waiting room round a small coal fire. Honor was sitting upright on a bench and Denholm, with his very long hair, was stretched out with his head on her lap. They were a beautiful couple.' It is another image that sticks with Honor:

> It was my introduction to the ways of the theatre. Actors spoke so openly to each other. One of the other understudies was Mary Norton, who was just finding her way as a novelist. With five children she certainly needed the money. I overheard her talking to Joan Hickson. 'Darling,' she said (from where I came from, no one ever said 'darling'), 'Darling, I can't tell you, I get pregnant *so* quickly, I don't even dare to hold my husband's hand.' Her boldness was a real shock to me.

When Denholm was sick with 'flu, he found Honor a willing nurse. Understudying Rachel Gurney, who enjoyed boisterously good health, she felt free to administer to the needy. But at Bolton, as she tucked Denholm into bed, there was an urgent call from the stage manager. 'Rachel's ill. You're on tonight.' What better training could a young actress desire?

For the first night at the Criterion, Nina threw a party. She

61

worried herself for days getting everything right, but when it came to opening the champagne, Nina retired to her room, the victim of one of her frequent migraines. Denholm assumed that arranging the party had been too much for her but Honor was more inclined to believe that it was the strain of willing her son to succeed.

As a career move, Denholm was nervous of being too closely associated with the sexual ambiguity that pressed on his own imagination. It was not until the seventies that Honor realised where his interests lay, a decade after Robert Flemyng, overhearing a conversation between Denholm, Max Adrian and Laurie Lister, realised for the first time that Denholm was bisexual. 'In those early years he took great pains to keep it to himself.'

Denholm also missed the Rattigan bandwagon which, pre-war, had been set rolling by a gentle farce, *French Without Tears*, and was now being propelled by *The Winslow Boy*. He coveted the role of the languid, jazz-loving elder brother, played on stage and screen by Jack Watling. Every other young actor known to H. M. Tennent was keen to take over from Jack Watling should he vacate the role, but he played to the end of the run. Denholm's chances seemed to improve when he was called to audition for the Broadway production. Some of his contemporaries, such as Leslie Phillips, who was then making his first starring appearance in the West End in the comedy *On Monday Next*, were quite certain that Denholm had landed the job. More than forty years on, Leslie, who became one of our close friends, remained convinced that Denholm was part of the Rattigan export to Broadway. He was such a natural for the Winslow boy's sibling. No such luck. After a nail-biting day, Denholm heard that it was not he but Owen Holder who would be sailing for America.

Denholm filled in time – and collected a few credits – by working with semi-professional companies like the Sunday Society, the Reunion Theatre and the Under-Thirties Group. The much sought-after objective was a one-off performance in the West End, where several theatres were dark and only too happy to earn rent for a single night. Tickets were sold to friends and relatives or given to passers-by but, for lack of something better to do, the critics turned out in force to size up the emerging talent.

The Wasted Years, put on by the adventurous Q Theatre, a tiny venue opposite Kew Bridge station, explored the not uninteresting question of whether a brilliant young pianist with an illustrious career stretching before him should be allowed to marry a woman ten years his senior. Denholm ladled on the anguish as the confused musician. It was sheer melodrama, but it worked. The audience loved it and so did the popular press. 'A promising newcomer' was the very least of the compliments thrown Denholm's way while the favourite review prophesied that he would 'one day be a star'.

The gentle upturn continued with a television deal. The audience was minute by today's standards but the transfer of *The Wasted Years* to the screen gave Denholm his second experience of working with cameras. (The first had been a small role in Barrie's *Mary Rose* in 1946.) In a live production, without breaks, he found himself on friendly terms with the technology. Unlike many actors who feared the medium, the sensation of performing to an unseen audience did not unnerve him, just as long as everybody knew their lines and kept to the agreed moves. Denholm was not happy when driven to improvisation.

He went back on television with another experimental production, *John Keats Lived Here*, a first play by Diana Raymond which came and went at Wyndham's one Sunday evening. A pedestrian script called for extreme measures. Got up in a light brown wig with more than a hint of red-gold, Denholm roared over the top, giving what he later described as the 'carry on camping' version of the poet's life. The BBC did not seem to mind. It had three drama slots a week to fill and without resources to commission writers it was entirely dependent for product on the theatre. This was in the late forties, remember, when original television drama was still a revolutionary concept. Trouble was, the theatre did not have that much to offer – hence the portrayal of Keats as his mother would never have recognised him.

The low point of theatrical output in a not very distinguished decade was 1947–8. There were those, like W. A. Darlington of the *Daily Telegraph*, doyen of the London critics, who blamed the war for the dearth of new writers. 'There are few subjects the contemporary dramatist can tackle without either pretending the war did not happen, which would be absurd, or by bringing the war in, which is not likely to be popular.'

In retrospect, it seems a feeble excuse of mediocrity. More to the point was the devotion of H. M. Tennent to a narrow band of writing and acting talent. The message from Binkie Beaumont, in so many words, was that if you were not with him you might as well forget about a West End career. After his much-praised debut in *The Guinea Pig*, Denholm had assumed that he was part of the magic circle. But a succession of disappointments was followed by a dreadful silence. No more auditions, no interviews, no cosy chats about this or that exciting prospect, no calls even. It was hard for him to know where he had gone wrong.

The gossip was of a botched night out. Binkie was famously homosexual. What if he had cast a lustful eye in Denholm's direction? Maybe the younger man had misread the signs or rejected his advances too emphatically. Binkie was too much the professional to make life-or-death decisions on the casting couch, yet it was well known that he took against some unarguably talented actors. There had to be a reason for being handed the black spot. It was political indiscretion that led to card-carrying communist Beatrix Lehmann being exiled to the provinces while Harold Scott was rash enough to show Edith Evans his collection of pornographic playing cards. Cyril Cusack's offence was more serious. Allowing himself a few refreshing lunchtime glasses, he threw up in a matinee, an act of spontaneity that even the most liberal of theatregoers was unable to accept as part of the action. Still, for one of such extraordinary abilities, it was a little much for Daphne Rye ever afterwards to refer to him as 'an actor called Cyril Cusack' as if the rest of his career was total anti-climax. Once sinned, never forgiven.

Denholm was not of this order. He may have dropped a few heavy bricks along the way but he always delivered the best that was in him and never openly flouted any of the Tennent commandments. So what was it that put him out of favour? Back-track to the prison camp and school, which in Denholm's mind were synonymous. Everything in life so far had set him against authority. Anyone who said 'Do this' was inviting Denholm to do the opposite. Binkie

Beaumont was used to giving orders. He ruled his young actors like he ruled the West End – as a dictator. Binkie knew what was best. There were those, like Richard Burton, who played along with 'big brother', whether in the person of Philip Burton, his schoolteacher mentor in South Wales, or Binkie Beaumont, who took over direction of his life when he came to London. With the innocence of untutored brilliance he was happy to go wherever he was led. Denholm did not like being told, and it showed. Unused to defiance, Beaumont was resentful in return, and he had the power to back his prejudice.

Any chance of reconciliation was made more remote by a failure of sexual communication. Binkie did not quite know what to make of Denholm, who was a great teaser. He took perverse pleasure in stringing along the theatre queens and then dropping them when he felt that the game had run its course. It did not take much to persuade Denholm to mimic Binkie as an effeminate grotesque – a devastating, some might say cruel performance which doubtless got back to the victim. It was almost as if he was inviting Binkie to do his worst. So Binkie did just that. Denholm was declared the outsider.

An older, if not wiser Denholm was able to turn the snub into a joke. 'I asked one of Binkie's closest friends why it was that Binkie didn't like me. This chap thought for a moment and then he said, very solemnly, "Well actually, he didn't think you were a very good actor." And I said, "Thank God, I thought it was something I said." '

There was a curious sequel to the falling out with H. M. Tennent. When Denholm was beginning to make his way in movies, London Films in the person of Alexander Korda offered him a long-term contract. Ever afterwards Binkie Beaumont, who was a board member of London Films, claimed to have played a part in delivering this prize plum. Even if the boast was exaggerated it is undeniable that he could have put a stop to the idea. In the days when the cinema industry was beholden to the theatre for so many productions, Korda was inclined to take Beaumont seriously. But the deal went through. Perhaps it was Binkie's way of proving that Denholm was, after all, in thrall to him, a means of bringing him to heel. Or maybe he just felt generous – though Denholm, for once, could never bring himself to believe that.

The real pay-off came in 1972, just a year before Binkie died. He rang Denholm after seeing him on television. 'I just wanted to say you gave a superb performance.' Denholm mumbled thanks. Except on formal occasions, they hadn't spoken in twenty years.

The dull days of the 1940s were brought to an end by Peter Ustinov, who, at twenty-seven, was already on his way to forging a one-man entertainments industry. As producer, director, writer, actor (for stage and film), joker and mimic, his worry was deciding which talent to pursue while others of his year were still trying to find out if they had talents that were worth pursuing.

Denholm was introduced to his brilliant contemporary by Penny Patenham Walsh, the girlfriend from his days as a trainee radio operator, who was now Peter's assistant. She persuaded her boss to spend a none too enjoyable evening at the Saville Theatre to see Denholm acting his heart out in *The Conqueror's Gate*. His self-sacrifice was not without purpose. Peter had recently secured the stage rights to a 1944 Swedish film called *Hets* in Sweden, *Frenzy* in Britain and *Torment* in America. Much praised as 'an effective study of the psychology of sexuality and cruelty', this was another school drama, but much grittier than *The Guinea Pig*. The villain of the piece was an authoritarian schoolmaster whose striking resemblance to Himmler was reinforced by his nasty sadistic habits. The director was Alf Sjöberg, then Sweden's leading film-maker, but more significantly the screenplay was the creation of Ingmar Bergman, who used the opportunity to strike back at the narrow puritanism of his own upbringing. The international success of *Frenzy* gave Bergman the chance to direct his first film. Peter saw himself in the role of 'Himmler', or, to use the equally appropriate nickname awarded him by his pupils, Caligula. He saw Denholm as the much put-upon older student who falls in love with Caligula's mistress.

Frenzy was the only play ever adapted by Peter and for him the experience was not a happy one. The concentration of the plot for the stage risked a headlong descent into parody, and that is how most of the critics saw it. What was terrifyingly real on film became hopelessly melodramatic with Peter, his humour never far beneath the surface, getting close to caricature.

But for Denholm it was a breakthrough. He readily surrendered his opportunity to play Marchbanks in a Q Theatre production of *Candide* to team up with other first-class young actors like Alan Badel and Joan Greenwood, not to mention the already famous Ustinov. He achieved respectable billing and complimentary notices for his nervy performance. His ability to show vulnerability and moral indecision in a way that attracted audience understanding, even sympathy, set him aside from his contemporaries, who were more likely to be seen as straight up-and-down heroes or villains. This was no guarantee of stardom, of course. But Denholm came to know that he lacked the heavy physical presence, 'the monstrous personality' (his own words) of, say, a Richard Burton. He didn't see this as any great loss. He was never strongly attracted to the warrior-king-type role that other young actors were ready to give their souls for. There is no question that he was turned off by Shakespearian idolatry and had no wish to attempt *Henry V* or *Hamlet*. The only Shakespearian role that truly appealed to him was Iago, but, sadly – because he was born to play the part – this was one ambition that always eluded him.

When *Frenzy* opened at the St Martin's Theatre, Denholm's future looked promising and full of interest. He could point to his name above the title. Not bad for a twenty-seven-year-old who had been thrown out of RADA. Of all the congratulatory cards and telegrams, the one he kept was from his mother.

> This is one of the proudest days of my life. All my love and hearty congratulations.

He also kept a printed exeat signed by Caligula permitting Denholm 'to be in London between First Night and Final Curtain'. Peter kept up the master-pupil joke for some time after *Frenzy* closed, ignobly, with fewer than fifty perform-ances to its credit. A party invitation from Denholm inspired a suitably pedantic response.

Senior Lavatory
Master's Common Room
Martin Luther Wing
Calvin House

My dear Vidgren J-E

It was indeed pleasant to hear from you so soon after the End of Term. I had thought that at this stage you would be fully occupied in your holiday task, the translation of divine Virgil's Georgics in the Archaic Norse, with little time for parties. However, you cunningly deprive your poor master of the withering criticism which perches shivering upon his lips by including Fru Vidgren's name on the invitation. 'Sly in school, sly out' says the old Viking proverb.

As for the imposition, it is a pity that you could find only room for eleven lines in lieu of the twelve ordained. You will therefore write out 'A Whip in Time Saves Nine' twenty-four times. I expect it to be ready for collection at the party. I will, of course, bring my black portfolio with me. It is doubly unfortunate that you have clearly received help with your work, as my home-detective set has revealed to me that of the ten thumb marks on the paper, only two belong to you. Of the others, one belongs to Ostergren, one to Sandman, one to Birdie, one to the waiter in the café, one to your young brother Olaf, one to your esteemed father, Chief Fire Director of Internal Waterway Sven-August Vidgren, one to Monty the cat, and one to, shall we say, an unidentified person. In this connection, may I ask you whether you have lately seen the girl who serves cocaine in the snack bar on the corner?

By the way – in confidence, Vidgren J-E, if we are to play the exhilarating and wholesome game of sardines, may I suggest that you need only do twenty-two lines of imposition if you can arrange it so that Bertha and I are placed in adjoining positions in the same tin. I badly wish to show her my appendicitis scars. In a yellowish light they look like a ploughed field. And no wonder. They were made by a veterinary surgeon suffering from acute agoraphobia because he was dropped in a field when very young. I love nothing better than to hold Bertha's head when she is being sick. When you are older, Vidgren J-E, you will understand these things.

Meanwhile enjoy the little time at your disposal before your inevitable expulsion. You will be pleased to hear that lessons in the Scottish and Pictish tongues will be taken by Professor Honeyman next term.

I remain, permanently

Caligula

Denholm scored two immediate bonuses from *Frenzy*. The first was some radio work with Peter and with Alec Guinness, the second a contact with producer Henry Sherek who, energetically promoting T. S. Eliot, was leading the fashion for verse drama. It was a new wave that would eventually carry Denholm to Broadway. It began rolling at the tiny Mercury Theatre in Notting Hill where the director, E. Martin Browne, was a great believer in the cross-current between poetry and theatre. Before the war T. S. Eliot's *Murder in the Cathedral*, which attracted the interest of theatregoers jaded by standard West End fare, had showed beyond doubt that E. Martin Browne was on to something. He launched off at the Mercury with a pretentious piece by Ronald Duncan, later a founding force of the Royal Court, called *This Way to the Tomb*. It was soon interred but inspiration returned when Christopher Fry was commissioned to write for the Mercury. *A Phoenix Too Frequent* was presented in 1946 and led on to Fry's great successes *The Lady's Not for Burning, Venus Observed* and *Ring Round the Moon* – the making of a love affair between Fry and the theatre which was to last until the English Stage Company seduced audiences to the Royal Court.

Denholm's entry into verse drama was courtesy of George Bernard Shaw. Though not himself a versifier – at least, not with serious intent – the ancient sage was a great declaimer who gave his actors long and meaty speeches. Anyone who could deliver a Shaw lecture on one of his pet subjects with passion and conviction had to be in line to cope with Eliot and Fry. For *Buoyant Billions*, Shaw's last and probably least successful play, Denholm was said by J. C. Trewin to 'rise without obvious labour to the flights of eloquence allotted to him', and was dubbed 'the best young actor' on show at the Malvern Festival.

Buoyant Billions was a weird experience from beginning to end. Denholm was troubled about returning to Malvern, a natural first choice for Shaw, then living at Ayot St Lawrence, who had premiered twenty of his plays at pre-war Malvern Festivals. But while Denholm had no fond memories to stimulate feelings of pleasurable nostalgia, he could hardly resist the opportunity to appear as the college Old Boy who had made good against the best efforts of his teachers to turn him into a gibbering wreck.

* * *

I went down to Ayot St Lawrence to rehearse with Shaw.

His house was in the worst possible period of Victoriana. He was just one long enormously tall *bone*, wearing a Norfolk jacket and a Panama hat, which he took off using both his hands. His head went on and on and he only finally got the hat off when his arms were fully extended! The gap from his eyebrows to the top of his head was incredible. He was ninety-three and I felt his tired old brain struggling for a *bon mot*. He couldn't just say thank you if you offered him a cup of tea or some sugar. He'd have to say, 'Sweet things are all a swindle,' and make a thing of it. But I was so busy listening to everything he said that I hardly remember a word.

Shaw presented Denholm with a signed copy of the play. 'Take care of it,' he ordered. 'You can sell it after I'm dead and make a lot of money.'

The critics were pretty well agreed that *Buoyant Billions* 'said a lot about not much in particular', though Shaw's strictures on atomic war and vegetarianism impressed the man from the *Daily Worker*. Not at all fazed by the almost unanimous thumbs-down, Shaw readily admitted that he was delivering merely 'the best I can do in my dotage'. But on the strength of his name, it was enough to ensure a West End transfer. *Buoyant Billions* opened at the Prince's, now the Shaftesbury Theatre, in October 1949. Denholm valued the experience.

The great thing about the English school of acting – certainly when I was young – was that you had to play Shaw, and Shaw is incredibly difficult to breathe to. The phrases have to be absolutely round for the right moment and the right word has to be picked out because it balances with something in the next, and it really has to be orchestrated. That sort of technique, that sort of training, helps you enormously.

Buoyant Billions was Denholm's introduction to Liz Prideaux, who, fresh out of repertory, was enjoying her first adventure in mainstream theatre as understudy to the star, Frances Day. The young Liz was very English, vivacious and jolly. Parties galore helped to move things along and well before the show met its timely end, Liz's mother was having tea with Nina at Lyon's Corner House, a sure sign of serious intent. But though Denholm was 'very special' to her there was, Liz says, 'something missing' in their relationship. Furthermore, Denholm's constant need for bolstering was ill matched with his inability to give much in return. It was a problem that had long staying power.

He was the young man about town with self-indulgence his foremost interest. He did not even have to bother to find a flat: a comfortable room in Nina's apartment was always at his disposal and his mother and Nursie were eager to wait on his every need.

Liz eventually married the film director David Villiers, who died young leaving her with three children to bring up. Their daughter Catherine had Denholm as a godfather, a responsibility he bore lightly until, as a teenager, she came for a holiday with us in Ibiza. Liz's two sons also came to the island but unannounced. Spotting Denholm in a restaurant they were taken on a guided tour of the bars which lasted most of the night. While the boys nursed hangovers, Denholm chased off to the airport. Somewhere the cameras were waiting for him.

4

Crossing the Atlantic

The high point of excitement in the short London run of
Buoyant Billions was the night word went round that Laurence Olivier was in the audience. Fortunately for Denholm's
peace of mind, he did not know that Britain's greatest living
actor was there to see him.

On the strength of Denholm's performance turned the
critical question of who was to play alongside Larry in the
latest Christopher Fry, *Venus Observed*. For several days
after Larry's visit to the Shaftesbury, Denholm was kept in
ignorance while his prospective employer weighed his own
judgement against the views of friends and associates. 'I'm
thinking of having Denholm Elliott; do you know him?' he
asked Douglas Wilmer one evening, adding, 'He's making
quite a little name for himself.' Recalling their RADA days
together, Douglas couldn't help but wonder at the ironies of
fate. As he reflected many years later, 'If, at RADA, anyone
had told me that I would one day be thinking back on
Denholm's distinguished career as an actor, frankly I would

have thought that person completely off his trolley.'

The summons finally came for a meeting at St James Theatre, where Larry used his dressing room as an office. Denholm was in a fair state by the time he arrived, half an hour early, for the appointment. Pacing up and down outside the theatre did not help his confidence. When he was eventually called he was almost tongue-tied. Larry had to do all the talking. He summarised *Venus Observed*. An elderly aristocrat with fond memories of an energetic love-life seeks a wife from the line-up of his former mistresses. After choosing the youngest beauty he loses out to his son, the role for which Denholm was pencilled in. Was he interested?

Twisting his hands in an agony of embarrassment, like a head waiter who had double-booked the best table, Denholm said yes, he would be delighted, honoured, overwhelmed.

Larry allowed him to ramble on for a few moments before interrupting. 'On second thoughts, I'm not sure you're distinguished enough to play my son.'

Denholm snapped out of his reverie. 'Of course,' he said, 'you're absolutely right. I quite understand.' And having spoken clearly for the first time, he turned abruptly and made for the door. A few clipped vowels stopped him in his tracks.

'Come back here, you silly boy. Of course you have the part.'

From that moment on, Denholm worshipped Olivier. Twelve years later when I came on the scene, Denholm was still the doting pupil, nervous of mistakes, eager for praise. These hang-ups were a mystery to me. When I first met Larry I had not seen him in a single performance, on stage or screen. While I recognised the power of the man there were other actors I had met who were used to getting their own way. My response always was to treat them as ordinary beings and not to take any bullshit. Larry never seemed to mind my less than deferential manner. He called me his 'free spirit' and laughed loudly when he heard that I had made a special effort to see *Wuthering Heights*, his 1939 classic, to check out what he had been like as a young man. I did confess that if I had known him then I would have been leading the groupies.

Larry had a wicked sense of humour which relied on his victims taking his sage-like reputation too seriously, as when he teased Denholm on their first meeting. Denholm was often on the receiving end of his jokes. In rehearsals for *Venus Observed*, Denholm occupied a coffee break telling the rest of the company of an emotional row he had had with a friend. 'And so,' he concluded grandly, 'I told him, "Go and fuck yourself." '

Larry's expression turned from indulgence to disbelief. He wagged his finger at Denholm. 'You must never say that to anyone. It's very rude.'

Denholm was immediately contrite, offering profuse apologies. His protestations were brushed aside.

'What you should have said was. "Would you *like* to go and fuck yourself." '

Before joining the Olivier entourage Denholm had to survive a month at Richmond, where he was given prominent billing in *The Foxes of Kildorgan*. This turned out to be a dubious compliment. For one thing he was woefully miscast as a revengeful lover. As Harold Hobson detected, Denholm was 'a player of élan and delicate sensibility'. Rampaging brutality was beyond his range. But he might have got away with it if Vivian Connell's melodrama had not been quite so obviously contrived. Driven to murderous intent, Denholm barged on stage waving, as audience memory has it, 'one of the most inaccurate guns ever known in the theatre'. Firing off a volley of shots without a single hit, a wild-eyed Denholm succumbed to a hunchback who leaped out of the service hatch and stabbed him to death. The agony on stage was as nothing to the suffering in the audience, where muscles were strained in the effort of trying not to laugh.

Venus Observed was altogether of a different order. Verse drama was not to everyone's liking but there was no doubt that Fry was offering a theatrical experience that was out of the ordinary. Even the critics who complained that he said nothing of contemporary significance had to admit to the charm and wit of his poetic banter. And he, with T. S. Eliot, proved that there were English writers who could take on Anouilh, Giraudoux, Sartre and others of the French theatrical establishment who were then widely regarded as the arbiters of dramatic taste.

The alliance of the 'pre-eminent wordsmith of the British stage' with the pre-eminent actor justified a generous production budget. And since Larry was himself the producer and director there was nobody to quibble over details. Denholm was marched off to Savile Row to be fitted for a rack of suits and to Lobb's for his first pair of hand-made shoes. Living up to his stage image he took to drinking at the Buxton, an actors' club long since closed, conveniently sited in the West End just behind the Haymarket Theatre, and dining at the Ivy and other fashionable restaurants where the up and coming mingled with the arrived. He was now firmly in the ranks of 'young actors to be watched' and was talked of in the press as a future star. While the critics had their doubts as to the staying power of *Venus Observed* (on the evidence of first-night applause Larry correctly estimated a six-month run) it was another forward step for Denholm, who collected a fistful of complimentary notices.

Buoyed up by his own success, Denholm was unaware of the pressures building up on his mentor. Not only was Larry carrying *Venus Observed* (at a substantial loss), he was also directing two other plays for Olivier Productions while keeping a wary eye on his volatile wife, Vivien Leigh, who was giving the performance of her life in Tennessee Williams' *A Streetcar Named Desire.* Add to this the well-founded suspicion of an incipient affair between Vivien and Peter Finch, another of Larry's protégés, and it is surprising that he had any energy left over for pushing Denholm along the golden path.

But I mustn't do what Denholm always did, which is to exaggerate Larry's sensitivity. For years Denholm praised his master's generosity on the first night of *Venus Observed* when, apparently detecting the young man's nervousness, he moved behind where Denholm was sitting to massage his shoulders. It was all done in character and the audience was unaware of any departure from the script. So skilful, said Denholm, and so considerate. But the truth came out one evening when Larry was with us for supper. 'Don't you believe it,' he said. 'I wasn't giving a thought to young Denholm. I was just playing for time, trying to remember my lines.'

In May 1950, Denholm received his first accolade. The Clarence Derwent Award was given annually by American Equity in the cause of Anglo-American stage relations.

Denholm came out ahead in the category for best supporting performance. He collected a £50 cheque but of more lasting value was the approving nod from American Equity. Denholm had an urge to cross the Atlantic but tough conditions were imposed on English actors who came looking for work. A Derwent Award was halfway towards a green card – and it was to prove its value sooner than Denholm could ever have expected.

There was a point in *Venus Observed* when Denholm and Larry crossed over in the wings. They were together for just a few moments while Larry went through the contortions of a quick change. It was all so functional, neither felt the need to say anything. But one night, towards the end of the run, Larry wanted to talk. 'Have you seen *Ring Round the Moon*?'

This was the Christopher Fry play at the Globe with Paul Scofield in the central roles of identical twins with conflicting personalities. Denholm said yes, he had seen *Ring*.

'How would you like to play the twins on Broadway?'

The question was left unanswered because Larry was on his way. 'Oops, there's my cue. Must rush. Talk to you later.'

There is no doubt that Larry pushed hard for Denholm to be given his crack at Broadway. The final decision rested with the producer, Gilbert Miller, but he and Larry were close associates. Miller had sold the lease on the St James Theatre in London to Olivier Productions and was soon to present Larry's *Caesar and Cleopatra* and *Antony and Cleopatra* to American audiences. A recommendation from Larry as to who should play what part was as good as a contract.

Before *Venus Observed* closed on 5 August, Larry passed

on four golden rules. 'Be sure to keep your feet firmly on stage,' he told Denholm. 'Put them down like you are putting them down on a sponge so that you have a grip from toe to heel.'

The second bit of advice came after Denholm had let his mind wander during what for him was a dull part of the play. 'Remember to fill the gaps. Always keep the audience's attention by thinking the role. If once you let the mask slip, the audience will lose faith and it's near impossible to win them back.'

The next item on the list of things to remember had a more general application. 'Astound yourself every day with your own courage.' It was a maxim often quoted by Denholm, who would add: 'There's nothing worse than watching bland acting.' Finally, 'If you want to get on,' said Larry, 'wear a buttonhole.' It was the only Olivier tip that Denholm declined. It was too ostentatious for his style. But, proud of his association with Larry, he was always ready to acknowledge his debt.

Five years after I worked with Olivier, I was still talking like him. In fact I did a bit of Shakespeare on the set for some of the actors and when I finished it, Harry Andrews looked at me and said, 'Thank you, Sir Laurence!' I could have killed him. I hadn't realised how much had rubbed off. Ian Holm was enormously influenced by him and talked like him for years. Doesn't now. I did too. A lot of actors I know talk like Olivier.

Along with three other English recruits to the American version of *Ring Round the Moon* (Georgina Cookson, Stella

Andrew and Michael Evans), Denholm flew to New York in early September 1950. It was his first time in a plane since his wartime encounter with the North Sea. Naturally, he felt nervous – not so much at the prospect of taking to the air again as at the thought of how he might be judged by American audiences. For every Broadway triumph, there were a dozen horror stories of English actors failing to connect – and for no obvious reason other than the inability to fulfil the image of what Americans thought the English should be.

Once in New York, nervousness gave way to excitement. The contrast with London and its mean look of post-war austerity could not have been greater. New York was young and alive. Ideas were shouted back and forth with infectious energy and the then typical English caution – thinking of fifty reasons why something should not be done – was nowhere to be heard. Denholm immediately fell in love with the place. No longer hemmed in by family or class convention, his personality thrived on the free choice of either joining in the fun or losing himself in the anonymity of the big city. It was a curiosity with Denholm that his need for privacy was never dependent on isolation. His greatest happiness was sitting alone in a bar or restaurant, preferably with a full glass, surrounded by hundreds of strangers, just watching and observing.

Everyday living in New York was a rollercoaster of new experiences. Being paid in dollars on a rate at least three times his market value in London, he could roam the stores of Fifth Avenue for easily affordable luxuries. It was a revelation that Americans ate giant-sized steaks as part of their ordinary diet and were inclined to leave any surplus on the side of the plate instead of eating every last scrap. Taken out for lunch by a journalist, Denholm ordered lobster, his first ever, and was surprised when that was precisely what he got – a large, entire lobster set before him. I think he had visualised a sort of fish paste on a lettuce leaf.

Bowled over by technical efficiency and speed of service, he told another reporter: 'I've just had my trousers altered. It took twenty minutes. In London I'd have to make an appointment to see the tailor just to join the waiting list.'

The publicity machine was kind to Denholm. Showbusiness writers took to this 'slender, personable young man' with his 'brown eyes, thin straight hair and beguiling smile'. He had the disadvantage of being too naive – or inexperienced – to know what the journalists wanted to hear and there were times when he strained hard to find something interesting to say about his life. A self-imposed ban on war heroics left one desperate interviewer revealing that 'thanks to his service with the RAF, he is a skilled radio operator'.

But the unashamed modesty was appealing and gave some good copy, as when Denholm admitted that at RADA he was 'conspicuous for my amateurishness'. He was frequently photographed going to and coming from parties, usually with a pretty girl on his arm.

Ring Round the Moon opened in New Haven and moved on to Boston before making its Broadway debut. The out-of-town critics were pretty well evenly divided between those who backed Fry as a genius and those who dismissed him as a pretentious charlatan. The play had highly fashionable credentials, being a free translation of Jean Anouilh's *Invitation au Château*. Fry had worked on it as a welcome diversion from the rigour of his own creation, *Venus Observed*, causing some distress to Larry, who had commissioned *Venus* as a fittingly glamorous opening for his reign at St James Theatre.

In the event, both plays were produced at around the same time. Fry's own description of *Ring Round the Moon* (whatever his failings he had an instinct for memorable titles) was a 'charade with music'. The setting was a grand hall at which French high society, pre-1914 vintage, paraded their decadence. The costumes were lavish, the stage designs opulent, like a sponge cake with a double layer of cream. Not least of the splendours were the between-scene curtains designed by Raoul Dufy.

Denholm played Frederic and Hugo, one twin smitten by love, the other determined to thwart it. He made Hugo, the evil twin, as much like the young Olivier as he could get without outrageous caricature. As for Frederic, he was pure Denholm: diffident, a little clumsy, unsure of where his overtures would lead him. His portrayals impressed the New York critics and he drew loud applause when he had to exit as Hugo and enter as Frederic, all in a matter of seconds, a feat made possible by a behind-scene track of rubber matting which enabled Denholm to cross the stage in a few frog-like leaps. The trick, he said, was to be able to reappear without panting. The other high spot of the evening was an extravagantly mannered dance between Georgina Cookson and Michael Evans who, flinging themselves about the stage, managed to conduct a high-flown conversation on life and loves at the same time.

The consensus was respectful, offering faint praise to a play that was thought to be 'more suited to the leisurely carriage trade than to the age of jet propulsion'. It ran for three months. 'So there I was,' said Denholm, 'at the age of twenty-five, or something, with my name in lights on Broad-

Denholm with his mother Nina and elder brother Neil. Denholm's earliest photo which is why he still has the top of his right thumb.

Denholm aged two.

Denholm saved pocket money for weeks to have this photo taken in his school cap as a present for his mother.

The only photograph of the family together, taken next to the Talbot Tourer in Jerusalem in 1933. It was the last time Denholm (right) and Neil saw their father alive.

Above left: Denholm in his first term at Malvern. Many agonising years were still to come.

Left: Taken in Blackpool when Denholm was seventeen or eighteen years old and learning to become a radio operator.

Above: Denholm just before embarking on his first operational flight.

Denholm (centre) with members of his bomber crew shortly before they were shot down over Germany in September 1942.

Denholm was a leading light in amateur dramatics at Stalag VIII B. This photograph, taken with a home-made camera, shows him (centre) in one of the female roles in *Twelfth Night*.

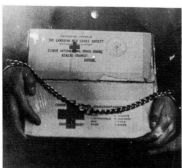

A typical Red Cross parcel held by a POW in chains. When the guards weren't there they learned very quickly how to pick the locks with a sardine-tin opener. (*Photo courtesy The Imperial War Museum.*)

An interior shot of a hut at Stalag VIII B Lamsdorf taken at Christmas 1943 and showing the three-tier bunks. Denholm lived for years in this environment. (*Photo courtesy The Imperial War Museum.*)

Back from the war. The young Denholm in *Don't Listen, Ladies!* by Sacha Guitry in 1948. The photo is inscribed, 'To Clever, Dear Denholm with love, Ada'.

Denholm's Broadway debut for which he won the Donaldson Award for his performance as the twins in *Ring Round the Moon*.

A treasured photo of Denholm with George Bernard Shaw rehearsing *Buoyant Billions* for the Malvern Festival in 1949. (*Photo courtesy Hulton Press Limited.*)

A scene from *The Sound Barrier*, 1951. Left to right: Ralph Richardson, Ann Todd, Nigel Patrick, Denholm.

Morell

is played by

DENHOLM ELLIOTT

Sub-Lieutenant—ex-barrister, very correct and assured, very English. His wit hid the unhappiness of his marriage to an actress who found an absent husband no handicap to a gay time. When the cruel sea claimed him he had little heart for struggle.

The Cruel Sea

Ealing Studios' film of the best-selling novel

A MICHAEL BALCON PRODUCTION

An interesting example of film advertising techniques _circa_ 1953.

The wedding of Virginia McKenna and Denholm. They were full of happy expectations.

From left: Alexander Knox, Denholm, Michael Hordern with Michael Redgrave on location for *The Night My Number Came Up*.

A silly moment with Peter Lorre during the making of a silly film. The first and last Smell-O-Vision film – *Scent of Mystery*, 1959.

Elizabeth Taylor (centre), Eddie Fisher (on her left, half hidden) and Denholm (to his left) at the premiere of *Scent of Mystery*. The smells of tobacco came out smelling like roses and vice versa.

With Dorothy Tutin in *Troilus and Cressida*. Denholm always did have great legs.

way, cartoons in Sardis, profiles in *The New York Times*, cocktail parties with the Duke of Windsor – all of which I took absolutely for granted!'

Denholm's last engagement, or so he thought, before returning home was to model for *Bazaar*, the glossy fashion magazine. He was photographed wearing a navy blue herringbone worsted ('$110 from Saks, Fifth Avenue') and a midnight blue Homburg. With cigarette delicately poised and one hand resting nonchalantly on a Brigg's umbrella, his portrayal was, by his own admission, that of a dodgy stockbroker who specialised in charming old ladies to invest in South American gold mines. Quite possibly it was his picture in *Bazaar* rather than his performance in *Ring Round the Moon* which inspired a call from a troubled theatre producer. He had a problem for which, he asserted, Denholm was the solution. A revival of *The Green Bay Tree* was struggling for survival. Its only hope of recovery was persuading its young male lead, an actor called Jay Robinson, to admit that the part would be better played by someone – the words were chosen carefully – who was more sensitive to the nuances of the play. As subsequently translated this meant an actor in the mould of Dorian Gray; corruption masked by beauty.

First produced in London at the St Martin's Theatre in January 1933, *The Green Bay Tree* had lost none of its power to shock. The breaking of the triangle between a middle-aged sybarite, his handsome 'adopted' son and the girl who wants to take him away was promoted as a dreadful warning against the temptations of luxury and idleness. But despite the protestations of the author, Mordaunt Shairp, a former schoolmaster with exaggerated claims to respectability, the predominant, if thickly veiled theme was homosexual love.

85

His resolute denial of a homoerotic interest was a critical factor (naive or calculating?) in circumventing the censors who, try as they might, could find no reasonable grounds for banning the play.

In London, as in New York, the representation of homosexuality on stage was utterly taboo. When, in 1946, there was an appeal by liberals to lift the ban, both sides shared the assumption that homosexuality was evil. The only point at issue was whether open discussion would help to save those who might otherwise fall into degradation. The view of a cross-section of the great and the good was that freedom of expression was 'more likely to introduce the subject to the innocent rather than accomplish the reformation of the pervert'. And so the ban stayed in force until 1967, when the Wolfenden Report accepted the obvious: that what consenting adults do to each other in private is entirely their own affair. Even then, the censor gave way only so far. Licences to perform were restricted to plays that dealt 'seriously' with the subject; violently homosexual plays would not be allowed and embraces between homosexuals were too awful to contemplate. These were the rules until stage censorship was finally abolished in 1968.

The Green Bay Tree escaped proscription because, as a spokesman for the Lord Chamberlain reported: 'There is no suggestion of physical homosexuality in it and indeed the play is inconsistent with it.' American moralists took the same line. The argument surfaced again for the New York revival in 1951, only now the author was not around for comment – he had died twelve years earlier.

The only thing Denholm knew about the play was that in the original New York production the role marked out for him had been played by Laurence Olivier. It was recommendation enough. Here was a chance to prove beyond doubt that he could tread in his master's footsteps.

There were a few details to work out before Denholm could succeed, in either sense of the word. The present incumbent, Jay Robinson, had to be handled tactfully, not least because Robinson Sr was the leading investor in the show. In the event, the actor withdrew gracefully confessing that 'the role requires an actor of more maturity'. Then American Equity had to be squared. The rule was for a British actor to go home after one engagement but for Denholm, it was waived. The reason given – nobody else so good was available – had interesting implications for Denholm's prospects as a transatlantic actor.

Allowing for the play's limitations, Denholm made a substantial meal of the role of Julian. Those critics who were persuaded to see the play for the second time in as many weeks heaped extravagant praise upon him. The *New Yorker* went as far as to say that Denholm was 'good, better than good, better than someone named Olivier once was'. But anyone who knew Denholm would have expected him to excel in a role that caught so much of his own character. He had no trouble in imagining being caught in a two-way stretch between a man and a woman. Nor was he in any doubt that a Julian could easily be seduced by riches. After his years behind the wire, Denholm had come to appreciate the good life.

But he was too late to save *The Green Bay Tree*. His co-star, Joseph Schildlsraut, a matinee idol from the twenties whose lasting role as Otto Frank in the stage and screen version of *The Diary of Anne Frank* was still ahead of him, was thought to be too camp as Dulcimer. As for the girl, Anne Crawford, another British import, fought and failed against leaden dialogue. There were nights, said Denholm, when Mordaunt Shairp's drama almost tipped over into hilarious comedy. Time was up for *The Green Bay Tree*. After twenty performances Denholm packed his bags.

He sailed home on the *Queen Mary* where he shared celebrity status with J. B. Priestley. The big talking point was the rapturous Broadway reception for the latest Rodgers and Hammerstein musical, *The King and I* with Yul Brynner as the king and Gertrude Lawrence as Anne. Denholm's homecoming coincided with the 1951 Festival of Britain. After a war-weary and dreary post-war decade, the festival was a government-inspired attempt to put some sparkle back into ordinary lives. Its centrepiece was the exhibition of British achievement on the South Bank of the Thames (the Festival Hall complex is all that is left), but celebratory events were staged throughout the country. One such was a new verse play from Christopher Fry, an extraordinary piece called *A Sleep of Prisoners*. Dubbed recently by the author as 'the production with which I have been most completely happy', *A Sleep of Prisoners* was not only set in a church, it was actually played in a church, in St Thomas's just off Regent Street. As a theatrical venue it was difficult to think of anywhere less likely to attract customers. Tucked away behind the shops, the passing trade was blissfully unaware of its existence and even those in the know were grateful for a street map to get them to their seats on time. But the originality of the idea, at a time when churches were rarely used for commercial performances, and the interest in seeing how Christopher Fry met the challenge, was enough to guarantee crowded pews. It was also enough to excite Denholm into immediate acceptance when he was invited to head a cast of four. Appearing with him was Stanley Baker in his first venture into the London theatre and, as understudy and stage manager, Peter Vaughan.

At this point in his career, Peter was not at all sure how he would survive in the business. Regional accents were not yet in fashion and any hint of working-class credentials was a liability. Denholm, on the other hand, had everything going for him. 'We saw him as the natural heir to Gielgud,' said Peter.

The storyline of *A Sleep of Prisoners* was suitably biblical. A varied bunch of war captives are locked in a church. Each has a dream which he plays out as a modern variation on an Old Testament story: David and Goliath, Cain's murder of Abel, Adam hearing the voice of God, and Abraham and Isaac. The underlying message is that Everyman is responsible to himself for the way the world goes, and it is only through the assumption of responsibility that mankind will find peace. For Denholm it was one of the great acting experiences. He was not religious, at least not in the conventional mode – unlike Christopher Fry he did not espouse the teaching of the Church of England (the play was written for the Religious Drama Society). But like anyone remotely involved in artistic endeavour, he acknowledged the rare moments of spiritual revelation.

Ronald Searle drew haunting skeletal figures for the programme cover. No drinks or ice-cream were served: such frivolities would have disturbed the mood of the play. Applause was not invited. At the end, the audience sat in silent approval. It was all very curious – and evocative. Long afterwards, Denholm remembered the power of natural light streaming through the stained glass window above the altars.

A Sleep of Prisoners was one of the few new plays to be presented in the Festival year. Mostly it was the classics that occupied the English stage. At St James, Laurence Olivier was offering Shaw's *Caesar and Cleopatra* and Shakespeare's *Antony and Cleopatra* on alternate nights with Vivien Leigh as Cleopatra in both plays and Larry as Caesar in one and Antony in the other. John Gielgud was at the Phoenix playing Leontes in *The Winter's Tale* while at Stratford, Richard Burton, who to date had appeared in only two modern-dress plays, was exercising his aggression as Henry V. For the rest, the French drama still held sway.

Denholm was not comfortable with the classics, which he thought heavy, nor with Parisian imports, which he thought mostly pretentious. He did enjoy Fry, though he was honest enough to admit that he was not always clear as to what Fry was getting at. It was the poetry that attracted him, the beauty of the words by a living master composer.

The magazine *Theatre World* published a readers' poll of the top dozen outstanding young theatre actors. Denholm came in at number eleven, just ahead of Peter Finch. The list makes interesting reading for retrospective talent-spotters.

Peter Ustinov	James Donald
Paul Scofield	Hugh Burden
Anthony Quayle	Robert Flemyng
Stephen Murray	Harry Andrews
Michael Gough	Denholm Elliott
Richard Burton	Peter Finch

While thinking of what to do next, Denholm was encouraged

to know that New York had not forgotten him. In May he had a letter from Peter Witt, his American agent, addressing him as 'Dear Old Cock' which said that the drama critics had nominated him as 'the most promising young actor of the past season'. Peter advised him to 'get a haircut so that the swelling of your head won't be too unusual'. In the event, he lost out to an actor whose style could not have been more of a contrast to Denholm's quiet subtlety. Eli Wallach, a devotee of the Method, took the award for his performance in Tennessee Williams' *The Rose Tattoo.*

Denholm had better luck with the Donaldson Award. In *Ring Round the Moon* he had achieved, said the judges, the 'best Broadway debut' of the year. A gold key with a little scroll attached – not unlike a gift from an expensive Christmas cracker – was presented to him by Yolande Donlan, who was a regular in London after her marriage to Val Guest.

In the last days of *A Sleep of Prisoners* two happily reconcilable offers came up. The first was a film role, for which he had to thank Olivier Productions. Though not directly involved, the company had on its board Alexander Korda, mogul film-maker and Britain's only serious challenge to Hollywood. Having seen Denholm in *Venus Observed*, Korda thought of him as a likely son for Ralph Richardson, who had just signed for *The Sound Barrier*. The second offer was a spin-off from *The Green Bay Tree. Third Person*, a new play by the American writer Andrew Rosenthal, had a smart-set war hero returning home with his young buddy who, as played by Denholm, 'combines sinister charm with childlike innocence'. Hints at a relationship closer than that normally allowed by military regulations brings out the fighting spirit in the wife. Armed with details of his unsavoury past, she succeeds in pushing the intruder out of her home.

Third Person opened at the Arts, a theatre which operated under club rules, theoretically putting it beyond the prurient gaze of the Lord Chamberlain. But in practice it was not thought politic to go very far beyond the guidelines set for the commercial theatre. In any case, the chances of the play making a profit depended on its starry cast, led by Roger Livesey and his wife, Ursula Jeans, going out on tour to return eventually to the glitzy West End. If the plan was to work, there was no prospect of boldly embracing the homosexual theme. Instead, a muted script was softened still further to protect the censor's delicate sensibilities. It was *The Green Bay Tree* all over again; the same blinkered arguments, the same insipid resolution.

There were cluckings in the press at the theatrical interest in affection (the word 'love' was never mentioned) between members of the same sex. But such mild reproofs as the conservative critics could muster probably attracted more business than it deterred. When they played Glasgow, Denholm took the entire cast to visit brother Neil, his wife Rosemary and three-year-old son, Myles, and their baby daughter, Susan. It was a rare moment of relaxation for Neil. In the week he was a chartered surveyor working in Glasgow but at weekends he was trying to run Dalreoch with its 1,100-acre estate in South Ayrshire, a windfall inheritance from his Great-Aunt Bea Mitchell which was turning out to be less of a boon than a burden. 'The rest of her fortune she left to other relations, but being so wealthy the rate of duty the estate had to bear was high and the land had to bear its share. My old grand-aunt had been in her eighties when she died and for years she had been unaware of the deterioration of the house. There was no mains electricity and water came by gravity from a small stream near the house.'

But Dalreoch brightened up when Denholm and his friends arrived. There was a great party and, says Neil, 'fans came over from the surrounding countryside to see them and obtain autographs. When this happened the rest of us rushed off to fish, leaving the house to the theatricals.'

Turning from stage to screen was no hardship for Denholm. The idea of doing a job and getting it out of the way instead of turning up night after night to repeat the performance appealed to him. And the money was better. A few encounters with television drama had put him on friendly terms with the camera and he had already made a brief contribution to a real movie. *Dear Mr Prohack* was nothing much to write home about. Dismissed by one hardened critic as a 'flat little comedy', the sole interest of the film now is seeing future luminaries going through their initiation – Dirk Bogarde, Glynis Johns and Denholm, all of them trying like mad to squeeze laughs out of a dull script.

The Sound Barrier, released in 1952, could not have been more of a contrast. Alexander Korda was only interested in big movies. He had made his name before the war with blockbusters like *The Private Life of Henry VIII* and *The Four Feathers*. For the early part of the war he was in Hollywood raising money and enthusiasm for pro-British movies, returning in 1943 to head up the MGM British subsidiary and to receive a knighthood for his services to national survival. With his central European background, his fractured English and his fondness for large cigars, Korda was the very model of a Hollywood producer, the antithesis in style to his contemporaries in the British film industry such as the puritanical J. Arthur Rank and the conservative, very

British, Michael Balcon. In the forties, when British cinema was at its zenith with sales of more than 30 million tickets a week, Korda revived London Films, the production company he had set up a decade earlier, to bring together the distribution network of British Lion, a modernised Shepperton Studio and the Rialto, a showcase cinema in Leicester Square. After a couple of flops – an unintentionally hilarious *Bonnie Prince Charlie* and a dull *Anna Karenina* which even Vivien Leigh could not rescue, Korda hit his stride with a succession of classics: *The Fallen Idol, The Winslow Boy, The Third Man, The Wooden Horse* and *The Sound Barrier*.

It was sheer luck that put Denholm into the film. His part was first offered to Bryan Forbes, who now takes some pleasure in having launched, if inadvertently, Denholm's film career. For Bryan, the circumstances were not happy.

I had only just got married to my first wife, Constance Smith, who was under contract to Twentieth Century-Fox. I was playing in *The Holly and the Ivy* at the Duchess Theatre, and it was there in my dressing room that I believe I first met Denholm. Subsequently, my wife was recalled to Hollywood for a new film, very shortly after our marriage, and immediately the provincial tour of *The Holly and the Ivy* finished I made plans to rejoin her. I remember that I went to see David Lean at his house and explained my circumstances. He generously agreed to release me from my contract, and I went out to Hollywood – a disastrous mistake, as it proved, for the marriage failed within a very short space of time. Denholm then took over the role and, ironically, also played my role in the film of *The Holly and the Ivy*.

I suppose at the time I felt a keen sense of loss at having a wrecked marriage and no work, but that was my bad luck.

Then in his early forties, David Lean, who also co-produced *The Sound Barrier*, was already established as a front-rank director of extraordinary range. To make the point one has only to balance his extravagant adaptations of the Dickens novels *Great Expectations* and *Oliver Twist* with the beautifully understated romance *Brief Encounter*. His mammoth productions – *Bridge on the River Kwai* and *Lawrence of Arabia* – were still to come but if the scale of *The Sound Barrier* was relatively modest the question it posed was big enough. In 1951 it was still a matter of intense debate as to whether any plane could travel faster than sound. Even now, when the matter is known to every schoolchild, the film, as scripted by Terence Rattigan, holds its dramatic interest as a combat between emotional instinct and hard ambition.

Ralph Richardson was the ruthless captain of industry ready to sacrifice even his son, played by Denholm, to his determination to make the first aircraft to break the sound barrier. The cast included Nigel Patrick, whom Denholm cordially disliked for his pushy arrogance, and Ann Todd, whom he adored, but from a safe distance because she happened to be married to David Lean.

Denholm was killed off in the first half-hour but the critics were eager to resurrect him. On an overdose of fear – of his father and of flying – it would have been so easy for Denholm to go over the top. Instead, he created 'a little gem' of a part and the magazine *What's On* returned to the film simply to give due credit to Denholm, 'a newcomer of great promise'.

Happily, the verdict was endorsed by director and producer. Summoning David Lean for a midway progress report over lunch at Claridges, Korda asked how Denholm was making out.

'He's going to be all right.'

Korda turned to one of his assistants who sat with notebook at the ready. 'Give him a contract.'

Reminiscing from forty years' distance, Denholm still could not quite believe his luck.

It was an incredible break. Contracts were about £5,000 a year then so it would be about £80,000 now. I never went on a tube train or bus. I mean, I was a bachelor changing my car when the ashtrays were full. And without any sense of it not being absolutely just and right. What shall I do today? Oh well, I might as well go to the south of France. And just get into a taxi and say, 'London Airport, please.' That sort of thing. Fantastic.

Korda was well known for his cavalier disregard for simple economics but even by his standards, signing up a young actor on a five-figure deal was wildly extravagant. On the other hand, his ambition to surround himself with a repertory company of future stars (as Binkie Beaumont had tried to do in the theatre) was entirely understandable. Trouble was, the British film industry was in no fit state to exploit the opportunities. It suffered from three debilitating weaknesses: chronic mismanagement, government meddling and American competition. It was the third weakness which attracted all the attention. With a yearly intake of some 400 American movies against home production of less than a hundred, the imbalance was plain to see. And it was this that led to the other two failings. With flat-footed subtlety, the government slapped a surcharge on Hollywood imports. Hollywood retaliated with restrictions on the distribution of British films. Then, to escape from the trade war they couldn't possibly win, the politicians exchanged the stick for the carrot, dropping the import duty and subsequent quotas in favour of subsidies to producers.

When he clasped Denholm in a golden handshake, Korda was already dependent on government hand-outs and it was getting harder all the time to raise finance for movies that were other than second rate at home and non-starters in the potentially lucrative American market. Ironically, Denholm's next film for Korda achieved belated recognition in the States, where it is still shown on Christmas TV as a post-luncheon digestive. *The Holly and the Ivy* was a straight lift from the theatre (courtesy of Binkie Beaumont), where audiences had wallowed contentedly in the soap-opera antics of a vicar who is dedicated to helping others but cannot face up to the problems of his own family. On screen, there was no disguising the thinness of the plot and its resort to easy sentimentality. Ralph Richardson and Denholm relived their father-son relationship.

Waiting for his next offer, Denholm concentrated on spending the money Alexander Korda was so thoughtfully ladling in his direction. He bought a new Triumph Roadster, a nimble two-seater which he drove erratically. The frequency of his accidents never ceased to surprise him. What he dismissed as bad luck was his failure to anticipate danger. Visiting his uncle's house near Henley, he picked up speed through the spacious grounds, whipped through the gates at the foot of the drive, and was distinctly irritated when the centre support caught the Triumph's low chassis and took off the exhaust pipe. He blamed the gates.

Another girlfriend entered his life. He met Sonya at an exhibition of ballet paintings by his cousin Thayer Lee Elliott. She was, and remains, petite and light, the very essence of a dancer, and with looks that immediately reveal an Oriental connection. They were together for almost two years before Sonya met and married Peter Wright, the Royal Ballet dancer turned choreographer who, as Sir Peter Wright, is now director of the Birmingham Royal Ballet. Sonya readily admits to an innocence that belied her chosen profession and it is not entirely surprising that she failed to notice that while she and Denholm were together he was conducting an affair with another dancer. Denholm kept him under wraps.

Peter Wright recalls: 'He was a good-looking boy and Denholm, too, could be very seductive. They had quite a fling together. All very discreet, of course. But it lasted about a year.'

For his next film, Denholm was put back into uniform and loaned out to Korda's arch-rival, Sir Michael Balcon, the maestro of Ealing Studios. By British standards, *The Cruel Sea*, based on Nicholas Monsarrat's worldwide bestseller, was big budget and quite beyond Korda's resources. His money, including a £3 million government loan, was fast running out and he was less than two years away from a painful conference with the official receiver. In 1954, Shepperton Studio, London Films and anything else that Korda could claim his own was taken over by the state-owned National Film Finance Corporation and regrouped under the umbrella name of British Lion. When this happened,

Denholm fully expected his lucrative deal with Korda to fail by default. But not a bit of it: British Lion went on paying his retainer until 1963 when the company was sold to a private consortium headed, ironically, by Sir Michael Balcon.

The Cruel Sea was Ealing's most durable contribution to wartime stiff-upper-lippery. Such was the appeal of Monsarrat's epic of naval heroism that it might easily have gone to a Hollywood studio. Certainly, tempting offers were made from across the Atlantic. But the author wanted a British production company and when Balcon shrewdly introduced him to Charles Frend, one of Ealing's longest-serving directors with several tales of heroism including *Scott of the Antarctic* to his credit, the deal was made. To compensate for the relatively modest payment up front, Monsarrat settled for a percentage deal. In the long run he probably made as much if not more than he would have earned from a Hollywood blockbuster.

The leading role went to Jack Hawkins. As Captain Ericson he was the epitome of sturdy British manhood and had already served his time in numerous gritty movies. Chief interest for the younger breed was the second-in-command, Lieutenant Lockhart, a part that was snatched from under the noses of his more experienced colleagues by Donald Sinden, who had never made a film before and who, to use his own words, 'had come from nowhere'. In the scramble for what was left – a rich assortment of character roles – Denholm came away as Sub-Lieutenant Morell, described in a publicity blurb as an 'ex-barrister, very correct and assured, very English . . . His wit hid the unhappiness of his marriage to an actress (Moira Lister) who found an absent husband no handicap to a gay time'.

Again, Denholm was the loser; again he did not survive beyond the first reel. But there was a difference. This time he was playing to an audience of millions. Now he really was a celebrity, recognised wherever he went, the darling of the gossip columns. It was the same for Donald Sinden and Stanley Baker (who had appeared with Denholm in *A Sleep of Prisoners*), and for a twenty-one-year-old actress 'of remarkable beauty and considerable histrionic ability' who played a Wren officer. Her name was Virginia McKenna.

5

The Cruel Sea

Virginia was known to friends as Ginny. The nickname was significant because it suggested a girl with a sense of fun, one who did not take herself terribly seriously – quite a contrast to her publicity image, which portrayed her as the English rose preserved in cold storage. Maybe it had something to do with her inexperience that she came over so frostily. She had no great love for the trappings of stardom and was inclined to underestimate what publicity could do for – or against – her. But occasionally she was moved to complain at her treatment. Soon after her engagement to Denholm, she rounded on a journalist who was feeding her platitudes of sober respectability. 'What a bore! Who wants to be a plaster saint at twenty-two?'

To see what Ginny had in common with Denholm, apart from a commanding screen presence, you need to look back on a childhood that must have seemed curiously familiar. Her family was comfortably middle class but by no means conventional. Both parents had carved out distinctive careers; her mother as a pianist and composer, her father as chief auctioneer at Christie's, where he once sold the Portland Vase. They separated when Ginny was four and for the next five years she lived with her father. 'He insisted I more or less only spoke when spoken to, sat up straight and ate everything on my plate and so on.' It was not much fun at the time but, as an actress, she came to be grateful for her early initiation into the virtues of self-discipline and good time-keeping. 'If you're late at the theatre or on set you soon get a bad reputation and may not be offered another part.'

At the age of nine, she exchanged parents. Anne Rudd, briefly Anne McKenna, was better known by her professional name, Anne de Nys. The Gallic connection was justified by a French mother who provided the teenage Ginny with annual holidays. When Ginny joined her mother, Anne de Nys had her own jazz group, That Certain Trio, which played at the Savoy and the Berkeley.

Like Denholm, there was at this point little in Ginny's personality to suggest an acting career. If he had a fondness for mimicry to his credit she rivalled him in modest achievement with brief appearances in school productions. Ginny had no burning desire to be an actress; if anything she wanted to write. But her parents fastened on to the only clear evidence of artistic ability and sent her to the Central School for Speech and Drama. That was as far as her father's guidance was able to take her. He died when she was seventeen.

The tragedy, though striking her when she was almost an adult, left her dangerously exposed to a strong-willed mother. Denholm, having suffered the same loss, if much earlier in life, was equally vulnerable to maternal wishes. When eventually the two matriarchs got together, liked each other, and saw the potential for a socially desirable match between their offspring, it was hard for either Ginny or Denholm to resist the impetus. The gossip writers made it their task to speed things along.

Ginny did well at the Central School and enjoyed her two years there, as she enjoyed her apprenticeship at Dundee Rep. None of the frustration or bitterness that poisoned Denholm's early career finds an echo in Ginny's experience. She even talks of the sadness at leaving Dundee – 'I cried bitterly, I loved it so much' – when, after six months, she was spotted by Daphne Rye and invited to join the Tennent cavalcade. Ginny's first West End role was in a John Whiting play, *A Penny for a Song*, directed by Peter Brook at the Haymarket. A memorable love scene with Ronald Howard got her noticed and though the play failed after six weeks she was soon back on stage, this time as Perdita in John Gielgud's much-praised *Winter's Tale*. She followed with two run-of-the-mill West End plays before being cast for *The Cruel Sea*.

While working on the film she was also rehearsing her first comedy role for Dodie Smith's adaptation of her popular novel *I Capture the Castle*. The cast was notable for its stars in the making: Richard Greene, Roger Moore, the fourteen-year-old Andrew Ray and a young Scottish actor, Bill Travers. 'I thought Bill was such a fascinating person,' said Ginny, 'with very profound views about life.'

But over at Ealing Studios, where *The Cruel Sea* was being made, there was another fascinating young actor. If Bill Travers was the rugged, outdoor type, Denholm was more at home in a smart dining room or a fashionable nightclub. He could be moody and withdrawn but on good form, he had wit and sophistication on his side. There is no doubt that Denholm fell desperately in love with Ginny. Encouraged on all sides to believe that this was a match made in heaven, he threw himself into an ecstasy of romance. Here, at last, was his paragon. It was hard for Ginny not to be swept along by the sheer force of his desire. He told the world how much he needed her. When Peter Skinner, his friend from the RAF, called in on him in his dressing room, he found the walls plastered with photographs of Ginny. Denholm talked of her incessantly. As one of the rare objective witnesses, it seemed to Peter that the actor's love was dangerously close to idolatry.

They married on a cold day in March. It was a conventionally middle-class occasion – the bride wore white for a family gathering at Holy Trinity, Brompton, an eminently fashionable church. The press photographers turned out in force for what the caption writers had already nominated the picture-book wedding of 1954.

The spell was soon broken. Ginny was incapable of meeting the demands made upon her. And who could blame her? I doubt that any woman could have satisfied Denholm's wholly unrealistic expectations. It didn't help that they had careers that were liable to take them off in opposite directions. Such were the pressures, there was not even a honeymoon. Any free time was spent house-hunting but there was not much of that because Ginny was on tour with *I Capture the Castle*.

Both were lacking any sort of real experience at making a relationship work; any relationship, and this one had more than its share of problems. In press interviews Ginny maintains that she knew nothing of Denholm's bisexuality. Allowing for the innocence of the age and Ginny's own protected upbringing, she nonetheless realised that Denholm's fondness for some men went beyond ordinary friendship. 'I recall saying once, protectively, that I didn't know, but I did become aware. In truth, I suppose I thought it was the result of being in a prisoner-of-war camp and would no longer be a problem.'

Since Denholm told me he never had any physical relationships with men as a prisoner, she perhaps put too much emphasis on his experiences in the prison camp. He genuinely expected that life with Virginia McKenna, by popular consent an alluring beauty, would be successful. It never occurred to him to talk about sex. He was madly in love and had put Ginny on a pedestal. She was a nicely brought up girl. This was the fifties, remember, when young people were held in social confinement. Ten years later, when I came along, the naivety was still suffocating.

According to Denholm, they never made love in any way that was satisfying or fulfilling for either of them. There are friends of both who have always assumed that the marriage was not properly consummated. I can only say that in our time together Denholm never, ever, discussed it.

In reality the marriage lasted six months; on paper it was three years – there were attempts to hide the failure. Denholm went to Glasgow for the Scottish opening of *I Capture the Castle*; Ginny returned the compliment when Denholm was in *The Confidential Clerk* at the Edinburgh Festival. She saw only the second half – during the first act, she was standing in for the cast of *The Cruel Sea* at an awards ceremony.

In their rare moments together there was nearly always a

row. Having put Ginny on that pedestal, Denholm was furious when he discovered that she was less than perfect. His rage fed on jealousy, knowing as he did that Bill Travers was ever near to console his wife in her marital troubles. But when it came to open confrontation, Denholm was no match for Ginny. When words failed her she was ready to express herself with a few well-aimed domestic missiles. Five minutes was all she needed to work her way through an entire tea service – less a single cup which Denholm managed to save, albeit temporarily: it was shattered against the living-room wall, along with other wedding presents, when the argument was resumed a week later. After a particularly bitter exchange – about what, Denholm could never quite remember – he walked out, taking with him the only momento of their joint life that inspired his affection: a porcelain cat.

His anger did not subside. When it eventually came to divorce, Denholm took, for those days, the unusual step of bringing an action against Ginny, citing Bill Travers, instead of saving male pride by accepting guilt by association with an unnamed co-respondent. The suit was undefended. HUSBAND SUES THE ENGLISH ROSE ran the *News of the World* headline. That was in 1957. A few weeks later, Ginny and Bill were married and remained happily so until Bill's death in 1994.

Even after the final snap of the cord, Denholm could not face up to what had happened. He simply blocked it from his mind. During our first couple of years together, Ginny was never mentioned. For me, she might have remained forever in limbo but for an accident of casting many years later which put her and Denholm in the same film. With our meeting made inevitable, Denholm wore a brave face but I rarely saw him make such a fuss.

In the wake of *The Cruel Sea*, Denholm was tantalised by provisional offers – contingent on the money being raised – to star in yet bigger and better British movies. Korda wanted him to play Lawrence of Arabia. The idea for a biopic of the wild Arabist had been around since 1935, when Leslie Howard had been mooted for the role. The twenty-year interval had not improved the chances of putting together an adequate budget, however, and it was not until 1962 that Lawrence's screen portrait was realised, by Peter O'Toole. It was a barnstorming performance and a deserved triumph, but think what Denholm could have made of Lawrence's sexual vulnerability.

By way of compensation, Denholm had to make do with a succession of also-ran parts, supporting actors who had already confirmed their star status and were regarded as safe box office. It was as much as the British film industry could run to. In *The Heart of the Matter*, an adaptation of Graham Greene's novel, he was the self-seeking colonial official who had designs on the police commissioner's wife. It was said that Greene was dissatisfied with his book. If that was so he must have been even less happy with the movie which, true to type, watered down the moral dilemma of a Catholic convert who commits mortal sin, including adultery, out of compassion for others. When, as a finale, the police commissioner (Trevor Howard) dies heroically in a shoot-out with villains instead of, as in the book, committing suicide, the audience is left wondering what all the fuss was about.

Another case of high expectations brought low was *They Who Dare*. With Lewis Milestone, the legendary director of *All Quiet on the Western Front*, behind the camera, a commando raid on the island of Rhodes (led by Dirk Bogarde) was expected to say something profound about the nature of war. In the event, we are told that war is 10 per cent action and 90 per cent boredom, which makes for a rather dull film. Denholm put the blame squarely on Lewis Milestone, who quickly tired of Cyprus, where the film was shot, and made no secret of his eagerness to get back to Hollywood. He didn't even stay to supervise the editing, probably because he knew the film was too long and that the inevitable cuts would confuse the storyline. He was right. The title played straight into the hands of the critics, who headlined their reviews, 'How Dare They?'.

The treadmill continued with *The Ringer*, an Edgar Wallace second feature with Mai Zetterling, and *Lease of Life*, Robert Donat's penultimate film which revived *The Cruel Sea* partnership of Charles Frend as director and Eric Ambler as scriptwriter. At forty-eight, Robert Donat suffered cruelly from asthma, which made him look older and more fragile than his years. Having been forced by illness to surrender the lead in *Hobson's Choice* to John Mills, this latest movie was his attempt to prove that he had recovered both his health and his box-office appeal. But neither Robert Donat nor the screenplay were up to the challenge.

The feeling of not quite having made it in films, despite consistently respectful notices, caused Denholm to think again about the theatre as a way of building his career. Now over thirty, he was nervous of losing credibility as a young romantic lead and uncomfortably aware that one-time equal rankers such as Paul Scofield, John Neville and Peter Finch were roaring ahead.

The West End, to quote *Theatre World*, was 'still looking forward to the advent of long-awaited new young writers for

108

serious theatre'. But verse drama remained fashionable and there was the latest T. S. Eliot almost ready for casting. The producer of *The Confidential Clerk* was Henry Sherek and the director E. Martin Browne, a long-time associate and friend of the poet. Both knew Denholm's work and admired him as a verse speaker.

He was cast as the aspiring musician, pushed against his will into a business career by his supposed father, a millionaire tycoon, until he finds out that he is destined to follow in the footsteps of his real father and, like him, become a second-rate organist. The message was simple enough: if you haven't the strength to impose your own terms on life then you have to accept whatever terms are offered you. Or, as the critic Milton Shulman put it in an unfriendly review, 'Don't keep hitting your head against a brick wall'. But this being Eliot, few could accept that there was not a more profound inner meaning to be detected. Denholm insisted that the play was about loneliness, an emotion that was second nature to the character he played. The dramatist refused to be drawn into the debate. The play, he told an interviewer, 'means what it says. If it had meant something else, I would have said so'. A Hollywood cartoon showed a couple emerging from the Lyceum Theatre in Edinburgh where *The Confidential Clerk* opened. The husband is saying to his wife, 'Disappointingly comprehensible, don't you think?'

To Denholm it ranked as one of the high points of his early career and he revived his belief that it was in the theatre rather than the cinema that he would consolidate his reputation as a first-rank actor. But while he enjoyed the challenge of verse drama – 'You have to get it right,' he said, 'there's no chance to improvise or cover a gaffe' – he knew that the theatre could not survive on Eliot and Fry. The still fashionable Rattigan was with H. M. Tennent, which put Denholm out of the running, and while his contemporaries made off with the classics – Paul Rogers as Macbeth, Michael Hordern as Prospero, Richard Burton as Coriolanus – he still could not see himself in the same company. His best chance was keeping in with his contacts in the hope that they would come up with something new.

Denholm stayed loyal to E. Martin Browne, introducing him to young actors he thought were worth a try. One of them was Charles Osborne, later to achieve fame or, as he might prefer it, notoriety, as literature director of the Arts Council and as a drama and music critic. On Denholm's recommendation, Martin Browne signed up Charles for the *York Mystery Plays*. Charles remembers Martin as 'a gentle soul'.

He found it impossible to come up with images of violence when he needed them. Rehearsing a scene in which three devils are dragging Lucifer back into hell, he took the four of us aside and said: 'It needs to be much more horrifying. Lucifer must be savagely man-handled in such a way as to shock the audience. He is, after all, being dragged into hell. It has to be awe-inspiring, tremendously frightening. I want you to convey a sense of . . . of . . .' He searched for the most violent thing he could imagine, and eventually produced it. 'A sense of . . . "Come on, chaps, let's scrag him." '

A true gentleman, then, but not a new-wave leader to inspire the affection of Kenneth Tynan and other young Turks calling for dramatists 'to speak directly to the people, in the language of our time, about the realities of our time'.

A better prospect was the twenty-four-year-old Peter Hall, not long out of Cambridge, who was now the prime mover at the Arts, the theatre club just off Charing Cross Road where Denholm had appeared in *Third Person*. Eager to make his mark, he saw the opportunity to present controversial plays that defied the edicts of the Lord Chamberlain. His first offence against the establishment was André Gide's *The Immoralist*, a Broadway adaptation which, on Peter Hall's own admission, made 'a banal novel even more banal'. But since it dealt with bisexuality, it pulled in the audiences and demonstrated the idiocy of the very idea that censorship was imposed by popular approval. The follow-up was another homosexual drama and, says Peter Hall, 'the first production I was completely proud of in my own right'. This was Julien Green's *South*, a 'delicately written piece, hardly daring to verbalise its feelings' which had already enjoyed success in Paris.

The play is set in the old South on the eve of the American Civil War. The leading character is a young Polish exile, an officer in the Northern army who is desperate for the approval of the aristocratic family with whom he is staying. After *The Green Bay Tree* and *Third Person* it was natural that Peter should look to Denholm to play the social intruder. The money was awful – luncheon vouchers for rehearsals rising to £8 a week after the opening. But with the Korda money he was not exactly hard up and with the earlier than expected closing of *The Confidential Clerk* he was open to offers. It seemed to him that Peter Hall was going places. He was not a wild innovator – nor, it must be said, was Denholm – but Peter's first instinct was to follow the crowd to Paris for plays 'which deal with contemporary problems'. As a career move it paid off with the discovery of *Waiting for Godot*. His introduction of Samuel Beckett to English audiences caused a huge fuss and made him famous. It also put him on course for the Shakespeare Memorial Theatre, now the Royal Shakespeare Company, at Stratford. When Denholm eventually followed him, disobeying his own first rule not to get involved in Shakespeare, it was to lead to a disaster which, coming on top of other reverses, set him back for years.

The line-up of admiring critics for *South* persuaded Denholm that the play would transfer. Yes, it was controversial and yes, it dealt with the subject most likely to offend the Lord Chamberlain's office. But *Third Person*, which made the transition with minor changes, had surely created a precedent. Sadly, it was not that easy. *South* was not a play that could easily be adapted by cutting out a few lines. The message was either clear or unclear: if clear then it would not get a licence, if unclear it would not get an audience.

The chances of *South* moving to the West End were further reduced by a newspaper strike. Endorsements from admiring critics were lost to posterity and public interest quickly faded. It was the same with an Ealing movie *The Night My Number Came Up*, in which Denholm appeared as a fighter pilot who had lost his nerve. The plot had an uncanny resemblance to Denholm's own experience. As a bomber crew sergeant he had dreamed that his plane would come down. The film had Michael Hordern telling the same dream to a friend (Michael Redgrave) who then experiences the prophecy. It was a first-rate cliff-hanger which ever afterwards was underrated because of its poor start.

Denholm had a fall-back offer if *South*, against his expectations, failed to transfer. On paper, it was the chance of a lifetime. John Gielgud was preparing to lead a seven-month European tour with a revival of his ever-popular *Much Ado About Nothing* and a new production of *King Lear*. He had chosen a golden cast led by Peggy Ashcroft and Claire Bloom. The director for *Lear* was George Devine, who, without knowing it, was soon to lead a theatrical revolution at the Royal Court.

Denholm was asked to play Claudio in *Much Ado* and Edgar in *Lear*. His well-known antipathy to Shakespeare melted before the compliment of working with John Gielgud, an undisputedly great actor whom Denholm easily identified with – his greatest admirers actually spoke of him as a Gielgud in the making. But while the offer was flattering, he did not seriously imagine taking it up – until *South* closed. It was then that he was feeling at his most insecure. His marriage was already floundering in rows and remorse. Denholm needed someone who was open, eager, assertive; Ginny wanted patience and gentle understanding. Their domestic crisis spilled over into their careers. While Denholm was beginning to feel that luck was running out for him – where was the big break he was so frequently promised? – Ginny's progress was smooth and apparently effortless. It was almost as if by not trying too hard she tantalised producers into coming to her. In 1956, she was to win a British Film Academy Award for her role in *A Town Like Alice*.

When they went off together on publicity jaunts it was Ginny who was the main attraction. For her the cameras snapped and the fans cheered. Denholm was invariably in the background, looking sullen. One of the rare occasions he asserted himself was at the opening of the summer fête at Bury St Edmund's, an otherwise minor event made memorable by his contribution. Ginny gave a typically gracious little speech but Denholm, noting that the staff and pupils of the local grammar school were heavily represented, spoke rather more informally about the iniquities of the classroom and of certain types of schoolmaster. 'Ignorant', 'prejudicial' and 'sadistic' were a few of the choice descriptions with which he favoured a startled audience. The rumour was that he had made free at the mayor's reception and that it was the drink talking. No matter. On that day a group of disreputable boys from the lower form of King Edward VI School swore to him undying allegiance.

While Denholm was mulling over the Gielgud offer, Ginny was at the Old Vic playing Rosalind in *As You Like It* and the Queen in *Richard III*. The admiration served up to her was a spur to Denholm's ambition. Why shouldn't he do Shakespeare? Maybe he had underestimated the classics as a qualification for stardom. But donning the tights was not his style, and six months on tour was a long sentence. He agonised right up to the last moment. Even after signing he was unable to stifle his doubts. It suddenly occurred to him that trudging around the Continent for much of the year was not likely to improve his chances of saving his marriage. Of course, he should have thought of that before, but where he could not be blamed was for failing to anticipate the extraordinary nature of the production he was joining.

Nothing quite like Gielgud's *Lear* had ever been seen on a European stage. It was a highly stylised version, fashioned by the American-born Japanese sculptor and ballet designer Isamu Noguchi. Unused to classical drama, he knew only that George Devine wanted to amaze audiences with a visual concept that matched the awesome power of Shakespeare's words. This he achieved magnificently. The set consisted of sliding blocks of contrasting shapes and colours; the costumes were kimono-style, unquestionably eye-catching but also heavy and confining, with wigs that were like oversized cream puffs. The offence against tradition was too much for some critics. Lear was given a cloak scattered with holes which grew progressively larger as the play proceeded, symbolising, explained Gielgud, the disintegration of the personality. 'I see,' said Emlyn Williams, after the first night, 'a sort of Gypsy Rose Lear.'

The strain on the entire cast was horrendous and there was near revolt when Noguchi, having achieved what he thought was a splendid transformation of English theatre, left the country on some other enterprise before the dress rehearsal. But by then, Denholm had long since given up. Unable to sympathise with any aspect of the production, he found it hard to adapt to the complexity of detailed direction favoured by George Devine and by John Gielgud, an actor who by dint of seniority could hardly be expected to keep his views to himself. Denholm was the sort of actor who liked to work out all his moves in his head. Mumbling his lines as he matched words with action, he rarely gave his best in rehearsal. This irritated Devine and Gielgud, who wanted to see more of the quality of performance while there was still time to make changes. Given the intricacies of the production, their nervousness was understandable.

Denholm's first attempt at Shakespeare since he had

played Macbeth in Stalag VIII B ended in humiliation. Ever reluctant to say anything against any colleague, John Gielgud is nevertheless driven to admit that 'Denholm behaved very badly in rehearsals, when he appeared to take very little interest in the two parts he accepted, and would not learn his lines or take direction.' The decision was made: Denholm had to go. He couldn't quite believe that he had been fired, even when Richard Easton was hired in his place. And even when the company returned to London after the European tour, Gielgud recalls that Denholm 'further embarrassed us by appearing at the theatre and hanging about in the dressing rooms'.

The truth, of course, was that Denholm had no idea where to turn. His marriage had collapsed and so, apparently, had his career. After his failure to meet Gielgud's challenge, he went off to Manchester to appear in *The Delegate*, a light comedy fronted by Naunton Wayne and Eva Bartok. It failed to come in to the West End, a predictable disappointment which only seemed to confirm Denholm's rapid demotion. John Gielgud was unforgiving – in the nicest possible way. 'When I worked with him, many years afterwards, we got on perfectly well, though I never felt really at ease with him. I thought he was acting extremely well. But he seemed to have a bad chip on his shoulder and was never a very congenial colleague.'

Many would disagree with this last comment, though not, perhaps, with John Gielgud's perceptive pay-off: 'Maybe his success came too late to please him.'

There is nothing on record to show what George Devine thought of Denholm, but it is a fact that Denholm's banner-waving as an actor interested in new drama was studiously ignored by the English Stage Company until 1972, when he was cast in John Osborne's adaptation of *Hedda Gabler*. By then, he had said many harsh words about the Royal Court. The English Stage Company was a very British institution in that its success was thanks largely to a succession of accidents. It was started by a schoolmaster and a writer who shared a vague idea that London should have a showcase for new writers. The name was taken from the already well-established English Opera Group. A wealthy businessman with no previous interest in the theatre struck a cheap deal on leasing the Royal Court after negotiations on the first choice, the Kingsway, fell through. George Devine was appointed artistic director. An ad in the *Stage* appealing for new plays brought in a clutch of well-thumbed manuscripts. Only one held George's interest. For £25 he bought the option on a play called *Look Back in Anger* by a young out-of-work actor, John Osborne.

It is part of the folklore of the theatre that Kenneth Tynan was alone in detecting the brilliance of *Look Back in Anger*. His ecstatic review in the *Observer* ('I doubt if I could love anyone who did not wish to see *Look Back in Anger*. It is the best young play of its decade') gave an almighty push to the new drama and the verdict of the overnight critics was friendly and encouraging. The fiercest opposition came from within the English Stage Company with Ronald Duncan, an exponent of verse drama, leading the attack on what he saw as the same old West End platitudes served up in a different guise. 'Instead of the Shaftesbury Avenue duchess fiddling with her flower vase we have Jimmy Porter picking his nose in public.'

This was Denholm's first reaction too. He railed against

the 'scratch your arse' school of acting and dismissed kitchen-sink drama. 'I knew where the kitchen sink was, all right. I just didn't want to sit in it.' It was particularly galling for him when Larry took the lead – and was a vast success – in John Osborne's second hit play, *The Entertainer*. Of course, Denholm was furious with himself for having antagonised George Devine. But he was also smart enough to realise that what was happening at the Royal Court would revolutionise British theatre. Fry and Eliot had already lost their appeal; Rattigan and Coward were on the slope. The post-war younger generation, politically aware, eager for change, rejected dilettante drama with its talent to amuse, and to say nothing in particular. The Royal Court of John Osborne and Arnold Wesker spoke directly to a new audience, and in accents not usually heard at RADA.

'I was "tennis, anyone?" ', said Denholm. 'My middle-class tone was despised. I was passed over. Actors like Peter O'Toole, Albert Finney and Alan Bates whizzed past me when I had been in the business for fifteen years.'

Actors who were used to waiting weeks or months to join the ranks of working-class bit-part players suddenly found themselves in hot demand. As Peter Vaughan says, 'We knew our time had come.' Much later on, he and Denholm shared credits in several productions which called for a strong, menacing presence (Peter) bearing down on fragile vulnerability (Denholm). But for now, writers could not think of ways to mix the two styles, and Denholm was out of fashion.

It was disappointment of expectations that he suffered, not real hardship. On the money from the Korda contract he was able to live comfortably and he felt no need to economise on his nights out at expensive restaurants and

West End drinking clubs. But he was increasingly conscious of time passing. The marriage he had confidently assumed would lift him to another dimension had, in cold reality, brought him lower than at any point since the war. It set him off on a wild pursuit of romance which gave him a diary full of lovers of both sexes but nothing in the way of lasting happiness.

There were offers of work, more, sometimes, than Denholm could handle. But the quality was suspect and very often it seemed that he was used because his recognisable name and face came cheaper than the usual celebrity rates. As he told Dan Farson, he would have been ready to take lesser roles in better plays or films but his agent resisted even when Denholm protested that if he was a concert pianist looking through a glass wall at a Steinway he would be desperate enough to play scales let alone Rachmaninov. 'I'd have played the butler, any damned thing, but he didn't understand.'

Not that Denholm's judgement was all that reliable. He and his agent were as one in wanting him to star in the movie *Pacific Destiny*, and they were both wrong. Nowadays, *Pacific Destiny* would be called *A Year in Samoa*. It was that sort of film based on that sort of book. Denholm had to follow in the tracks of Sir Arthur Grimble, a colonial civil servant whose memories of governing a tropical paradise appealed strongly to armchair romantics. The best that can be said of the film was that it was fun to do. Denholm used to say it was like being sent on the holiday of a lifetime with all expenses paid.

Among the small cast was Michael Hordern, already playing the curmudgeonly elder. He recalls:

We were staying in a ropey old hotel called Aggie Grey's Guest House, which was the model for the one in the musical *South Pacific*. Aggie Grey was a half-caste lady of great character who ran the guest house rather like the matron of a boarding school. We were taken under the wing of a Polish chap who was a resident of the guest house, had made it his home and knew a good deal about the island and surrounding waters and took us out 'goggling'. It was an island with a lovely coral lagoon all around it, about four or five feet of deep, warmish water full of sparkling little coloured fish. Clambering over the reef you suddenly found yourself in very deep water and the sparkling little fish were replaced by monsters – sharks and all sorts. The Polish chap instructed us to punch any sharks on the nose and if we met an octopus to turn it inside out. So, trying to remember which was which and not punch the octopus on the nose or try to turn the shark inside out, we swam into the Pacific with our snorkels, following our instructor like ducklings. At night there were village dances around fires. The Samoans' singing reminded me very much of the marvellous choral singing of the Maoris.

The revelation for Denholm was the liberated view the Samoans had of sex. It didn't seem to bother them in the sense that they didn't worry about how people had sex, or how often, or with whom, just as long as they enjoyed it. Denholm went wild. Years of frustration and guilt were lifted from him. In a far-off country with money to spend and a romantic cachet attached to his craft, he found himself happily besieged by eager young girls – and boys.

Stories of what was going on in Samoa got back to London, where the gossip writers waited eagerly for Denholm to return home. The hero of their picture-book wedding had some explaining to do. They reckoned without Denholm's skill (and priceless asset in later years) of turning away unwelcome questions with such concerned innocence as to disarm the interrogator while remaining friendly. To the admiration of his colleagues, it really did look as if Denholm had got away with it. That was before they knew of the arrival of Princess Mary Papali'l.

Sensual libertarians the Samoans may have been, but they were also possessed of a strong sense of bonding. The expression of love was not just for a night out under the stars. For a Samoan romantic there was nothing strange in journeying round the world to be with the man she loved. Mary wanted to marry the handsome English actor. Back on home ground, Denholm was not at all sure what he wanted. On a practical level, since he was already married there was no immediate prospect of a second wife. But even when Ginny was removed from the frame – and this could be only a matter of time – he was not eager to fill her place, even with a Samoan beauty of high birth. The renewal of responsibility terrified him and, anyway, his few weeks on a Pacific island had shown him what there was to be gained by remaining free. He loved Mary but he could name quite a few others he loved, or thought he loved.

There was another question. How would the family, especially his mother, see this? Around this time, she was on an extended tour of Africa, winging back letters that revealed her to be an enthusiastic traveller.

My dear Denholm,
How *did* you find that Xmas card? I have hooted with laughter ever since receiving it and last night in the hotel, at dinner, I looked at it again and everyone thought I must be mad as I was quaking with giggles. The expression on the Claus face is the most vocal thing I have ever seen. I am writing from the hotel in Livingstone where we are stopping for a short time for coffee and 'pennies' after our excursion to the Victoria Falls. I never thought I would live to see them and they are quite fantastic. We flew over the Falls before landing and saw a beautiful rainbow in the spray. The spray can be seen for miles like mist rising from the valley. I can't help wondering what Livingstone must have felt when he discovered them. Believe it or not, a charming woman sitting next to me in the plane is a great friend of Mary Norton and a great admirer of Dr Nicol. Of course, we have talked and talked and will meet in London I think to have a reunion with Mary. So glad you are busy. I am looking forward to seeing you again. Must end now as we are off once more to catch a launch down the Zambezi to an island where we have tea (lunch on the launch). I am told you are lucky if you're getting anything to eat on the island as the baboons snatch your food from your hands.
Your Mama xxx

Denholm was not misled into believing that Mama's African adventure, however exciting, would enable her to adapt to having a coloured girl as a daughter-in-law. He was himself aware of the power of that most stifling of middle-class inhibitions, the fear of what other people might say. The reserve that had fallen from him in Samoa was now, once again, building up like a protective shield. In trying to rationalise his feelings to his princess, he was helped by her dawning awareness of some of the drawbacks of living in England. Like it could be very cold in winter. She had followed Denholm, recalls Michael Hordern, 'carrying, I believe, just a shopping bag with her essentials'. Denholm bought her clothes but they were not greatly to her liking. She began to pine for the simple life.

While the private romance was being played out, Denholm's agent was deputised to present the public image. 'There is no love affair,' he told the press and, holding a straight face, 'Princess Papali'l is over here to study English. She will return to Samoa as soon as she has passed her examination.' The official version was reported deadpan, giving great pleasure to the many who could read between the lines. There was no follow-up. The story died when, soon afterwards, the disillusioned lady went home. Denholm was lucky. The experience should have warned him not to make vague promises in bed. But that was a lesson he was never able to learn.

The Oriental look continued to feature heavily in his love-life. He was often seen with Tsai (otherwise Jacqui) Chan, star of *The World of Suzie Wong*, who, in turn, was often seen with Anthony Armstrong Jones, now better known as Lord Snowdon. And there was a second Polynesian who managed to unsettle him. He met Eileen when he returned to Samoa for a short holiday. Though born on the island, she too was on a flying visit. Her home was New Orleans, where she had a husband and a young son. She was back in

Samoa to see her parents and to tell them the good news that she was expecting a second child. None of this deterred her from falling in love with Denholm or him from falling in love with her. Their affair continued by correspondence with Denholm fearing what might happen if history repeated itself but doing nothing to prevent it. Eileen came to England in 1960 and she and Denholm lived together for several weeks when he was fast falling to the lowest point in his career. It wasn't long before she recognised that her heart was back in New Orleans; and it wasn't long afterwards that she followed it.

Denholm was obsessed with the fear of losing control of his life. From his declaration of undying allegiance to Ginny he had swung to an extreme of random affairs, offering and expecting love with every encounter but panicking if the question of marriage arose. The wild gyrations of his career – high hopes and crushing disappointments – did nothing for his peace of mind. He did still try for interesting work with interesting people who were not afraid of new ideas. So strong is the hold of the Royal Court on the mythology of British theatre that it is easy to forget that beyond Sloane Square there were other writers, producers and actors with something worthwhile to say. The margin of luck was often narrower than we assume.

A fair example was Leo Lehman's play about the treatment of political refugees – highly topical in 1956, the year of the crushing of the Hungarian Revolution. The slightly unfortunate title, *Who Cares?*, was resisted as an obvious put-down – the topic was too serious for levity. Instead the critics ran with the debate on how far a liberal sympathiser, in this case an academic who takes in a young refugee, should

124

go in helping a political dissident. Alec Clunes, who had been director of the Arts Theatre when Denholm was in *Third Person*, was the professor and Denholm the unsettling house guest. The play had its defects, not least a romantic sub-plot which distracted from the main argument. But as a first play (Leo Lehman was only twenty-r ne and himself a Polish refugee who had spent the war on the run) it clearly showed great promise. Denholm was sure that it could lead somewhere. That it failed, never to be heard of again, was a back-handed tribute to *Look Back in Anger*. With John Osborne having transferred from the Royal Court to the West End, audiences had their ration of political debate.

Another unexpected flop – unexpected then, that is, if obvious now – was *The Long Echo*. Loosely based on the Burgess and Maclean spy scandal (again, how topical could you get?), Leslie Storm's play centred on the woman who was left behind. Denholm was the go-between – whether romantic idealist or ruthless manipulator was never made clear – who had to persuade the defector's wife to follow him through the Iron Curtain. Having earned the best notices in *Who Cares?*, Denholm was savaged in *The Long Echo*. The critics said he was acting down to a bad script.

In 1957, Denholm was back with Peter Hall, the only serious rival to the innovators at the Royal Court. Peter had already made his name with *Waiting for Godot* and *Waltz of the Toreadors*, both of which had transferred to successful West End runs. Now he was to try his luck with a convoluted piece by Tennessee Williams called *Camino Real*. It was the first production under the banner of the grandly named International Playwrights Theatre, Peter's attempt to make the world his stage. The money was put up by Lars Schmidt, a Scandinavian impresario. The chief drawback to *Camino Real* was that it had already failed on Broadway where, on the author's own admission, 'people stamped out of the theater and demanded their money back'. This was no proof of a bad play but *Camino Real* was, by general agreement, a difficult play.

The build-up to opening night was a publicist's dream. The writer, trailing controversy, flew in to deliver his views on life and art; Peter Hall, the golden boy of the theatre, was encouraged to speculate on his future and a starry cast, which included Diana Wyngard, Harry Andrews, Elizabeth Seal and Denholm, was paraded for the cameras. Late of the family musical *The Pyjama Game*, Elizabeth Seal was cast as a Mexican prostitute who believes that her purity is renewed every full moon. In what must be one of the happier examples of typecasting it put her in line to play the lead in *Irma La Douce*.

Returning from America where he had played in a television production of Anouilh's *The Lark* (an early colour production), Denholm was met at Waterloo Station by Elizabeth Seal and a contingent of photographers. The reception, even if carefully prearranged, with Elizabeth wearing a captivating smile that suggested more than what was, in fact, a nodding acquaintanceship, took Denholm by pleasant surprise. Could this be the change of luck everybody said would eventually come his way? The answer was a resounding No. While the direction and acting were praised, the play itself died. Even the *Stage*, the trade paper of the theatre, in those days not usually given to unfavourable reviews, was compelled to admit that *Camino Real* 'was not Tennessee Williams at his best'. Other critics expressed themselves more stridently. 'Too arty, too feverish, too decadent', wrote John Barber, while Kenneth Hurren declared it to be 'a work of such paralysing vacuity that I am resentful of having to discuss it'.

An awful silence fell on the box office. Taking a favourite line from the play, Denholm said he felt 'like the milk on the doorstep when people have left for the summer'. He did register a compliment from the author. How clever he was, observed Tennessee Williams, to put on an Australian accent. It added greatly to his part. Denholm guiltily accepted the praise. Only he knew that he was trying to speak American.

He stayed with Peter Hall for two Anouilh one-act plays, *Madame de Bouvier* and *Traveller Without Luggage*, the first a curtain-raiser written specially for the Arts Theatre production, the second a more substantial piece in which Denholm played an amnesic soldier in a tug of war between several families, each of whom claims him as a long-lost son. In a process of self-discovery he hates what he finds out about himself. 'For long periods he was wearing an expression of puzzlement, of straining at memory and trying not to remember,' wrote an admirer, 'a difficult assignment which he is well equipped to meet.'

Denholm revelled in the power that Anouilh presented him to hold an audience. After *A Sleep of Prisoners*, these were among his finest moments in the theatre, moments when he felt an almost divine inspiration.

But I couldn't hold it. I felt my ego was in the way. I felt it was all up to me to sustain this rattling silence which had enveloped the audience. When you get on to this level with them, it's almost nothing to do with you.

127

It's a state that you're in. I couldn't sustain it. I wanted to do something vulgar to break it, to give them a chance to breathe again. It happened both times, I'm convinced, when there was a high barometric pressure. I'm a great believer in people's spirits being lifted or depressed by high or low pressure. I don't think you can get these moments of catalytic inspiration, the spirit that comes through you and you're taken, unless there's this barometric situation. When the clouds are heavy and low, everybody's spirits are down, down, down.

The experience of acting in *Traveller Without Luggage* convinced Denholm of the virtue of intimate theatre and, by extension, of television.

The great thing about television is that you don't have to throw your energies so far, you see. If you are in a large theatre you have actually got to bellow. And the actual act of bellowing destroys this delicate crystal of the idea and the thought. And of course, with a television camera, you can chuck it two feet or less. You have a microphone two inches away from you, you can breathe, so you can almost think it, and almost without speaking, as it were, because the camera sees everything. Once you've come to terms with cameras. And that takes a bit of doing. You have to hide from them because you know they see everything.

Denholm's grappling with the complexities of Anouilh and his satisfaction at having achieved the extraordinary suggests a singlemindedness that is at odds with the turmoil of his personal life. The simple truth is that he was at last able to relax outside the theatre because he was looking forward to several lucrative weeks in Spain.

Whatever appeal the assignment had, mind-stretching it was not. *Scent of Mystery* had a single distinguishing feature that set it apart from all other movies: it was the first – and last – 'smelly'. With cinema audiences falling drastically in the face of competition from television, producers were racking their imaginations for sales gimmicks that would attract customers back to the big screen. Some ideas, like Cinema-Scope, proved their worth and made a lasting impact on film-making. Smell-O-Vision, and its rival, Aromarama, most definitely did not. As *Variety* had predicted, the smelly was nothing more than a passing whiff.

The equipment for Smell-O-Vision, which pumped out aromas into the auditorium to suit the action or mood of the film, was expensive and unreliable. For *Scent of Mystery*, audiences were invited to participate in the detection of the villain by identifying the smell of his pipe tobacco. Trouble was, when it came to the denouement, pipe tobacco smelled like – well, whatever it smelled like, it wasn't pipe tobacco. Mike Todd Jr, in a vain effort to match the entrepreneurial flair of his father, presided over this eccentric experiment with good humour and a readiness, not at all common among producers, to take responsibility for failure.

It must be said that the achievement of great acting was not one of his priorities. The cast was chosen on a permutation of famous faces and modest fees so that, for instance, Peter Lorre, well past his prime but instantly recognisable, filled the undemanding role of a Moroccan taxi driver. He, at last, was on screen much of the time. Other well-knowns made fleeting appearances: Diana Dors, Leo McKern, Liam Redmond, Peter Arne and Michael Trubshawe, he of the handlebar moustache, the all-English character actor who, even now, is instantly associated with upper-class military roles. Even Elizabeth Taylor, the director's stepmother, made a surprise guest appearance. Denholm took top billing.

While he was enjoying the Spanish sun, Denholm had a cable from Peter Hall, who was now firmly in charge of the Shakespeare Memorial Theatre at Stratford. Everyone recognised Peter as an entrepreneur of huge energy but his capacity for innovation, and his achievements in a single year, were to leave the theatre establishment breathless. His coup was to lease a second theatre, the Aldwych, as a London base, a move that was opposed by West End managers, who were fearful of losing their monopoly. They were outmanoeuvred. Reaffirming the breakaway from the provinces, the Shakespeare Memorial Theatre became the Royal Shakespeare Theatre, host to the Royal Shakespeare Company, a title, as someone told Peter Hall, that had 'practically everything going for it except God'.

To give cohesion to his bold enterprise, he wanted a permanent repertory of actors whose work on a range of plays, at Stratford and at the Aldwych, would be supported by guest stars. Here again he found himself at odds with the West End. But the plan, much the same as that favoured by George Devine at the Royal Court, made commercial sense as the only way of competing with Tennent's. Binkie Beaumont recognised the threat. Having been persuaded on to the Stratford board of governors to reassure actors venturing out of London, he now resigned in protest against Peter Hall's refusal to keep to his home ground. It was not as if the newcomer was limiting himself to Shakespeare: young dramatists like John Arden, Robert Bolt, Peter Shaffer and John Whiting were commissioned to write plays for the Aldwych. Gone were the days when all roads led to Tennent's.

Word went quickly round the business that the RSC had a fistful of contracts to hand out. It did something for Denholm's self-esteem that he was among the first on Peter Hall's list. And he was in very good company: Richard Johnson, Ian Bannen, Eric Porter, Clifford Rose, Ian Richardson, Patrick Allen and Paul Hardwick were among the talents attracted to Stratford. Peter Hall certainly knew his actors.

To balance the compliment of being asked, a compliment that more than made up for his rejection, real or imagined, by the Royal Court, there was Denholm's old prejudice against Shakespeare, lately reinforced by the falling-out with John Gielgud. Tipping the scales was Denholm's nervousness at all the talk of long-term commitments. In his professional life he had already become something of a loner. He did his work to the best of his ability and circumstances and played fair by his fellow actors, but he was a long way short of handing over his entire life to the muse. There were few actors among his close friends and he was not given to agonising assessments of his performances. A job was a job was a job. He wrote back to Peter politely turning aside the offer with excuses of other commitments.

It is a fair measure of Peter's regard for Denholm that he did not take no for an answer. Instead, he went to Denholm's agent, Philip Pearman, appealing to him to use his influence in favour of Stratford. This put Philip in a difficult position. His clear preference was for Denholm to pursue his film career – that was where the money was – but knowing that *Pacific Destiny* had faded and that *Scent of Mystery* was not about to win any Oscars, he couldn't be sure that Denholm would hold his market value. It would be foolish to reject Stratford out of hand when there was always the risk of not having any other choice. Philip wrote to Denholm at his hotel in Malaga. The letter is dated 29 April 1959.

My dear Denholm,

Peter Hall tells me that he has cabled you offering you Troilus (in *Troilus and Cressida*), Bassanio (in *The Merchant of Venice*), Hortensio (in *The Taming of the Shrew*) and Speed (in *Two Gentlemen of Verona*). I do not think anyone can do anything with Troilus and if his casting of Pandarus and Helen really is what he intends at the time of going to press, I think the lovers can very easily get overlooked.

Peter Hall says he hopes I will be 'on his side' about this offer to you, but really I must be on yours, obviously, and I cannot think that it is a good follow-up to the film! We did rather go into this before you went away and agreed we could always put the blame on British Lion for your refusing a season at Stratford, without anybody getting offended.

If I were you, I would stall and say that you cannot make up your mind until the end of your film in Spain and by that time you will know very probably how the film is likely to turn out for you and this may help your decision re. Stratford.

The advice was sound but it left Denholm the delicate task

My mother – the baby – being held by my grandmother, while my grandfather in the rocking chair looks on, in front of the family home in Wilmington, North Carolina, 1905.

My terribly elegant grandmother – my Mom's mother.

My father Ted with my Mom in their engagement photo, outside the family home in North Carolina, with a Model T Ford in the background.

My father Ted Robinson Jr at work in 1949. By this time he had five children to feed.

Ted (temporarily a movie critic) with Wyatt Earp alias actor Hugh O'Brian.

My twin Mark, cousin Tommy, little sister Joyce and myself on the beach in North Carolina.

My twin brother Mark and myself. I was 'roped' to stop me from taking unannounced trips.

Our Uncle Arthur's jeep in Long Beach, North Carolina. Mom on front, Ted standing at the back and my older sister Joanna in the front seat with various cousins in 1951.

Susan desperately seeking work as a model, 1961.

Denholm in the coat with the fake-fur collar he was wearing when I met him. He was appearing in *Write Me a Murder*, New York City 1961.

In the Libyan desert in *Station Six Sahara*, just before we were married. I was nineteen, he was thirty-nine.

Denholm and me on his thirty-ninth birthday with, from left, Peter van Eyck, Carroll Baker and Mario Adorf.

Celebrating his fortieth birthday on location with me and Alan Bates during the shooting of *Nothing But the Best*. I gave a surprise party later.

Jennifer just out of hospital, 1964.

Exchanging roles in *Ring Round the Moon* with Farley Granger on a
National Repertory Company tour, 1964.

Denholm was one of the first readers on BBC's *Jackanory* series and this
studio-bound publicity still marked the occasion. (*Photo courtesy British
Broadcasting Corporation.*)

On location in Stockholm in *The Sea Gull* with, from left, James Mason (in the wheelchair), Simone Signoret and Vanessa Redgrave.

The cast of *Too Late the Hero*. Denholm, seated centre, with, among others, Michael Caine, Cliff Robertson, Ronald Fraser, Harry Andrews, Ian Bannen and Lance Percival.

We decided to split up in Los Angeles where Denholm was completing studio work on *Too Late the Hero* in 1969. Our separation lasted one week.

of compiling a letter to Peter that was a long way from acceptance while stopping just short of rejection. He did what all actors do in these circumstances. He raised the ante. Troilus and Bassanio were too low down the pecking order of Shakespearian roles to be really tempting, he told Peter. When would he get the chance to play meaty characters like Iago or Richard III? As for Speed in *Two Gentlemen of Verona*, the part was much inferior to that of Valentine. If he was in that production, Valentine he would have to be.

The response from Peter was a model example of the art of subtle persuasion. He agreed with alacrity to Denholm playing Valentine if that was what he wanted, and made numerous other suggestions in an attempt to meet his demands. 'All this *is* blackmail,' he concluded, 'and because we know each other so well, it's better that your next refusal is unjustified! Just write "Dear Peter, No," and I shall understand. But *do* do some Shakespeare soon, though I shall be furious if it is at the Old Vic!'

Denholm could never explain convincingly why, in the end, he said 'Yes'. His seducer had a shining reputation which attracted outstanding talents but there was more to it than that. Denholm's failure to achieve the stardom he had craved as a protégé of Ustinov and Olivier; the hazardous state of British theatre and cinema, which offered few decent roles for actors who were putting on the years; the need to feel wanted, always a strong motivating force but made overwhelming by the final break with Ginny: all these emotions must have tugged at him. But the deciding factor could equally have been something quite simple, like a favourable comparison with Rex Harrison that Peter slipped skilfully into his letter. Whatever the reason, Denholm was hooked. He spent much of the next year wriggling painfully.

Looking back on Peter Hall's first year at Stratford, what he achieved was barely short of a miracle. But his credits were chiefly organisational. The weaknesses revealed themselves onstage, in full view of customers and critics. In a premiere season described by Peter himself as one of 'bumps and disasters', the hardest bump and the epic disaster was the opening production. As one of the *Two Gentlemen of Verona* (by his own wish he played Valentine), Denholm was defeated by his lines, by his costume, which made him look hilariously and inappropriately camp, and by the tendency of Derek Godfrey, as the other gentleman, to lose track of what was going on. Chatting to Diana Rigg in the wings, a miserable Denholm, wrapped in a raincoat, predicted 'The audience will piss on me.'

The best that anyone could say was that Denholm was miscast. He was simply not the swashbuckling character liable to find himself leading a band of outlaws. But the critics were not out to find excuses for Denholm. A relatively mild review concluded that the best performance was given by the scenery; elsewhere the distinction was given to Duff the dog who played Crab the dog. For his second turn, Denholm passed unnoticed as Bassanio. All eyes were on Peter O'Toole as a businessman's version of Shylock, convinced of the logic of his own accountancy. Denholm had expected to support Paul Scofield, but Paul had pulled out at the last moment. As an inspired second choice, Peter O'Toole was high on his triumph as Hamlet at Bristol and as Private Bamforth in *The Long and the Short and the Tall* at the Royal Court. It is not hard to imagine how Denholm reacted to the cast change. All he had in common with the newcomer was a fondness for hard liquor, a slender bond which snapped when O'Toole was scared by his doctor into cutting out booze. Instead, he made great show of downing large quantities of milk.

The O'Toole personality was of hurricane force and could be just as destructive. It got so that Denholm could hardly bear to be in the same room. 'I get awfully nervous with the kind of actor who looks as though he might be about to hit you, even though he never does.' It didn't help when rumours started flying that O'Toole had been picked for David Lean's epic *Lawrence of Arabia*, a role for which Denholm had been heavily tipped not six years earlier. Onstage, Denholm found it 'very, very difficult' to work with the younger actor. 'He acts at you and it becomes a sort of battle. He is just completely overpowering.'

In London he would have had diversions and friendly shoulders to cry on but at Stratford he was expected to lead a monastic life. 'It was,' he said, 'my idea of hell, stuck in a cottage in the middle of a ploughed field and having to work every day with people who talked about nothing but the Bard.' He was not averse to working for little money if the project attracted him (many of his later films prove that), but at Stratford the combination of hard graft and low reward demoralised him. 'You never get any spare time; you're rehearsing from dawn to dusk and then you play the evening and the curtain comes down five minutes after the pubs have closed. And you don't get enough money to live on.'

But that wasn't the whole story. What Denholm held back from journalists was the single biggest cause of his unhappiness. For much of his year at Stratford he was living with

Eileen, his Samoan lover who had left her husband and family in New Orleans to be with him. It was the worst possible time and the worst possible place for the inevitable agonising about their future. Unable to resist an expression of love, Denholm knew that he was making trouble for himself but went ahead anyway, defying Peter Hall to find fault. As Denholm told it to me, Peter was unsympathetic, accusing him of allowing his private life to interfere with his work, even making snide references to Eileen and remarking on her unsuitability as a consort to a distinguished actor. Her appearance at a rehearsal led to a huge bust-up, with Denholm accusing Peter of behaving like a schoolmaster (the strongest insult he could muster) and Peter threatening to blackball Denholm for future work. But there were those, like Diana Rigg, who felt that Denholm was trying for a row to work off his frustration with a dying affair. Away from Samoa, the delectable Eileen had lost her bloom.

Truth has as much to do with feelings as with words. Whoever said what and to whom, Denholm felt patronised by Stratford. He knew that he had made a stupid mistake in letting romance overrule practicalities; he knew also that personal troubles were damaging his professional reputation. But he could not bring himself to admit the fact. He simply wanted out.

A letter from a friend in New York gave him the will. He had always managed to get work in America; the pay was good, and the excitement of the city would come as a welcome antidote to rural seclusion. He went out and bought himself a one-way air ticket. He was just two months away from meeting Susan Robinson.

Part Two

6

Desperately Seeking Susan

5 January 1961 is a date that comes easily to mind. It was the day that Denholm asked me to marry him. I was rehearsing a show, nothing very grand, and another song. It was early evening and snowing when Denholm came round to the theatre. I must have been in chatty mood because I remember that I did most of the talking as we walked, arm in arm, out on to the windy street and battled our way round the corner to a greasy spoon café.

We had hot coffee in front of us and I was still rabbiting on when Denholm broke the flow. 'Listen to me,' he said. 'I've got an idea and I want to know what you feel about it. I think we should get married.'

There is nothing much else I can tell you about that evening. Except that I did say Yes. And that I had to go back to rehearsal. I sang 'Lorelei'.

Did I know what I was getting into? The question never occurred to me. I was nineteen, naive and madly in love. The next step was to tell my parents.

We were not what you would call a conventional family, thank God. My mother, Sally, one of seven children, was brought up a strict Catholic in a well-off Southern family with servants to do the cooking and washing. She studied art, became a fashion illustrator and a more than competent watercolour artist. My paternal grandfather edited the *Cleveland Plain Dealer* and my father, Ted, was brought up surrounded by writers and journalists, so it was natural for him to step into the shoes of his own father. He did make a form of protest when at sixteen he ran away from home and got as far as France before his parents found him and brought him back. I don't know what age he was when he began his career in journalism but he did tell me that he started as a police reporter.

My parents met while my mother was on a study course in Province Town, Massachusetts, where my grandparents had a summer home. In spite of the fact that my father was agnostic he had fallen in love with a Catholic and agreed, in marriage, to let his children be brought up as Catholics. Sally and Ted produced five children, including twins, me and my brother Mark who, defying chronology and confusing friends, always claims that he is ten years my junior.

Mark and I were conceived in New York City and born in Cleveland. This being 1942, Ted was persuaded that New York might become prey to a Japanese air attack. His wife, he decided, would be safer further west, while he stayed behind and looked after my two older siblings (with the help of one of my mother's family servants imported from North Carolina). Ted was then a journalist for *Time* magazine. He was also a manic depressive and in between working for *Time* and *Newsweek* over the years he suffered several nervous breakdowns. This meant we spent our formative years commuting between New York City (good times) and North Carolina (bad times). In the good times, when Ted had a regular pay cheque, we lived comfortably with plenty to eat. When he was in the throes of depression, standards plummeted. It made all the difference between steak one day and baked beans the next. It came to the point where I couldn't face a tin of beans without feeling ill. It was a fact of my life that Denholm found hard to accept. For him, baked beans with sausages and eggs constituted the best meal on earth.

I went to school at the Sacred Heart Academy in Washington DC. My parents decided that North Carolina at that time did not offer enough in the way of high school education, and the fact that my mother's sister was living in Washington contributed to the decision to uproot the whole family in the interests of a better education. My father was now working for *Newsweek* in New York City, which was only two hours away, and that meant he could be with us at weekends.

I hated the uniform, a rough, shapeless serge, and found the ritual, including morning confession, for which I had to invent sins, faintly ridiculous. My lasting resentment was that my teachers – all nuns, of course – ignored my desire to learn languages. Instead, they noted that I was a good basketball player. Much against my will they made me captain of the team with time off to practise. As a result, I missed out on French and Spanish. A few years later, circumstances gave me a second chance, and although it was a struggle I am now happy to speak in Spanish. Needless to say, I no longer play basketball.

From my early teens I was a sucker for showbusiness and,

through Ted's connections, I was able to find the antidote to classroom tedium on *Saturday Night Jamboree*, a television show for rockers and rollers led by Johnny Cash, and on its Wednesday counterpart, *Record Hoppers*. Whenever I went to the studios I had a chaperone to watch over me, to take me there and bring me back. How times change.

My first, modest success as an actress was in *Riders to the Sea*, a play that was entered in an inter-state competition. I carried off the award for Best Supporting Newcomer. Ted was in the audience to share my triumph. His pleasure at seeing his daughter walk away with the prize made it a good moment to pop the question. I told him I wanted to go to drama school. He didn't even pause to think about it. 'OK,' he said. 'If you want to act, act.'

So I signed on at the American Academy of Dramatic Arts in New York. My mother was nervous at letting me loose in the big city but had to agree that Washington had made me streetwise. I was still recovering from a beating up (eight girls, one boy) which left me with scars on my face and crowns on my teeth. After that, New York held no terrors. I knew how to look after myself.

Where I came adrift was in not knowing how the other half lived. As a good convent girl my knowledge of sexual matters was slight and what little I thought I knew came from those romantic novels which held back on the practical details. Love was an idealised state of being. Sex didn't really come into it. Following through this curious logic, it is hardly surprising that I failed to draw a line between different expressions of love or between heterosexual and homosexual love. Love was a bond; it kept people together. That had to be good.

I was storing up trouble for myself and no mistake. As I was soon to discover, the girl I shared a flat with – 63 West Side, just up from Columbus Arch – wanted more from me than best-buddy companionship. Misreading all the signs and unaware that I was causing her pain, I allowed a show of affection that must, to her, have promised far more than I was ready to deliver.

I was every bit as naive in my efforts to understand Denholm. He was never anything but totally honest. It was just that I failed to get the point. A few days after he had set the church bells ringing in my head, he took me out to a small restaurant where he knew we wouldn't be recognised by friends or, in his case, fans. He started immediately by saying 'I've been in love with other women, of course.' He was very patient, building up to what he really wanted to say. 'But I want you to understand something. I've had male lovers. Does that shock you?'

No, it didn't shock or surprise me. I could have given him chapter headings to any one of a dozen Mary Renault novels which showed that love between men or love between women came high on the list of human virtues.

'Why should it worry me?' I asked. 'The women and men you have loved are part of you. If it wasn't for them I might not love you as much as I do.'

If I had been a little older and wiser I might have pressed the inquiry. If a man falls in love with another man how does he show his love? When and how does spirit become flesh? Denholm made no attempt to enlighten me. He assumed I knew more than I was letting on. I was a good enough actress to put on a convincing show of worldly sophistication.

I have done with excuses. If I come across as a dingbat,

so be it. I was only nineteen years of age, for God's sake. And it was barely opening time for the liberated sixties. But even if Denholm had spelled out every detail of the love of man for man, I would not have doubted his love for me. I was flattered by his honesty. What would have shocked me was that, in telling me of his homosexual affairs, Denholm was confessing to what was then a serious offence, a crime for which he could have gone down for a lengthy prison sentence. No wonder he was afraid; no wonder he kept the door closed on his other life.

We decided not to tell anyone of our engagement – at least, not immediately. 'The last thing we want is a lot of unnecessary fuss,' said Denholm. I agreed. A quiet engagement and a quiet wedding suited me fine. 'Of course, we have to let a few friends into the secret,' he added.

One of the friends Denholm told was the actor Edward Mulhare. The venue he chose for his revelation was P. J. Clark's, a restaurant highly favoured by showbusiness people and, naturally enough, by showbusiness journalists. The need to share good news overcame discretion. He did not even bother to check who was sitting at the next table. It was only when he had made a clean breast of his secret and was receiving Edward's loud and hearty congratulations that their neighbouring diner turned and introduced himself as Leonard Lyon, the *New York Post* gossip columnist. The formality was unnecessary – Denholm immediately recognised one of New York's leading gossip writers. He did try talking his way out of trouble by openly admitting to Lyon that our engagement was no more than an understanding between us, that he had not yet performed the ritual of a prospective son-in-law in asking my father for my hand in marriage. It wasn't enough of a reason for Lyon to hold the story.

The first I knew of all this was the following morning when I sat up in bed to take a call from my father.

'Congratulations!'

'What for?'

'You're getting married, aren't you?'

'Yes, but how did you know?'

'Everybody knows; it's in all the morning editions.'

I was distraught. 'You mean that's how you found out? You read it in the papers?'

'No, not at all. Denholm rang me at first light to ask my consent. I told him that if it was OK with you, it was OK with me.'

My mother was less easy-going. We went, with Ted, to Washington to meet her over lunch. Denholm was at his charming best but Mom, the good Catholic, was none too happy at having a divorcee in the family. Later, I found out that a family friend who was also a priest had settled her conscience with the severely practical advice that she might as well give her consent because if she didn't, I would go ahead with the marriage anyway. If this was an argument of convenience, the judgement we received from a Catholic bishop in New York was even more so. It was his distorted view that if we could persuade Ginny to declare that she didn't really mean it when she said 'I do' on taking Denholm as her lawful wedded husband, then the Church would give me a special dispensation to marry the man of my choice. I began to think that my family religion was stronger on hypocrisy than it was on theology.

But I was thankful that the get-together with Mom had

passed off without the expected conflagration. It was a help that Ted was in one of the happier phases of his life, considerate and constructive with me and supportive of my relationship with Denholm. He seemed to have emerged unscathed from the nervous breakdown he had suffered ten years earlier when, for two awful months, he had gone missing. He had simply walked out of his office one day and not come back. What made it all the more terrifying was the planning he put into his escape, even going as far as to disguise himself against the risk of being spotted before he had got well away. When he was found and brought home he submitted to electric shock treatment, a remedy for mental disorders that we now know not to be all that it was cracked up to be. But, as I say, in the early sixties Ted was at his best, a popular and successful journalist who had climbed back to be a senior editor on *Newsweek*.

After Denholm was introduced to Mom, Ted made only one mistake and it was hardly his fault. By way of paternal compliment, he put his arm round me and commended me to Denholm. 'Not bad for a nineteen-year-old, is she?' The reaction from Denholm was one of amazement which, in turn, confused Ted. I was alone in knowing what was wrong. In my efforts to impress my fiancé, I had advanced my age by two years. I shouldn't have worried: the younger the better was Denholm's motto. He loved the idea of an untutored personality he could mould to his ideal. As for me, I was ready enough for the challenge while I was on home ground. It was different when I had to get used to a new culture, but the revelation that was England was still to come.

There were still a few problems to sort out. One of them

was sex, but not in the way you might think. Denholm was my first and most considerate lover. He wined and dined me for weeks before we actually made it into bed. And then it was more by accident than design, I think. The unwitting agent of our desire was a kitten called Blipper. It got its name from the way it moved across the apartment in a succession of short jumps – blip, blip, blip. One evening, when we were sitting over drinks, Blipper went on the rampage, zigzagging across the living room – blip, blip, blip – and over the feline border into the closed territory of my bedroom. A cat chase started with Denholm under the bed and me on the bed, then me under the bed and Denholm on the bed, then both of us on the bed. After that we rather forgot about Blipper.

The reverie was broken by the sound of a latchkey. I sat bolt upright. My flatmate had returned. There was a five-minute gap between her entering the living room, doubtless surveying the bottles and glasses with a disapproving glare, and us emerging from the bedroom. That was when the problems started.

Denholm left soon afterwards, stunned by silent disapproval. The row that ensued, violent in its intensity, with a fair amount of tableware smashed to bits, was my first indication that my body was in demand on both sides of the sexual divide. It was all too much for one so young. I was streaming tears when Denholm picked me up the next day. He wanted me to move in with him and I agreed. After all, we didn't have long to wait before we would be married.

Wrong again. Denholm wanted to change the wedding plans. He was bothered by the public takeover of our engagement – goodwill cables; flowers delivered to the stage door, often from total strangers; photographers waiting for us whenever we opened a restaurant door, coming or going. Half fearing the reply, I asked him what he wanted to do.

'Why don't we let things quieten down for a bit? There's no rush to get married. We could live together for a few months until the pressure's off. Then we could marry quietly, without all the fuss.'

I agreed to the postponement on condition that we could square it with Ted. After sharing his pleasure at the prospect of an early wedding, and knowing something of his mercurial personality, I feared disappointing him. I should not have worried. For one thing, I was not the only one in the family heading for the altar. My brother Mark was planning a wedding before the end of the year. Here was more than enough to divert parental attention from my affair.

Furthermore, I had underestimated Ted's liberal tendency. This became clear when I over-prepared for a meeting with him to discuss the live-in option. We gathered at his favourite restaurant, the Escargot, just off Broadway and next to the theatre where Denholm was playing in *Write Me a Murder*. It took us some time and numerous Manhattans (Ted's drink), Tom Collinses (me) and Denholm's vodkas and tonic before I could bring myself to utter the dreadful words. 'Denholm and I have decided not to get married immediately. But we don't want to live apart. So when Denholm goes back to England, I'll be going with him.'

Very slowly, Ted put down his drink. He leaned back in his chair and breathed out a great sigh. 'Thank God,' he said. 'I never believed you had that much common sense.'

But before we could order another round, he added a rider. 'Whatever you do, don't tell your mother.'

Bringing Mom into it reminded me that Denholm had not yet involved his family. What did his mother know of our quixotic arrangements? In his letters, Denholm must have made a passing reference to me in early November because Nina wrote back to say, 'I am so glad you have, at last, found a woman.' But she was quickly diverted by a recent visit by Neil to London. The other family preoccupation was Denholm's reunion (social only) with Ginny. She and Bill Travers were over in New York for a play in which Bill was appearing.

I am so glad you and Ginny and Bill met. It must have cleared up so many apprehensions. I am hoping to see Ginny soon as she said she would come and see me when she returned to England and I saw in last week's *Sunday Express* a photo taken of her at London Airport on her return from America. I'm sorry Bill's play didn't have a good run. In this photo you could see Louise in the car. She looked very sweet but Ginny looked terribly thin and tired – no wonder after that journey with two children . . . I had lunch with Ginny about ten days ago. It was so nice getting all the 'wrinkles' straightened out but I was quite shocked when I saw her looking so dreadfully thin as it makes her looked strained. She was probably a little nervous but was very sweet to me.

It was not until late February, two months after our engagement was sealed, that Denholm confessed all with a letter to Nina followed by a formal announcement in *The Times*. Nina's spontaneous delight at the news was an enormous relief to Denholm.

My dearest Denholm,

Your letter came this morning and I am *thrilled* to learn of your happiness. Please tell your sweet Susan that there is a *very* affectionate and warm welcome awaiting her here. AND ask her to congratulate you from me on being such a lucky man! I must have a party when you arrive. You may not remember this but many years ago I said to you 'Don't marry until you are about 35–38 and then I hope you will marry an American girl.' That was the pinnacle of perfection and now you have the perfection. Too excited to write more.

Love to you both,

Mama

Having broken the ice, Denholm then went to the other extreme, plotting to get Nina over to New York to meet me and my parents. He was thwarted by illness on both sides of the great divide. Nina again:

I am so sorry to learn from your letter that Susan has been rushed to hospital for an appendix operation but I hope, by now, she is feeling much better. I am afraid I cannot manage to get over before the play comes off. It would be such a terrific rush plus vaccination, etc. and I am just out of bed after spending two days there with a rotten bilious attack and tummy 'flu which is what a number of people are having right now ... When and where are you going to be married? If you let me know the date of your arrival and where I can get the key to your flat I'll see there is a 'WELCOME' for you and Susan. Champagne etc. Good idea?

Tons of love & xxx

Mama

There followed a month-long gap when we were trying to get our act together. The wedding was on, the wedding was off. We were travelling together to London. No we weren't. On 12 April, Denholm had an anguished letter from Nina. 'Haven't heard from you for *ages* – Mama. Remember me?'

Our failure to communicate was no great mystery. It was simply that events were conspiring against us. When *Write Me a Murder* eventually closed, Denholm was cast in a movie called *Station Six Sahara* to be shot on location in Libya. I would have gone with him but there was family pressure on my side to stay on for Mark's wedding. Everybody had been so understanding towards my problems, I could hardly resist. Bolstered by good wishes on all sides, Denholm took it in his stride. 'I've got it all worked out. I'll go ahead, you follow in three weeks. Nina will meet you in London and put you on a plane to Tripoli. It's simple. There's nothing to it.'

Denholm flew to London in the last week of April after helping me move out of my apartment into the Woodward Hotel.

Then, silence.

We are talking about the days when communication between America and Britain left a lot to be desired. You couldn't just pick up a telephone and start talking. Trans-atlantic calls had to be booked well in advance through the operator and they cost a bomb. Anyway, Denholm was not easily contactable by telephone. I wrote letters, three in as many days, and spent a lot of time moping around a friend's apartment. I had never felt so empty in my life.

After about a week of no news I persuaded Ted to take

me out to supper for the dubious reward of listening to my worries. Had Denholm changed his mind? Was there someone else? Why hadn't he been in touch? He'd promised to write immediately he got back. Showing remarkable patience, Ted waited until I had finished before coming up with a practical suggestion. 'We'll go back to *Newsweek* and put a call through to London. Talk to Denholm's mother. She'll know where he is.'

The very idea made me tremble at the knees – how on earth would I explain my predicament to a future mother-in-law I had not even met? – but Ted's commanding tone forced me to a decision. We managed to get through without too long a wait but while the telephone was ringing in London it suddenly occurred to us why there was not a long queue of callers ahead of us waiting to use one of the few available transatlantic lines. London time was five hours ahead of New York. I snapped the receiver back on to its rest, imagining as I did so my future mother-in-law struggling from her bed at an ungodly hour.

Feeling more frustrated than ever, I went home, where there was a message to ring Ted. 'I've got another idea. Send Denholm a wire. Just tell him you miss him and want news. That should do it.'

It did. A reply came the next day. 'All well. Letter on its way. Love.'

It was enough to be going on with. As he promised, the letter explained all. He had been spending time at what he liked to call his 'country place' on the Thames, near Richmond. Without having seen it, I had in mind a log cabin surrounded by trees. In reality, it was more of a shack, buried in the undergrowth of Ham Island. But as Denholm said in his letter, it was a shack with 'big possibilities'.

I found a robin with six young sitting on her nest in the middle of my sitting room. So all day she has been flying in and out of my window with worms and popping them into six wide-open mouths; quite fearlessly. I thought she was going to give one to *me* for one moment! I've got the wind things up. They tinkle away all night. We'll have to work hard to make the place liveable. Could be fun.

Forgive my silence. I've been readjusting myself to this land of mine – which I *HATED* for the first three days – it's improving though. I do hope you like England – I'm afraid it's going to seem very strange and quiet after New York. Still you're young and adaptable. I'm glad you've got the pants fixed round that *SUPERB* Bottom. I've written to Tommy Hammond [an agent with MCA]: Don't Forget to confirm your booking – that is to tell me *soonest* what planes you are booked on – (flight and airline numbers) time of take-off and time of arrival – *this is very important*. Also get a visa from the Libyan Embassy. Try to book on *BOAC500* 19 May, New York-London and on 21 May *BOAC915*, London-Tripoli, arriving Tripoli midnight and I'll meet you. My mother will *meet* you here outside Customs on the 20th . . . So to London-to-Tripoli-to London. OK?

Love to Ted and the family and lots of Congrats to Mark and Kisses for your Mum and a Big Kiss on your Botty from me and See you Soon.

Having been starved of information, I was now overwhelmed. The very next day, I had another letter.

The plan is changed a little. You will NOW be met at London Airport (in Immigration) by a representative of ARTHUR HOWLETT'S Travel Agency. They will put you in a car (they have your photograph and anyway will meet you shortly after you leave the plane) and take you to my mother's apartment.

Also Very Important, you *MUST* have a letter from your Father giving his written permission to your marriage. (In English Law the father's Consent is needed if you are under 21). The letter should be a formal Declaration and witnessed by a NOTARY or better still, *Witnessed by the British Consul* in New York. And dated . . . Without this we can't get married – so get it!!!

Don't forget to tell me which planes you are coming on.

Love XXXXX
Denholm

Along with the letter came a clipping from the *Evening News* diary page reporting Denholm's return to London and his preparation for *Station Six Sahara*, his 'first English film for some years'. The interview ranged from Denholm's £100-a-week contract with British Lion, which had only seven months to go, through to his forthcoming marriage to 'devastating twenty-year-old, slender Susan Robinson'. I liked that bit even if it was a little unnerving to find that Denholm was planning a wedding in Tripoli. If he wanted to cut back on the guest list he was certainly going the right way about it.

Happy to know that our relationship was secure, I shot off an instant reply which betrayed my fluttery state of mind, though I had to wait for my flights to be confirmed before I could mail it. Tommy Hammond, who was arranging the flights, hadn't called back, so, restless with the excitement of it all, I went over to the Strollers and had dinner with a friend and then sat around with colleagues and friends from the show until one in the morning, talking and drinking.

In fact it took two more days to sort out the tickets. I was to arrive in London on 19 May – the day after Denholm had left for Tripoli – by the night plane (eleven and a half hours in the air), and fly on to Tripoli on 21 May. I was still short of my Libyan visa and my permission to marry. As the days passed, Denholm bombarded me with reminders of things to bring, people to see and practical instructions.

10/5/62
Hello Darling. Leave my suitcase at my mother's flat and bring cool things, and one warm thing for evening. Don't bring to Libya more than $30 *IN CASH* or £10 sterling *IN CASH*. Leave rest, if any, with my mother. Travellers' cheques are OK.
Love Denholm.
PS BEST to Ted. Bring camera to Libya.

As they always say, it is the unexpected that throws the best-laid plans. In my case, it was a mugging.

I was relaxing in a cinema when the friend I was with suddenly shouted that my handbag had been snatched. Turning, I caught sight of a man hurrying up the aisle. In ordinary circumstances I might have let him go; even in the half light I could see that he was more than a size for me and I was not into karate lessons. But this bastard had my passport and my travellers' cheques. If he got away there would be no telling when I could leave the country. The panic thought of another three weeks in New York drove me to desperation. I gave chase.

What followed in the next ten minutes was straight out of the Keystone Cops. As I ran out of the cinema, a bystander pointed down the street. 'He went that way.'

Those were the very words. They were heard by a cop who flagged a taxi, pushed me into the back seat and shouted at the driver – but, yes, you've guessed it – 'Follow that man!'

He was still running when we caught up with him but when he saw the cop, he just stopped and waited. While the two of them were going through the old routine, I was looking for my handbag. It was nowhere to be seen. Frustration was building up to a flood of tears when a woman, leaning out of her window, called to me from across the street. 'He threw something under that car.'

She was right, and I was reunited with my most treasured of possessions. But not for long. I had to hand it over to the police. I would get it back, I was told, when the case was heard. I was in agony until I heard that we would be in court immediately after the weekend. It looked as if I would be able to catch my night flight to London after all.

Only one more week to go, but I couldn't actually believe it until I was on the plane. It seemed like an eternity until the following Saturday. I wished that Denholm was going to be in London when I got there. I was delighted that by now we both had Mom's blessing. I guess she accepted the facts and resigned with a smile. Ted had an awful lot to do with it, bless him. He was wonderful, and Denholm had really won his heart. My last letter from Denholm before he left for

Tripoli arrived, full of our soppy but cheerful endearments.

> I posted a letter last night to the Woodward Hotel (for lonely and desolate Grunks) with a press clipping about us. So get it. Thanks for the 4 letters I got today! With the Flight Nos. etc. So now I can make *certain* you'll be met. Sorry about the Negro incident – you must have been scared to death, poor little Grunkette. I wish I'd been there to be scared with you! Thank God he was caught anyway . . . The Shack is beginning to look less awful. There will still be lots for us to do. Especially in the garden (GARDEN!!!!JUNGLE). The river is filled with wild duck – heron, swans, moorhen and all around are robins, chaffinch, crow and swamp grunks. I'm off Thursday so I'll be at the airport (Tripoli – Libya) to meet you. See you soon my little pretty one, and keep that Botty warm for me!
> LovexxxxxxxxDenholm

I did get a card, posted express, from Heathrow, reminding me of essentials such as a transistor and cigarettes and 'your botty', and a wire from Tripoli: 'Please bring my fawn jacket and pants. Hot days. Cold nights.' He could be vague, but my Denholm was never one to lose all sight of the practicalities.

I togged up in all my finery for my first-ever flight. The sense of occasion demanded that I looked my best. It never occurred to me that sitting bolt upright in a cramped seat for close on twelve hours might sully the image. I left the plane in London looking like a rag doll.

I fell for Nina immediately. Round and comfortable with pearls and sensible shoes, she was the ideal mum, welcoming and reassuring. I had no trouble in spotting her in a crowded reception hall. She was standing next to a uniformed driver who was holding aloft a clipboard on which was written in commanding letters 'MRS ELLIOTT'.

Bubbling with information (on the left this, on the right that), yet eager for news, Nina's conversation was an unbroken stream until we got to Marble Arch, where she stopped the car and whisked me off to Lyon's Corner House for a light lunch which I could hardly eat, I was so tired. Then we were off again, this time to her apartment in Drayton Gardens, a smart residence in fashionable Chelsea, where I was introduced to Nursie, who put me into my first featherbed and tucked me up under my first eiderdown. Heaven! I slept right through until the following morning. When I came round it was to hear Nina and Nursie in whispered consultations as to whether, as an American, I would prefer coffee or tea for breakfast. I called out that I would like tea, a choice which made me a convert to Earl Grey.

There was not much time for sightseeing. The car taking me back to the airport slowed outside Buckingham Palace for me to witness the Changing of the Guard. Then we were off again. I felt like the proverbial American tourist on the Cook's tour. If it's Tuesday it must be London.

The flight to Tripoli was second class in every sense. Before we took off I fancied I could hear the pilot winding up the elastic. Passengers were offered a choice of drinks – flat Coca-Cola or water. We landed in the middle of the night on a strip of concrete in the middle of a desert. The doors opened to a blast of hot air. It was like walking into a fully heated oven. At the foot of the steps was a jeep and standing in the back of the jeep, in well-worn khaki trousers and shirt, was Denholm. We hugged all the way to the hotel called – wouldn't you know it? – the Palace. As Denholm was the only member of cast or crew with a partner in tow, we had a spacious if sparsely furnished room dominated by a large bed.

The filming of *Station Six Sahara* was in the desert, several miles out of town. In the evenings we would come back to the hotel covered in a fine sand which gave the illusion of an amazing tan – until it fell off in the shower and disappeared down the drain. The set was a simple construction of huts to represent a pumping station for an oil pipeline. In command of this outpost was Peter van Eyck, doing his bullet-head Prussian act, his expression fixed in a sneer. The contrast between his screen personality and the real Peter could not have been greater. Out of character he was courteous and sympathetic with a distaste for raw temperament and confrontation. He was a meticulous dresser even in casual gear, setting off snow-white hair with a suitably contrasting pink or blue rollneck. Very attentive to me, in the nicest possible way, he promised me a huge surprise when we returned to London. In a hundred years, he said, I would not be able to guess what it was. He was right. The surprise turned out to be an introduction to his teenage daughter, who just happened to be my spitting double. Talking to her was like an out-of-body experience.

Of the rest of the cast, Ian Bannen was way off the wall. Maybe it was an extension of him hamming it up in front of the camera to try to put some life into a dismal script. Or perhaps our nervy relationship was more to do with him becoming a Catholic at the time when I was drifting away from the Church. In any event, he certainly spent a lot of his time telling the rest of us how to run our spiritual lives.

It wasn't long before we all realised that *Station Six Sahara* would not be anything to write home about. The budget was peanuts but that would not have mattered so much if there had been any semblance of a believable storyline. The plot, such as it was, turned on the disruptive power of a beautiful woman over an otherwise all-male community. The *femme fatale* was Carroll Baker who, after six other movies, was still trailing seductive glory from her portrayal of the child wife of a cotton miller in *Baby Doll*. She was an accountant's choice to head the cast, a bait for an American distributor and typical of British Lion's talent for getting it wrong. For this movie her entrance is spectacular, if eccentric. She appears out of the night in her Chevy convertible, horn blaring, and crashes into a pile of oil cans, the only sizeable obstacle within a hundred miles. Thereafter, the excitement fades into a succession of anti-climaxes. A scene in which Miss Baker has her clothes torn off was censored into oblivion.

There were more thrills off the set than on it. One day we were caught up in a sandstorm otherwise known as a gibley, which made it sound like a cocktail. It would be hard to think of a more unsuitable association. Actors and crew huddled together in a makeshift breeze-block hut. We had one table and three chairs. Time passed slowly until someone suggested a matchbox race. The idea was to catch some flies – there were plenty of them around – and to divide them up into teams of three of four for each empty box. The box ends were then left ever so slightly open to encourage the flies to attempt escape. The flapping of their wings moved the boxes along the tabletop. The first box to fall off the edge was the winner.

The gibley died down towards evening but when we emerged from our shelter it was to find that the desert had changed shape. The whereabouts of the road was anyone's guess. It took several hours to find our way back to the outskirts of Tripoli where, at the sight of the first bar, we shouted at the driver to stop. 'No need to wait,' we said, 'we can walk to the hotel from here.'

Mistake! I was dressed in hat, jacket, desert boots and – an unintended transgression – trousers. It seemed that our local Arabs had never seen a woman in trousers before and were upset at this attempt to widen their sartorial frontiers. As we started back to the hotel, there were unfriendly shouts from passers-by who began following us. We walked faster. Our pursuers kept up the pace while gathering more support along the way. We ran. They ran. We made the hotel at a sprint to be told by a smiling receptionist exactly why we were the object of hate and ridicule. So tolerant, these Arabs. I wondered what would happen if we liberated women started chasing the veil and bedsheet brigade through Central Park. But political considerations aside, I did resolve never again to venture into Tripoli without being 'properly' dressed.

A few days later the troops were out in force, though not for my contravention of any rule. This time it was much more serious, a national revolution, no less. There were armed soldiers all over town and all over the hotel, where they watched suspiciously as we ate our meals as if we might be about to stage a counter-coup with knives and forks. Denholm let slip the sacrilegious thought that we would do better to forget *Station Six Sahara* and point the cameras at a real-life drama.

No one had a good word to say about our movie. Even

Seth Holt, the director, felt we were on to a bummer. He soon lost interest entirely and took to the bottle for consolation. As the hot, sweaty weeks rolled by without any sense of achievement, Denholm let his frustration show. He told a visiting journalist, 'If things don't work out over *Sahara*, I'll up anchor and live and work in America permanently.'

Elsewhere he extolled the financial advantages of an expat. 'I can claim tax allowances on both sides of the Atlantic. And the allowances in America are enormous. They even allow money for presents to directors and producers. You can give a director a cigarette case encrusted with emeralds and it's deductible.' This insight into actors' dealings with the Inland Revenue was passed on in a telephone interview. When it was over, Denholm worried like mad that he had overstepped the mark of discretion. Eventually, he rang back with a plea to drop the quote or add a rider. The journalist agreed to the rider: 'Mr Elliott added that he had not given any director a cigarette case encrusted with emeralds.'

With filming on *Station Six Sahara* to be completed at Shepperton Studios we returned to London, resolved on a quiet wedding. But there were more forms to fill in and more parental signatures needed. It was as if I were a child bride and Denholm didn't help when he was quoted as saying, 'I feel a bit as if I were her father.'

Right up to the last moment, when we were standing together outside Kensington Register Office, I feared disappointment. I had cabled Ted for some additional facts and figures on my upbringing but he was on vacation somewhere in Massachusetts and couldn't be contacted. I had no idea if the information demanded was critical or not. Would they slam the door in our faces? I felt slightly hysterical as we were shown into a waiting room where Denholm, catching my mood, had a fit of giggles. I took to biting my cheek in an effort to keep a straight face while Denholm assumed a fixed grin which gave him a spaced-out look.

Nina was one of our witnesses. She gave me a gold ring which had been passed down through her family. It was a typically warm-hearted gesture which sealed my fondness for her as much as my love for Denholm. Our second witness was Denholm's agent, John Findlay, who was married to Googie Withers. After the ceremony, we went back to John's flat to celebrate with champagne left over from a party he had given the night before.

A proper honeymoon had to wait until Denholm was free from *Station Six Sahara* but we did spend a few days at his cottage on Ham Island. It was every bit as primitive as his letters had suggested; more so, in fact, because it did not even have running water or electricity. Other residents on the island were nearly all weekenders escaping from the urban crush. Some of them enjoyed the wild in more senses than one. A famous gynaecologist and his wife who lived nearby were inclined to give summer parties in the nude. And it wasn't for health reasons, either. As he said, 'My interests are purely sexual.' Holding him off was my first experience of the swinging sixties, London-style. I had plenty more practice in dealing with predatory males. The Bunch of Grapes in Knightsbridge, a favourite pub with Denholm and a popular meeting place for actors, I wanted to rename the Bunch of Grey Apes. In comparison, my life in New York had been sheltered.

As we settled down together and I came to know him better, I realised that Denholm was always hyper-sensitive to criticism and quick to take offence – both signs of his chronic insecurity. He also drank quite heavily when he was not working. If the drink was talking and Denholm took a dislike to someone or something, it was invariably my job to act as peacemaker, apologising in the morning for indiscretions the night before.

Station Six Sahara turned out to be as bad as we feared, though the German production company which put up part of the money was hopeful that Peter van Eyck would carry the dubbed version to a modest profit. Denholm was in despair, and with the British Lion contract ending he started worrying about where the next cheque was coming from. His fears were much exaggerated, although, at the time, not knowing much about how the acting business operated, I shared his frustrations. All I can say is that he had a steady stream of offers from television which kept us in reasonable comfort.

What is true is that he was almost convinced that he had missed his chance of a big break. The curiosity is that his break had already come, it was just that he hadn't noticed it. In *Station Six Sahara*, Denholm played his first unromantic loser. As he described the role: 'I play a pompous, weak, opinionated creeper. There is very little to say in his favour.' With his pencil moustache underlining a sickly smile, 'the Major' came across as a second-rater who had had a good war and was now desperately trying to live up to that fleeting reputation. The film sank without trace but Denholm's part in it lived on in the memories of casting directors. Henceforth, he found his greatest success as a failure. It was, as he said, the ultimate joke.

7

Nothing But the Best

Denholm's first idea for an extended honeymoon was to take me to France. He spoke the language and he loved the country, particularly the south, where he could relive happy memories of boyhood holidays. My fascination was for Spain. It was only a little further on, I reasoned. If we were to drive 600 miles down to the Pyrenees, why not go a bit further and see what it was like on the other side of the mountains?

We loaded up in his Mercedes SL 190, an open-top sports job in gunmetal grey with red upholstery, and made the first leg to Paris. The admiring glances we collected along the way were entirely for a car that personified every young man's romantic dream. Love came easily with a Mercedes drop-head. He told me how much luck it had brought him in the past.

From Paris we took a succession of short sprints to Barcelona and from Barcelona we went by ferry to Majorca, where we had an open invitation to stay a few days with friends. When we turned up unannounced at their door, it was not them but their parents who were installed. No problem, we were welcome to stay – except, as we soon discovered, the two oldies were in a state of permanent conflict, baiting each other to rows of ferocious intensity. It was like squatting in a war zone. Making our excuses, we called in at the first travel agency to book ourselves back to Barcelona. Incredibly, there on the noticeboard was a letter addressed to Denholm. It was from our Majorcan friends to tell us that they had gone over to the island of Ibiza, presumably to escape from their parents. We were welcome to join them.

The adventure was irresistible. Neither of us had even heard of Ibiza. As far as our imagination ran, it was a pile of rock somewhere out there in the Mediterranean. Its importance in those days can be judged by the extent of communications with the mainland – one boat a week. And today was the day. At first we assumed we would have to leave the Mercedes in Majorca. But, no, there was space for a car somewhere between the crates of live chickens and the sheep pens. We bought our tickets and, because this was an overnight trip, reserved a two-berth cabin which turned out to be designed for one berth for a very small person.

To say that our fellow passengers were of peasant stock is no insult. Dressed in the style of a mediaeval painting, they stayed close to their animals and provisions. The journey to Majorca was evidently a big event in their lives, the equivalent of an excursion to the big city. It was clear that Ibiza was not an advanced society.

The next morning we were out on deck in time to see the island come into view. As we approached the harbour, the sun was rising over the battlements high on the cliff above Ibiza Town. It was quite the most gloriously exhilarating sight. When we looked at each other, we both had tears streaming down our cheeks.

To the latest generation of visitors who have seen expanses of the Spanish islands transformed into costa del concrete, it may be hard to imagine Ibiza as an undiscovered idyll. But in 1962, just before the dawn of the tourist package economy, it was still quiet, gentle and unspoiled. There was little traffic (given the state of the roads we might usefully have swapped the Mercedes for a donkey), the beaches were empty and accommodation – a converted barn or a deserted farmhouse half hidden in its own olive grove – could be rented for a few pesetas. The pace of Ibiza's development has been given a vivid perspective by the writer Juan Lluis Ferrer, who asks us to imagine the whole of the island's history compressed into one hour.

> The Carthaginians would have arrived in the first five minutes and the Moors ten minutes later. The Catalan invasion happened at half past, and at quarter to the Corsairs took to their *xabecs*. Four minutes to the hour and Ibiza saw its first feeble glimmer of electric light. With thirty seconds to go the island's first hotel was built. And in the last second of the hour there has sprung to life a monstrous industry capable of handling 100,000 tourists at any one time in 700 hotels and 3,000 bars and restaurants.

Nevertheless, we were not the first of the showbusiness crowd to find Ibiza. The Danish balladeers Nina and Frederick were already installed; from the States, Howard Sackler, writer of the smash hit *The Great White Hope*, attracted a contingent of East Coast celebrities. The rich and famous rubbed shoulders with the hippy crowd who were in search of purity of spirit. A third group of foreigners consisted of those who operated on the fringes of legality and beyond the reach of the longest extradition treaty. Elmyr de Hory, subsequently famous for his art forgeries, was in residence along with Clifford Irving, who was nearly to get away with a fake biography of the reclusive millionaire Howard Hughes. When Orson Welles came to Ibiza to make a biopic of Elmyr he cracked, 'I came to Ibiza in search of a forger and I find myself surrounded by them on all sides.'

On our first visit, meeting the glamorous names of Ibiza was the least of our interests. What we saw was a glorious simplicity that we could measure against the false gods of glamour. Finding ourselves in Ibiza did not stop us worrying but it certainly made the worrying more bearable. Denholm came to a decision. He wanted his own place in Ibiza. Nothing extravagant, just a room or two we could call a home from home. We found an ideal spot overlooking the old harbour. Unfortunately, the house Denholm set his heart on was already occupied, and the owner was averse to moving out. A lengthy negotiation, conducted in a medley of languages, ended with an inspiration from Denholm to buy the space above the building to add an extra floor. Stunned by the originality of the idea, the owner agreed a price and we set off to find a notary to put his legal stamp on the purchase of air. There was also the little matter of getting what was then quite a large sum out of Britain at a time when there were strict currency restrictions.

After a succession of misunderstandings, and after Denholm had engineered a transfer of cash to a Spanish bank, the deal fell through. We almost gave up on Ibiza. In the heat of disappointment, Denholm decided unilaterally that Morocco was a far better bet for a holiday home. With his money returned to him in used notes, he packed a couple of small cases and stuffed his pockets with illegal currency before setting off to Gibraltar to make the crossing to North Africa. He went through passport control and on to Customs, where a formidable-looking officer was checking every third or fourth passenger. The nervousness of a first-night performance had nothing on this. Getting caught for doing something wrong didn't bother Denholm but his respect for money made him sweat at the risk of having his hard-earned cash confiscated. It must have been his day for looking honest because when his turn came the cases were given the traditional chalk mark of Customs acceptance without search or question. Denholm gathered up his possessions and moved smartly only to be brought to a halt by a sharp word of command.

'Señor. Stop!'

The smuggler turned to face his accuser. He was greeted with a broad grin.

'Señor, that is the wrong way. You are going back into Spain.'

So the money went to Morocco, but not for long. I had not taken to North Africa and Denholm was put off by the tendency of young Moroccans to mark every Westerner for a profitable mugging. Returning to Ibiza, we consulted the oracle. Sandy Pratt had been a resident of the island since 1955 when, as a law student from County Meath, he had found in Ibiza the perfect excuse for not returning to 'deadly studies' (his description) at Trinity College, Dublin. Instead of becoming an advocate – and his powers of conversation suggest that he was a loss to the profession – Sandy opened a bar. Built out of a derelict chicken house in what was then the tiny fishing village of Santa Eulalia, Sandy's Bar was a long way short of the Ritz. But he set a standard in friendly informality that proved irresistible. You were in need of an accommodation address? Sandy could provide it. You wanted to call home? The telephone at Sandy's Bar, one of the very few on the island, was at your disposal. It was almost incidental that he could mix a scintillating cocktail. A great collector of gossip, Sandy was a mine of information on what property was available, on its likely asking price and on the reliability of the seller.

It was Sandy who urged us to look for a place away from the coast. He could detect signs of a burgeoning tourist economy. When the hotels and discos began to sprout there would not be much left of the quiet life. So we explored the hills above Santa Eulalia. The few houses were either working farms and not on the market or deserted cottages tucked away out of the reach of the sun. That was not what we wanted. But we did find a patch of land that was ideal for building our own south-east-facing villa. The plan had the virtue of matching outgoings with income since instead of handing over a lump sum we could pace our investment according to means.

This time the deal did go through. We were in for a long haul but the achievement made the hard work and the frustrations worthwhile. Our home in Ibiza was to become a major preoccupation of my life and it will crop up frequently in the rest of this story.

Back in London I went for a routine medical and was told

170

that I was pregnant. That was the first bit of good news. Then Denholm was sent a stunning script. *Nothing But the Best* was a screenplay by Frederic Raphael, then a young and barely discovered talent who had managed to hit the tender reflexes of the 1960s upwardly mobile culture. The role pencilled in for Denholm was that of a seedy aristocrat and con artist hired by a young social climber (Alan Bates) to teach him the tricks of the establishment and help put him at the top of a City property company. As the hero on the make puts it in his approach to his oily associate, 'You've got something I want. Style.'

Something worthwhile had come out of *Station Six Sahara* after all. Denholm had proved that he was not just a pretty face and, for the first time, directors were taking him seriously as a character actor. It was farewell to top billing (except for television plays) but it was also a heartfelt welcome to a far more satisfying and fulfilling career. 'There are two types of people,' he said. 'There are stars, and there are actors. If you are a star then one has enormous personality. Clint Eastwood and Joan Collins know exactly who they are. I get up each morning wondering what I am.' He found it a pleasurable, if often bewildering, sensation.

Nothing But the Best was very much a film of its time – a *Room at the Top* with laughs, as a critic described it. While satirising the get-rich-quick mentality familiar to anyone who lived through the eighties, Frederic Raphael also targeted the social pretensions of the upper classes who had to have their prejudices massaged before they were ready to let an outsider board the gravy train. Pitched forward twenty years, the character played by Alan Bates would have been able to satisfy his greed unaided. By then, sheer ruthlessness was enough.

It was a quality team that came together for the movie. Apart from Alan and Denholm, Harry Andrews and Millicent Martin were in the upper reaches of the cast and the director was Clive Donner, who had edited the comedy classic *Genevieve*. With a little help from American friends, a more than adequate budget was put together by David Deutsch for his own company, Domino Productions.

Though Denholm was nervous when he saw the rough cut – he had doubts about the story hanging together convincingly – the edited version was greeted enthusiastically on both sides of the Atlantic. Clive Barnes called it the 'most stylish British film comedy since *Kind Hearts and Coronets*'. It certainly made Alan a star but not, thankfully, a hostage to the Hollywood studios. He remained very much his own man. He was fifteen years younger than Denholm but they complimented each other wonderfully. Though they came from different backgrounds – Alan had his northern vowels to prove it – they had shared memories of schoolboy loneliness. The pull of acting was, as Alan put it, an expression of something suppressed, something which you can release if you have the gift to do it. 'I know, if I get up there, I'll be able to scream and shout and express myself.'

Alan at least had the distinction of having finished his time at RADA but there had been no prizes for him and he had been the last of his year to get a job. His break was the English Stage Company and a new generation of writers who rejected the carefully modulated tones of the West End. Alan was a prototype of earthy regionalism; just what they wanted. With his own career lifting out of the doldrums, Denholm could afford to be magnanimous, especially to an actor like Alan, whose talent he admired.

The main challenge for me at this time was adapting to the English way of doing and saying while trying to reconcile myself to the strict upper-class conformity of Denholm's family. Nina was generosity itself and was forever covering up for my indiscretions. But Neil and Rosemary had never before encountered anyone quite like me, determinedly cheerful, outgoing and independent. They probably thought of me as a cross between Calamity Jane and Little Orphan Annie. At my first family dinner party in London, I stayed rooted at the table when the other female guests departed from the room to leave the men to gossip over their cigars. Having committed the gaffe I made matters worse by refusing to make a belated exit. Denholm thought it was hilarious, even when the party broke up early.

I was never jealous of Denholm's later infatuations for the simple reason that I knew – I absolutely knew – that I was central to his life. On the rare occasions Denholm showed jealousy it was often for the silliest of reasons. When he turned forty I decided we would celebrate in grand style. Choosing my moment, I filched his address book to compile a guest list and chose all his friends, including his ex-lovers. I needed help, so I hired a young guy to cook. While we were cooking Denholm came home unexpectedly. His key was hardly out of the latch before I had grabbed my co-conspirator by the hand and pushed him into the kitchen closet. For Denholm I had the unfriendliest of receptions. 'What are you doing here?' I did not mean to sound quite so unwelcoming but I was unable to hide my impatience for him to go.

'I'll be back later,' he promised.

'OK,' I said, 'but not too early.' That wasn't what I meant, either, but he took the hint and left. He must have spent the next couple of hours creating for himself a drama of betrayal and adultery. When he returned he was in a fine old state, angry and distraught, ready to have it out with me about the affair he was now convinced I was having. What he was totally unprepared for was a chorus of 'Happy Birthday to You' from around thirty friends who were packed into the living room. He stood gaping with amazement and then burst into tears of relief and happiness.

Denholm's triumphant comeback in *Nothing But the Best* brought in a shoal of scripts. Of his next batch of film work, his cameo as the seedy abortionist in *Alfie* still attracts admiring recognition whenever the movie is shown on television. He was getting into middle-aged stride. In *Nothing But the Best* he was still playing the young man; for *Alfie* he aged appreciably. It wasn't entirely an act. As he admitted, 'I had been a reasonably attractive young actor. But now my face just fell off the bone.'

The change gave him a depth of character entirely lacking in his earlier roles. For Graham Greene, who had seen his potential in *The Heart of the Matter*, Denholm had made an important discovery. It was 'the loser beneath the skin'. At his best, Denholm revealed a 'suffering subtext', a hopelessness with dignity that attracted audience understanding and sympathy. Setting a pattern, he managed to attract good notices even when the movie fell short, as in *Here We Go Round the Mulberry Bush*, Clive Donner's 1967 follow-up to *Nothing But the Best*, for which Denholm was cast as the permanently sloshed father of one of the hero's girlfriends.

The downside of 1963 was the misery of two baby deaths. In February I gave premature birth to twins, a boy and a girl. My gynaecologist was away at the critical moment and when I was taken to Westminster Hospital, I was handed over to a doctor who seemed to be unaware that there were twins in my family and indeed that I was a twin myself. He gave me something to induce labour. The boy died two hours later; his lungs were not properly developed. The girl died shortly afterwards from 'no apparent cause'. The room I was in was next to the nursery. I could hear babies crying. After one night Denholm took me home, where I went to bed, and there I stayed. For how long I have no idea; it might have been days but more likely weeks. It was like living in a dark cave. I just wanted to cut myself off. Denholm was incredibly attentive, sitting with me, holding me when I cried.

He kept from me his own troubles, including a play he was rehearsing which fell apart when the director wandered off in an alcoholic haze. Then one day I simply got up and started busying myself around the apartment. When Denholm came home he found me as I had been before the birth – chatty and interested and eager for a laugh. If he was surprised he didn't show it. Neither of us made any mention of the cause of my breakdown – not then and not for years afterwards. My way of coping with our loss was to pretend that none of it had really happened.

One of the advantages of being an actor in demand is that you have a better chance of matching what you want to do with where you want to do it. Denholm was keen to return to the theatre but, given our domestic trauma, he also wanted to move us beyond familiar surroundings. The best cure for me, he decided, was a complete change. The opportunity came up with an offer to join an American touring company. This was no ordinary touring company. Its full title was The National Repertory Theater and as part of the Kennedy-led cultural renaissance it had congressional funding and presidential endorsement. It was a great compliment to Denholm (and says something of his appeal in America) that he was wanted as part of an illustrious team led by Farley Granger, famous here for his film roles, notably in *Rope* and *Strangers on a Train*, but best known in the States for his stage and television work. The quartet of regulars was completed by Eva le Gallienne, doyenne of American theatre, and Anne Meacham.

The project was only in its second year but had already attracted high praise for a varied and exciting programme. The schedule for its second season was a national tour of *The Seagull, Ring Round the Moon* and *The Crucible*. Meaty roles for Denholm included Trigorin in *The Seagull*, an experience that was to put him on the track of other northern European plays and led him to his finest stage work performing Ibsen and Strindberg.

We both shouted yes almost before Denholm had finished reading the telegram of invitation from the NRT. There was not much time to get ourselves together and when we left for New York to start rehearsals in September 1963, it was poor Nina who was deputised to settle affairs in London.

The tour started at the University of North Carolina, where the four principals were billed as artists in residence. This meant that they had to perform during the day to packed lecture halls. It was great fun and the adrenaline was in perpetual motion. Over the next year we were to visit twenty major cities to reach a total audience of some 350,000, of which a quarter were college and high school students. We usually stayed a week in each venue but now and again we held on for two weeks and in Chicago, three. Wherever we went we were treated like royalty. The NRT was seen as very much the President's baby so for every opening night the local dignitaries turned out in force.

The company became like a family with nightly gatherings after the show, invariably in our rooms which, as we were a married couple, were larger than the others. The first thing we did when arriving at a new hotel was to change the lightbulbs. They were always too bright. Low-wattage yellow was more suited to post-performance relaxation. The booze was set out, and anyone who felt like a party was welcome to join in. It was a happy tour with very little bitching.

In Boston, I was told I was pregnant again. I also found out that Denholm and I had different blood types – he was O positive, and I was A negative – which in those days caused problems with pregnancy. Of course we were worried, but I decided unilaterally that I would not cut out from the tour. If I went back to London I would only spend time staring into space, but if I carried on as if nothing had changed I would have plenty to occupy me. And somehow I felt that if I was with Denholm and the others and I did lose the baby, it would not be as bad as before.

What I could never have anticipated was the extent to which events outside my own little concerns were about to occupy all our lives. The climax of the tour was a White House dinner hosted by President Kennedy. It was to be the seal of approval on two years of achievement and a powerful boost to the company's ambition to found a national theatre for America. The day before the celebration we were playing Philadelphia. The President was in Dallas, Texas. We were with Farley in a taxi when the news came over the radio that

J.F.K. had been shot down. Farley stopped the taxi; we all got out and started running as though that would change everything. There was no performance that evening; we just sat and talked. The sadness was not for one man but for a brave hope that had died with him.

We went by coach to Washington, not for a celebratory dinner but for a funeral. Afterwards, Denholm and I were asked by the British ambassador, David Ormsby-Gore, to have lunch at the embassy. As close friends of the Kennedy family, the Ormsby-Gores had the late President's children, Caroline and John-John, staying with them. During lunch, we were joined by John Mitchell, who had already started his investigation into the assassination, later known as the Mitchell Report. It is curious what one remembers from moments of intense emotional crisis. The conversation over table is as nothing; doubtless we talked in platitudes. But I do recall that when we were having coffee in one of the anterooms a peacock settled on the balcony. The ambassador asked me if I had ever seen two peacocks mating. I had to admit my ignorance. He then gave me a detailed and colourful account of what I had missed.

We finished the tour in the spring of 1964 with a short run at the Belasco Theater on Broadway. The plays opened to terrific reviews and healthy advance bookings. By now I was seven months pregnant and when Denholm landed a film job in Italy, I was urged to stay behind. After all, Denholm would be back in plenty of time for the birth and I was not short of friends to look after me. At weekends I shared the Long Island home of Frances Ann Dougherty, a co-producer of the NRT, with Farley as a regular visitor. Ted was telephoning almost daily to check how I was and the post brought news and encouragement from Nina.

I was so pleased to read your PS to D's letter and to know that you (and 'weeny') are behaving yourselves. I am longing to see you all, but will have to be patient before I can see No. 3 (Pa. Ma. & *IT*). It will be thrilling to find your house furnished when you return. That will make you feel even more A.T. Home in England. I hear that the bathroom and 'water-loo' have been put in order during your absence. It would have been depressing to return and find them still in that disgusting state. What a meeting we will have. So much to hear. So much to tell you. Until then, dear Susan, I send you both my love,

Nina (very soon 'Grina')

Towards the end of the seventh month of my pregnancy, Farley offered to drive me back to New York after a weekend in Long Island. But the doctor advised against the car. Too many stops and starts, he warned. So instead I took the train. Maybe the doctor hadn't travelled recently by rail, or maybe it was my day for the learner driver. In any event, three hours later, when we were rattling into Central Station, I was all ready to go into labour – six weeks ahead of forecast. Farley, Bob Calhoun and Frances Ann kept a bedside vigil for two weeks, showering me with treats while the medics slowed down my reproductive processes. Ted took responsibility for keeping Denholm up to date. His state of nerves can be judged by his complaints about his own rare lack of professionalism. 'I can't learn my lines,' he wailed over the international telephone. 'I'm too worried to think straight.'

Beginning to feel guilty about the amount of attention being lavished on me, I persuaded my minders to return to Long Island. 'Nothing's going to happen for a while,' I assured them. 'I'll give you plenty of warning of the event.'

That very weekend, on 8 June 1964, I gave birth to Jennifer Sarah Elliott. My daughter weighed in at precisely two and a half pounds, the size of a bag of sugar. Farley and Ted were both at the hospital first thing on Monday morning, both claiming paternity so that the nurses would let them into the intensive care unit to see the baby. The real father was still in Italy screaming for news. As soon as word got through, he flew to New York.

Once Jennifer was strong enough and out of the incubator where she spent the first six weeks of her life, the three of us flew back to London and our new home in Albert Street, Camden Town. We barely had time to draw breath before Denholm was summoned to the States to start filming *King Rat* and for an MGM film test. He knew that the chances of it leading anywhere quickly were remote but he was keen to be on file, as it were, and the trip to Los Angeles was good for making contacts. We had had so little time together, we decided that all three of us should go. Nina, as usual, was left to take care of domestic arrangements.

My dear Denholm,
I was more than delighted to get your letter yesterday – with the enclosed photograph of Jennifer. She has grown quite 'chubby' since I saw her and is obviously becoming strong if she can 'hold her own bottle'. That's very good but can she hold her drink? That is even more important! Susan looks enchanting in her topless

dress holding the bottle of vaseline (Jennifer's first solid food!) and J. appears to enjoy her new diet. Susan is saying 'open your mouth Jennifer – say Ah' and Jennifer is doing just that.

I went to your house last Tuesday with Nursie and I turned off the radiators in the rooms where they were 'on' as we have been having another heatwave and the temperature of the rooms was terrific with no air coming in. I was afraid of dry rot. In fact, I opened the window in the very top room – not more than half an inch to let a tiny current of air in. I'll go again this afternoon and close it and probably turn on the radiators, or anyway the moment it begins to turn cold.

To me, Nina was chatty about her news but at the same time gave more than a hint that she was beginning to feel her age. What I did not then know was that she had already been diagnosed as having cancer.

Dearest Susan,
I wish I could be with you but I have not been fit lately and although it's nothing serious I don't feel up to journeys (even quick ones by air) and doubt if I will go to Cuckney [Neil and Rosemary's home] for Xmas. I was so pleased to get your letter. I can't hear news of you all too often. It is the one real joy of my life and when I get photos *as well* I am 'younger than springtime' with happiness. I have been hoping to hear about the MGM test but as I haven't heard I imagine Denholm didn't get it but it will come, it will come – in time. I have been rather gay just lately and last Friday, Rose-

mary came to stay with me for a night as we were going to a cocktail party given by her brother Peter (I don't think you have met him) on board *HMS President* at King's Reach on the Thames. It was a great party and I enjoyed it very much but didn't go on afterwards to supper as Rosemary kindly invited me to do. I came home, went to bed and read a nice book. Rosemary went off with her family. I feel that she has so few chances of coming up and having a bit of a 'fling' in London that it would have spoiled it for her if I had wanted to come home before the end of everything. She would have felt she must come too. Anyway, Peter drove her back here about midnight so I think they must have enjoyed themselves. Some bridge too I have been playing but find it a bit of a 'Bind' sometimes. Neil arrives today as he is seeing an ear specialist tomorrow. He is getting a little deaf and has a 'singing' in his ear that annoys him. Your darling sweet baby. *How* I long to see her. My father's family all had VIVID blue eyes and were not only beautiful but *very* gay! I wonder if Tiny one will be the same. I think so. All my love to you, D. & J.
    Nina

And, again to Denholm; ever the optimist, the urger on to greater glory:

My dear Denholm,
Your letter received this morning has delighted my heart and my thoughts are all with you at this moment wondering and hoping about the result of your test with

MGM. How simply wonderful if you get it. Do please let me know as I am always thrilled to hear of your success. Certainly you deserve all the good luck in this way. You have never given in when things looked gloomy and your courage is reaping its just reward now. I simply *ADORE* the photos you enclosed. Nursie wants some! and Susan looks so lovely and happy – bless her. I love her not only for her very sweet self but also for bringing such happiness into your life. So much of your success has been due to her love and encouragement.

Flying back to London with Jennifer I was shocked to find how frail Nina had become. But rereading one of my old letters to Denholm, I must have thought then that she did not realise how ill she was. I am now more inclined to believe that she was not letting on as much as she knew.

Dear Pot,
I took Jennifer over to see your mother, after we had a sleep. She seems in marvellous spirits and it is obvious she knows nothing about her condition. She can't wait for you to get back and she is thrilled with Jennifer, who grrred and eeeked and smiled at her. Nina has lost weight but not so much that she looks ill. In fact, she looks very good. She coughed only a few times, and she said that it has improved. She thinks she has a kidney infection that is causing a pain in her back. Neil was there but we couldn't talk until today when I called him at Cuckney. He is very upset (and really sounded like he would cry if given a push) because he thinks you think he is terrible trying to settle Nina's affairs. He said

he would do nothing to let her know how seriously ill she is. I explained to him that our main concern was to keep her from knowing for as long as possible and to make her as happy as possible until the doctors feel they have to tell her. He said that this has been his *main* concern too, and that he didn't like having to go through the cold-blooded mess of paperwork and that he is absolutely emotionally and physically exhausted trying to do his very best and keep Nina from any worry too.

I did sympathise with Neil. It was hard enough trying to bring some semblance of order to family affairs without having Denholm trying to manage details from a distance. I fed him just enough information to deter him from worrying. At the same time, I had to go through the ritual of reassuring him that I had a tight grip on our finances.

I went over to pick up the car today and there wasn't any petrol in the tank and the indicators wouldn't work. So, I *made* them fix it (free of charge) and have a man deliver it here to 75 Albert St tomorrow morning. Tut-tut.

I had to delve into our American money at the airport at Washington because they charged me *$72.00* overweight. I made him give me a receipt because I think something is fishy. I only had to pay $14.00 from Calif. to Washington – and the difference isn't all that great from Washington to London. I didn't have one tiny thing extra, either.

About two months before she died, Nina asked me round

to her flat 'for a private chat'. She sat me down, looked at me levelly and said: 'I want you to have some money.'

Choosing her words very carefully, she went on: 'I want you to stay with my son. But only because you want to. And because you love him. Not because you can't afford to leave.'

I argued that she was worrying unnecessarily. But as always with Nina there was no denying the force of her argument or the power of her persuasion. I accepted the gift. The sum she had in mind was £10,000. It was ages before Denholm found out. I kept the money in a separate bank account, building up interest until I saw the possibility of using it in a way that would benefit us both, and would have pleased Nina. I spent the money on completing our bedroom in Ibiza.

Not used to being caught out on the state of our finances, Denholm was incredulous. 'Where did you get the money?'

'Nina gave it to me,' I told him. 'But just remember, if we split, I get the bedroom.'

There is not much remaining in the way of letters or diaries to remind me of events leading up to and just beyond Nina's death. But it is interesting that of all the letters of condolence Denholm received, the only one he kept was from Ginny.

Dear Denholm,
Your letter arrived this morning, and although you didn't think it needed an answer I just had to drop you a line.

It is strange because your mother has been on my mind for some while – I had a long letter from her last January from Liverpool to which I replied, and she told me then that she had been very poorly.

Your news this morning was very upsetting. She was

one of the people I loved and admired very especially. I do hope she did not suffer too much, Denholm. Please accept my deepest sympathy.

I would just like to add how pleased I am to read the splendid reviews you have been getting recently and how much we have enjoyed watching you on the tele.

I do hope you and your family are well and happy.
Love, Ginny

With that letter Denholm kept a postcard he had found in Nina's flat which Ginny had sent from Kenya.

My dear Nina,
I am wondering if you have safely returned from your trip to the Far East. It must have been somewhat of a sentimental journey for you – did you visit the places you used to know? We are all in Kenya to make a film of *Born Free* – about Elsa the lioness. We arrived by boat in June and it is somewhat vague as to when we will return. It's meant to be January, but somehow I doubt it. The children are thriving and William, nearly six, is a passionate fisherman, there being a well-stocked river at the bottom of our garden. Denholm seems to be very successful – I do hope he is happy too.

Fondest love, Ginny.

Nina did not live long enough to greet our second infant Elliott. Mark Mitchell Elliott was born on 23 January 1967, curiously enough on our second tour with the National Repertory Theater. It was another premature arrival, this time in San Francisco. The birth itself was a joy but the circumstances surrounding it were not quite so happy. For one thing, Farley Granger was no longer with the company. Furthermore, since the death of President Kennedy the steam had gone out of the NRT along with the conviction that an American national theatre was only a matter of time. Now all concentration was on keeping the show on the road.

Of the three plays – *Tonight at 8.30, The Imaginary Invalid* and *A Touch of the Poet* – Denholm was least at home with the O'Neill. He felt the production was under-rehearsed and while the tour was manageable, he approached the opening night on Broadway in a mood bordering on terror. Stage fright took hold, that grasping at the throat which makes each word an act of will. It was, as he said, the first time he 'had noticed the floorboards' and years on he would shudder at the memory.

8

Ibiza

Trying to raise a family is hard enough. Trying to raise a family with a husband who lives out of a suitcase adds to the complications. But to do the job with a peripatetic actor who subscribes to the chaos theory of household management calls for superwoman.

I started out on my vaunted ambition with a strategic withdrawal. There was no way I could continue with my career. I did take on one or two things, like a send-up of *The Wizard of Oz*, but it was more for fun and for keeping my hand in than any serious intent. A second decision followed naturally. If anyone was to hold together the nuts and bolts of family life, it had to be me. Raising the children and keeping the home going and managing Denholm was a juggling act I revelled in.

I took my time closing in on the piles of letters to be answered and bills to be paid. Denholm hated all paperwork and was capable of misinterpreting the simplest written instruction. But while he was relieved to have his life organised for him, he was a great believer in sod's law. Something, he imagined, was bound to go wrong. He was unable to break free of money worries, even when we had plenty. He was forever handing out titbits of advice on how to save a few pounds, or a few pennies. But with gentle persuasion, for the most part, he let me get on with it. Denholm was not a rich actor but we were comfortably off. His worst fears of what might happen after the British Lion contract money dried up were never realised. His earning power stayed healthy.

Of several projects that combined pleasure and profit, *King Rat*, a prisoner-of-war drama adapted from a James Clavell novel and directed by Bryan Forbes, stands out. John Mills led a contingent of British character actors – Denholm, Alan Webb, Leonard Rossiter, James Fox, John Standing, James Donald, Michael Lees, Gerald Sim – and one rising star, Tom Courtenay, as captives of the Japanese invaders of Singapore. The casting was impeccable, though Hollywood investment in the movie pressed for a stronger American presence. It says something for Bryan's persistence and powers of persuasion that he got his way, right across the length and breadth of the cast list, starting with the then little-known George Segal as the American Corporal King whose devious wheeler-dealing gives him effective command of the camp. Bryan selected George Segal in defiance of pressure to select an actor of proven bankability such as Frank Sinatra, Robert Mitchum or Burt Lancaster, all of whom could well have turned in a splendid performance but were too far into middle age to be truly convincing.

It was a weird experience for Denholm to find himself back in a PoW compound, not least because the reconstruction of the notorious Changi Jail was so utterly convincing. All the actors were under strict orders to slim down to bare subsistence level and, for further realism, their suitably ragged uniforms were soaked in oil and water before every shot.

The production went smoothly. Denholm even managed to patch up his quarrel with James Donald. There was only one awkward moment. In the final scene when the prisoners were released, Bryan wanted them to show complete incredulity. To get the desired effect from Denholm, the director shouted at him, 'Your wife Susan and your daughter Jennifer have died!' He achieved more than he had bargained for. For a few dreadful moments, Denholm really believed we were dead. His reaction on camera showed a despair beyond acting. Then he was furious and shouted: 'You paid me to act, so for Christ's sake, let me act!'

King Rat was a hit everywhere except the States where, in those fiercely chauvinistic days, audiences could not stomach an American anti-hero. Denholm was in Los Angeles when the studio registered the first downbeat reactions to the movie. Simultaneously, *Nothing But the Best* was released in the States. If Denholm hoped for better news on this front, he was quickly disappointed. The reviews were favourable but audiences stayed away. Stung into retaliation, Denholm went to the head of the studio and asked if there was anything he could do to boost the movie.

He said, 'Sure, sure,' and sent me to the head of publicity, who never took his feet off the desk and suggested a publicity gimmick of impossible vulgarity. So, at my own expense, I took a full page in the two Hollywood trade papers with my picture and one-line quotes from wonderful reviews in *The New York Times* and *The Times*. Underneath I added: 'You're about to see Denholm Elliott in one of the most charming, witty films of the year.' The film went on the following day and came off at the end of the week. I then took two more pages and did exactly the same thing except I added, 'You've just *missed* Denholm Elliott in the most charming, witty film of the year.' And this they could not understand. That anyone should spend their own money pushing something you couldn't see if you wanted to. So they brought it back into fifty movie houses and it's been on American television ever since!

Other less satisfying movies followed in quick succession – *The Spy with a Cold Nose*, in which Denholm worked with Robert Flemyng for the first time since they had appeared together in *The Guinea Pig; The House that Dripped Blood* (no prizes for guessing the genre); and the truly and utterly dreadful *Percy*, the everyday story of a penis transplant. After that little effort Denholm voiced the fear that he would never be seen again but he was too well known for stealing the notices from glossier co-stars to be out of favour for very long. Some movies he knew to be turkeys from the first day of the shoot but he had a fascination for trying to make something out of nothing and good money was always a consolation. When asked by a bemused journalist about one of his more outrageous roles, he replied, 'I don't have my files with me so I can't remember if I took the part to pay the gas bill or the phone bill. But I'll let you know.'

On television, Denholm regularly headed the cast list in productions that allowed him to extend his range. It was the pleasure of the new that chiefly attracted him. He could never understand actors who feared over-exposure. For him the opportunity to reach mass audiences had great appeal. He took to regarding the small screen as the only genuinely popular theatre. 'I like television work very much. I consider it the National Theatre much more so than the real thing across the river.'

In the years ahead much of Denholm's best work would be for television, though ironically these plays are less often repeated than hours of dismal movies. In the late sixties, his favourite appearance was as the eponymous villain of *Dracula*, in which he had to age and disintegrate before viewers' eyes, an artifice now made commonplace by Steven Spielberg's special effects but in those days a tricky exercise made possible only by liberal use of gel and dry ice.

After Denholm's agent, Tim Wilson, died, he joined forces with Dennis van Thal, who had looked after the British Lion contract players, when Dennis decided to set up his own agency. London Management was a team effort; Dennis's partner, Jean Diamond, was a power pack of energy who managed to talk on three telephones to three continents to do three deals all at the same time. She and Denholm hit it off immediately and she changed our lives from the moment she took over. She painstakingly and purposefully nurtured and built Denholm's career financially and established him as a transatlantic name. She could make contracts from which even Houdini couldn't escape. Jean became not only one of our closest friends but part of our small family. As practical as she is, she and I also share a strong belief in each person's power to heal and in mind over matter. Every morning, at the crack of dawn, she exercises her horses before driving to the centre of London. The three of us have spent many hours in laughter (and some tears) over plates of pasta (hold the mushrooms and green peppers), and bottles of champagne, Jean's only vice. Denholm loved and adored her. It was a friendship that lasted for twenty-five years, and she is still holding my hand now.

Around that time Denholm found land on Ibiza, in the hills outside Santa Eulalia, where we decided to build our villa. We would take a picnic basket, wine and two-year-old Jennifer and sit for hours planning which terraces would hold which bedrooms and how big the living room would be. While trying to be responsible parents we were still party animals and concentrated our minds on the number of people we could fit in comfortably. It never occurred to us that it would become anything more than a holiday home. Denholm was a mad-keen gardener and not a tree was cut down unless it was absolutely necessary. For each one we did have to cut down he planted two more. A hammock swings between the two trees under which we made most of our plans during the three summers it took us to complete the dream. The view from there is still just as stunning.

Our Mercedes SL 190, a fuck-me two-seater drop-head, gave up the ghost after two years' driving from London to Ibiza and over roads that were not much more than dirt tracks to meetings with our architect, Danish George. In fact we had to pay danger money to a friend named Wanted John to take it back to London, where Denholm traded it in for two Minis. The dealer got the best of the transaction and it marked the end of an era.

People on the island rarely used surnames at that time: instead we invented nicknames to distinguish between people with the same first name. So as well as Danish George and Wanted John there was H-less Jon – Jon Pertwee, who for years thought we were calling him Ageless Jon – and Pretty Pat, Ugly Pat, Writer Cliff (Irving), Cliff the Dog (he had a large black poodle). But Denholm was always Denholm and I was always Suzy Elliott or Denholm's Suzy.

The moment Danish George called to say the house was ready Denholm jumped into our trusty Mini and dashed to Ibiza to put in beds and prepare for my arrival. On his first night he lit the living room with an abundance of candles (we lived without electricity for eight years) and got ready to settle down for the night on a mattress on the floor, with, of course, a bottle of wine, when he encountered the ghost. Denholm was a non-believer in the supernatural – at least he was until that evening. He said that he felt rather than saw it at first. He turned and saw the vague shadow of a man standing in a corner of the living room. Initially he was scared out of his wits but then anger took over. After all, here he was in the first home he had ever built with his hard-earned money and he was damned if any ghost was going to spoil it for him. He stood up and shouted at the apparition: 'I don't know who you are but I'm damned well not moving out, so you better leave or get used to the idea and learn to live with me.' The ghost would appear periodically over the years to one of us, but eventually his visits stopped. Writing this now it has just occurred to me that the same corner of the living room is the place where I put Denholm's bed in the final weeks of his life so that he could look out on his garden. It is where he died.

The house, or perhaps it is the land, seems prone to strange happenings like the visits of the ghost. Years later, I came into the kitchen area one evening and found Eleanor, who lived in and helped me with the children, looking straight ahead, talking as if in conversation but to herself. When she finished I asked her what she was doing. She said, 'I'm talking to my father. Didn't you see him?' It took us a few moments to realise that something was definitely wrong – we both knew that her father was living in Ireland.

She said he had told her that she wasn't to worry: he was not in pain, he was all right. A quick dash to Sandy's Bar and a telephone call to her mother revealed that Eleanor's father had died a few hours earlier. It was straight out of the *Twilight Zone*, except that it really did happen.

Growing up and into my late twenties I often had what I now know are called 'out of body' experiences. I thought them quite natural and assumed that everyone had them. I loved the feeling, and would lie on my bed, relaxed, waiting to drift. It was wonderful floating somewhere near the ceiling looking down at my body on the bed. Then I found out that not everyone had these 'trips' and I began to think maybe I was weird or that something was wrong with me. I became totally inhibited and prevented them from happening again. It's a pity. Even now that a lot has been written about other people having such experiences, I simply cannot reach the point where I can take off as I used to do. I used to talk about it with Denholm but it kind of frightened him, so I stopped.

Denholm didn't really like indoor plants and therefore wasn't very good with them but his love for the garden was so great that he could and did make plants grow out of stone. Our land on Ibiza is all chalk and rocks, yet our garden is a proud tribute to his talents as a gardener. Denholm liked nothing better than digging deep into a sack of manure with his bare hands and distributing it to his beloved plants. He was like a child in a sweet factory if he came across a fresh, steaming dump of horse manure left by a local farmer's horse. Out of the car he would jump, shovel in hand, to cover the boot of the car, grinning from ear to ear as though he had just won an Oscar. I only objected when he used the car in which I had to take the children to school and neglected to cover the floor with paper first. Horse manure and morning hangovers don't mix well, believe me.

Twice a year, we would visit my mother's home in Southport, North Carolina. The house sits on land five metres from the Cape Fear River which leads into the Atlantic Ocean. The ground is 100 per cent sand; the river and the ocean are saltwater. Every year there are hurricanes, which usually arrive after long, hot summers when the temperatures soar to over 100 degrees. The fact that Denholm turned that pile of sand into a garden which passers-by stop to admire is nothing short of a miracle. He always talked to his gardens in London and Ibiza, but in this case I seriously think he threatened it.

On Ibiza, he planted oleander, roses climbing up trees, roses climbing over walls, hibiscus, tobacco plants, pampas grass. In one area he made a wall of cypress trees, put in a fountain and jokingly called it the D.E. Memorial Garden. When he knew he was dying he asked to be buried there. Our nineteen-year-old dog, Puppy, is the only animal allowed there. He said she had earned the privilege after so many years' faithful service.

We had many animals over the years, most of them Puppy's offspring but there were also cats, rabbits, mice and birds. One of the cats, an alley cat, began to give birth while I was in town and Denholm sent the handyman racing after me. When I arrived home I found Denholm pacing up and down the living room, motioning me to be quiet. There, on the only really comfortable chair, was the mother cat. Denholm said that he had put on boiling water but didn't know what to do next. He thought it might help to soothe her if he put on classical music. As each kitten was born he named it after the music that was playing. Hence we had kittens called Depussy, Cat Stevens, Beethoven; and also one named Marilyn after Monroe because it was blonde and very beautiful.

Denholm bought me a black hare on a trip through Barcelona. It was a baby and we trained it to live in the house. He had a special place designated as his lavatory and amazingly he did use it. He had the run of the house, and he often joined us in the living room after dinner and jumped on my lap to be stroked, to the utter astonishment of any guests. He behaved just like a dog, running to the front door expectantly when he heard a car pulling up. While we had workers around building our pool I had to put him in a large cage to protect him from becoming someone's dinner. He literally screamed at me. It broke my heart. When I came out to see him in the morning he had eaten his way through the wire. I never did see him again but I have seen a lot of little black rabbits running around the land over the years.

On one of their trips to Ibiza the Oliviers, Larry and his wife, Joan Plowright, came to the house for dinner. I think Larry had problems with his leg – whatever it was, I know he had to sit at the end of the table during dinner with his leg up on a bench to rest it. Amid the usual dinner-time chat

Larry said to me, 'I do believe we have an uninvited guest.' There, sitting on its hind legs looking expectantly up at Larry, was a fieldmouse. It was not at all frightened, just hungry. Larry leaned down and gave it some bread. The mouse very nonchalantly wandered off with its prize.

Denholm wasn't very sympathetic towards mice in the house. He got up and fetched a mousetrap to set nearer to the door, which was open. While he was down on his hands and knees setting the trap, he accidentally kicked the door closed with his foot. There was a sickening crunch. The mouse had been watching from the hinge side of the door and was no longer part of this world. I knew he was devastated, but his only comment was: 'Ha, fooled you.'

I bought myself a present from Denholm on the only birthday he missed in the thirty-one years we were together. I had commitments on Ibiza and he was in Australia filming *Bangkok Hilton*. I had already visited him for two weeks and it was a long way for him to fly back just to be there on my birthday. He called instead and said 'Go out and buy yourself something you really want from me to you.' I said I already had, and thank you very much. I had given myself a cockatoo. I have always loved those birds: if you get them young enough you can train them brilliantly. Whenever I am away a Spanish friend comes up to the house to look after him and now he is bilingual. His name is Cock-o – not very imaginative, but it suits him.

I will never forget Emma, who was a London pet. Jennifer's birthday was a few weeks off. She had asked Denholm for a hamster as her present so off they went, hand in hand, to the Parkway Pet Shop in Camden Town, carefully questioning the assistant and choosing the exact one she wanted.

Denholm was terrible at keeping presents a secret once they were chosen, as is Jennifer. Neither of them could wait to hand it over the moment a gift was decided upon. So it was that they brought home Emma, three weeks before Jennifer's birthday. Her cage and all the paraphernalia that goes with a hamster was duly deposited in the warmth of our only bathroom. And there it was that on our return one evening we found six little droppings with a life of their own in the cage with Emma. To this day I am amazed that not one mother called me in anger when, on Jennifer's birthday, I carefully boxed six little bundles to be taken home by the lucky little party guests.

As Denholm got more work, we were, over the years, able to add to the house. I really hated going to beaches with the children, who would end up covered in tar and get sand in all their orifices. Denholm loved swimming and so I asked him if we could build a pool. He said first we should dig for water. The well-digging was to be carried out while we were in London and I asked Tony, who was in charge of operations, to send us a telegram the moment they hit water. Meanwhile I went to the pool-builders and asked them for a standard contract, which I took to London and kept by my side at all times. The telegram arrived while I was in the bath. Denholm came in and read it out. 'Eureka! Four and a half tons an hour.' I reached over to my bag, pulled out the contract and said to Denholm, 'Well, you promised that if we hit water, we could have a pool. Sign here.' He was so excited that he signed without a murmur. I waited until he was upstairs again, then dressed, shoved the contract into the already prepared envelope, dashed across the street, my hair still dripping wet, and posted it. I knew that I wouldn't be able to go against him if he changed his mind. This way it was done and couldn't be altered.

The next morning he said, 'Susan, I've been having second thoughts about the pool.' He thought it was very funny when I told him what I had done. 'You really are beginning to know your old man, aren't you?' he said. He never regretted that move and used to get more out of the pool than I did.

However, in order to have such new acquisitions we had to have electricity, and to solve that problem Denholm bought a second-hand ship's generator. He conveniently never seemed to be within shouting distance when the time came to put on the lights, the filter for the pool or the pump for the well. I don't know anyone who knows what it takes to operate one of those things apart from perhaps an old merchant marine and myself. There is a handle halfway down the machine which you have to get turning at breakneck speed until it reaches a certain tempo, at which point you reach up with one hand – still turning the handle, of course – to flick a switch, which, in turn (if you're lucky) kicks the engine into action. What it usually did at the same time was to throw me against the wall with its sheer force. My knuckles were covered in scabs most of the time. When we finally did get mains electricity a Mormon gentleman who had recently moved to the island with his eight wives asked if he could buy the generator. I would have paid him to take it away – as it was, I gave it to him. How to make enemies ... As it happened, though, he sent his wives over with a special request. They asked if I would like to become wife number nine. Of course I had to point out that although I recognised the gesture as a great privilege, I was in fact already married.

The first eight years of our married life were great fun, a whirlwind of parties, films, touring and babies. Living as we did between Ibiza, London and the USA, it was quite normal for us to up sticks on the spur of the moment with the children in tow (and later a nanny, too) to be with Denholm. Denholm and I decided that the only way to keep us together as a family was to take it with us. I enjoyed it – it meant I didn't feel left behind and was part of the action. It never seemed difficult, nor indeed wrong. Other people thought our relationship bizarre, but then, of course, they could never have lived our lives. To us it was what we knew and how it was, and it became quite natural. Years later, Jennifer said that perhaps the only way I let the children down was in making our nomadic lives appear so ordinary that they didn't know other people lived differently.

I think my acceptance of our way of life had a lot to do with how I was brought up as a child. My family was forever moving between New York City, North Carolina and Washington DC, and in the earlier part of my childhood we had moved to Osining, then to Briercliff, White Plains and Yonkers, New York. I have soothing memories of travelling on overnight sleepers between these places and North Carolina. There are times when I have difficulty sleeping that I rock myself to sleep in the motion of a moving train. In Ibiza I sometimes get up in the middle of the night and go down to my boat to sleep.

On some occasions during the early years, because of Jennifer and Mark's education and, of course, the expense of moving us around the globe for what might be less than six weeks, I had to stay in one place without Denholm. We decided that if work took him on location abroad and we couldn't go with him it would be easier and more fun for me (and the kids) to be in Ibiza rather than London. The island was, and still is, a woman's island. People consider it quite normal for a woman to sit alone in a café or bar and don't assume she's on the make, as would be the case in most other parts of the world. Furthermore, the Spanish tend to take their children out with them, often until 10 p.m., to enjoy the social life on offer. If a film location looked as if it was going to extend into what we called the 'danger zone', then I would travel to wherever Denholm was filming in order to break up the time separating us. However, it didn't take me long to learn that in order to establish my credentials (however temporary the competition), it was best to make my entry at the very beginning of a location shoot rather than in the middle when, to use one of Denholm's favourite expressions, I was in danger of being made to feel like a spare prick at a wedding.

Visitors came to Ibiza from all over the world and from all walks of life. They still do, but now the island is much more crowded than it was in the sixties and seventies. Our side of the island, Santa Eulalia, and in particular Sandy's Bar seemed to attract all the artists, writers and actors. This had a lot to do with Sandy Pratt himself, a highly intelligent, well-read and witty Irishman. There were days when his bar seemed to contain more personalities per square foot than Broadway and the West End put together. Terry-Thomas and his wife, Belinda, and two sons, Cushan and Tiger, followed Denholm and myself, Nina and Frederick, Leslie Phillips, Caroline Mortimer and Robin Maugham. Later came April Ashley, John Hurt, Diana Rigg and Philip Saville, Nigel Davenport and Fiz, Debbie Leng and Roger Taylor, of Queen, and then Maria Aitken and her mother, Lady 'Pempe' Aitken, who still travels back and forth as often as a fiddler's elbow, transplanting half of England's 'green and glorious' into the red soil of Spain, with amazing results.

Maybe Sandy instilled a touch of fear as well as respect in his young disciples, but even after the children were dragged around the shops and then to Sandy's for the 'well-earned' Bloody Mary, you would never find anything less than impeccably behaved children. As for the adults, it took one, just one, quiet word from Sandy – who always took the offender to one side and never humiliated him in front of others – to straighten out any anti-social behaviour. They didn't get many chances, either – and believe me, no one wanted to be banned from Sandy's.

One of our favourite sayings was: 'I'm just going to check the post.' It could take five hours but at least everyone knew where you were to be found if necessary. Of course, Santa Eulalia did have a Post Office but at least at Sandy's the only thing you had to queue for was the Bloody Mary while you collected your post or took a phone call.

One of Sandy's more hair-raising moments was in fixing up a retreat for the Oliviers, Larry and Joan and their entourage of children and nanny. It was Denholm who encouraged them to sample the delights of Ibiza but I don't think he really believed it would ever happen and when they actually arrived he was a nervous wreck. His worries that Larry and Joan might not have a good time were entirely groundless (except for a few days when Joan had a battle with what we called 'Franco's revenge'). One night Nina and Frederick invited us all to their house for dinner and the best chocolate mousse I have ever eaten (she says it's because of all the alcohol). When the evening broke up Denholm and Larry were legless, but since we all arrived 'in the country on back roads' Denholm didn't feel he was incapable of driving. We shot off down the dirt track and it wasn't until we landed on the other side of the main road in a ditch that we all realised we had headed off in the wrong direction.

Larry decided to drive a few nights later when the four of us went into Ibiza Town for dinner. A very strange optical illusion occurs (irrespective of whether you are sober or drunk) at a certain point on the way to the harbour whereby, even though you are approaching the town, it looks as though it is moving away from you. On this occasion we were so engrossed in this phenomenon that Larry missed the bend and we ended up in the muddy banks of the Ibiza Harbour.

On Joan and Larry's second visit Sandy arranged a hire-car for them and he and I went to form part of a welcoming committee. As the procession of cars left the airport with Sandy in the lead, Larry's car overtook us and as they passed, Larry wound down his window and shouted at the top of his voice: 'First stop, Sandy's Bar!'

I was surprised how easy-going Larry could be. He was not at all as formidable as Denholm's apprehension suggested, though of course I usually saw him when he was at his most relaxed. I did tell him many years later that I was really glad I met him first in Ibiza rather than first seeing all his films because I would have gone into a dead faint otherwise.

There was a big change, though, towards the end of his life when he was suffering from a catalogue of illnesses, any one of which would have felled a lesser man. His fortitude was magnificent but he could sound off in sheer frustration, and without warning. Joan invited us to have supper together with a small group of their friends. I was sitting to his right.

He began to talk about death and oblivion. By now I was living in a private hell of my own, in fear of losing Jennifer to hard drugs, perhaps an overdose, and having just discovered that Denholm was HIV positive. I was only just beginning to realise that I might lose my lover and husband and my beautiful daughter. 'I understand, in my own way, what you are going through,' I said to Larry.

He rounded on me. 'What do you know? How can you possibly know about death and dying?'

It wasn't a question. It was more of an accusation. I was just short of bursting into floods of tears.

After a prolonged silence, at least at our end of the table, he said, 'Are you all right, my darling?'

Of course I wasn't all right but there was nothing I could say to change anything. Joan came to our end of the table and with difficulty helped Larry up and they left the room. She returned after some minutes and the dinner resumed.

It was the last time I saw either of them. I wish I had been able to let them know I really *did* understand.

But that is not the way to remember that extraordinary man. He was such a life-force, capable of great generosity and possessed of an almost childlike delight in giving surprises. Joan was in the theatre on one particular evening and Larry rang to invite us to his London flat for a Thanksgiving dinner in the style of the old South – turkey, succotash, sweet potatoes and pumpkin pie. This he had cooked himself, but an even greater compliment to me was the knowledge that he had gone through the business of producing this elaborate meal despite enduring a crippling disease in his hand which exposed all the nerve endings and caused excruciating pain. His only acknowledgement that he was suffering was that when he came to carve the turkey he used an electric knife. It was typical of the man that he wrote to thank me for going to see him and for being 'so sweet and brave to eat my cooking'.

Forget the jump in population and the profusion of souvenir shops, the charm of Ibiza was that wonderful sensation of stepping back into another century. But there were occasions when its remoteness could be a terrible drawback. I am thinking particularly of the tragedy that overtook my father and the sad fact that I was the last of my family to hear of his death. My brother Peter did his best to get hold of me, leaving messages at the Post Office and the hotel to say that he would ring at a particular time. But the calls never came or they came when I was somewhere else. An all-important telegram went astray. I did get the follow-up. It read: 'Funeral went well. Love Family.' That was all. Now I was frantic, booking calls to New York, Washington, North Carolina, any of the places where somebody might be able to tell me what had happened. I didn't even know *who* had died. The sheer frustration was driving me to panic when Denholm appeared on the island. His arrival took me by surprise. He had several weeks to go in North Africa working on the movie *Maroc 7*. He could not possibly have finished this far ahead of schedule. But, of course, he was home for a purpose. My brother Mark had succeeded in reaching him on location and Denholm had immediately flown to Ibiza to break the news.

Ted had killed himself.

I suppose I should have known. There was always a chance that a black mood would take him beyond endurance. Once before he had prepared himself for the finale, tidying up his affairs with minute attention to detail to minimise the inconvenience of his passing. That was just like Ted. To worry about the little things but to leave out of his calculations the huge sadness that his death would bring. At this first attempt, his plans were thrown by the sheer chance of Mom noticing that he had transferred a large amount of cash to her bank account. Assuming it to be a mistake she rang Ted to tell him that she had moved the money back again.

This time she did not immediately spot the change in her fortune. By the time she did realise what had happened, Ted had jumped from the twenty-eighth floor of the Manhattan Towers. After the funeral, Mom put a block on her memories. All of Ted's photographs and letters were packed away. Many years later I came across some of the pictures in a bottom drawer and asked her why I hadn't seen them before. She said that she had cried so much whenever she saw a photo of Ted that she couldn't stand the pain any longer. Even when she told me this she began to cry again.

Mom is still alive. At eighty-nine she divides her time between New York City and visits to her home in Southport. Although she doesn't get out as often as she would like she does manage to get to the Catholic church twice a week and to the café across the street from her flat, where she indulges in her favourite pastime – watching people, smoking, and drinking coffee. In the evening she has her Bourbon with water. She splits one jigger into two drinks to make them last longer. She's a real character and Denholm loved her. He also loved my sister Joyce, and he often said that if he hadn't married me he would have liked to be married to Joyce. I was very flattered because Joyce is outrageous and stunningly beautiful.

Thirty years on I have to ask myself whether we were right to bring up the children the way we did, hopping back and forth between Ibiza and London. I think the answer is yes, but there was no other choice anyway in view of Denholm's job. I think that today many young men take a bigger part in the actual routine of childcare. Denholm would never have been a 'typical' father anyway, because he wasn't a 'typical' person. He was off the wall and eccentric, but as a father, he loved Jennifer and Mark very much. He was better at communicating with them when they were in their teens and older. They laughed a lot together and he treated them more like friends than his children. But when they were little and I had to run to the corner shop for something I had forgotten for dinner his method of watching the kids for a minute was to sit them in front of the telly with a box of his favourite chocolates. I didn't often leave him alone with them at the single-digit ages but each time I did I would come back to find their faces smeared in chocolate and their appetites sated.

Mark and Jennifer were both born prematurely. This was due to the difference in blood type between Denholm and myself, which we didn't find out about until after I had lost the twins and became pregnant with Jennifer while on tour in the States. Both the children have Denholm's O positive while I am A negative and therefore both wanted out at about seven months. Jennifer made a quick recovery (although she was born looking as though she had come straight off the ski-slopes, as my father put it – I didn't have the heart to tell him she had jaundice) and in six months had caught up to the normal weight for her age. Mark, on the other hand (my biggest baby, weighing in at three pounds), took longer and also had the added problem of a hormonal imbalance which caused a growth deficiency. From an early age he would suddenly vomit and then go into a coma. At first he had incredibly high fevers as well. A whole catalogue of diseases were diagnosed by many different hospitals but they were all wrong and the poor child had to suffer many painful tests while the experts tried to determine which label to put on his problem. I was even told by one very well-known children's hospital one night when I rushed him in, that he had spinal meningitis and wouldn't last the night. Thank God, I knew they were wrong. The main worry and the reason why we always had to have professional nannies travelling with us was that if he should happen to have one of these 'fits' while Denholm and I were out for the evening there was a real danger that he might choke on his own vomit and we would lose him.

One evening in Ibiza we had a local girl come up to sit for a while with Jennifer, who was at that time eleven, and Mark, who was eight and by that time was passing out less than once a year.

When we arrived home that evening there was the most horrendous smell in the house. We let the girl go – she was herself only eighteen years old – and then I went to check where the smell was coming from. I followed it to Jennifer's room. She was huddled in a corner of the room. The stench was the smell of fear. As I stood there trying to get my wits together a glass that was standing on the floor shattered into a thousand pieces. The sheer force of energy in the room had caused that and the fear had been triggered by the babysitter, who had decided that for a bedtime story she would read out loud to Jennifer excerpts from *The Exorcist*.

Jennifer's personality as a fun-loving, carefree little girl went away forever that evening. We tried everything. I thought if I could get her involved in lots of exercise it would help so I took her to learn to ride, and then to tennis lessons. She got involved with a very nice couple who lived nearby who were into religion and would go with a group to Ibiza for sing-song meetings. I explained to the woman the trauma Jennifer had been going through and asked her not to throw guilt and devils at her. She was quite sympathetic. I think my efforts might have done some good but I know that Jennifer never fully recovered from the experience.

I had always forbidden the kids to go and see any films that would be frightening. Years later they confessed to sneaking out to see all sorts of horrors. It is for that reason from my own self-knowledge and because of what happened to Jennifer, that I totally agree it is a huge mistake to televise violent, frightening films that can be viewed by young children or even young adults. It might not influence all of them, but it can completely change the lives of a small percentage – and not for the better.

In their early years Jennifer and Mark went to a school on Ibiza rather grandly known as the International School where the teaching was perfectly adequate for a basic education. They also became bilingual. But when they hit eleven or twelve we had to decide whether to put them through the Spanish secondary system or send them to schools in England. It did not take us long to make up our minds. The children needed to broaden their horizons. They were already showing signs of becoming bored. Both were liable to withdraw into their own fantasy worlds, which suggested that their undeniably lively imaginations were not being sufficiently stimulated by life around them.

We did not, as many imagine, opt for an English boarding education as a way of avoiding the drugs problem in Ibiza. It is true that by the late sixties the drug scene was open and active. The authorities took a liberal view, as they did on most things, and you did not have to go far to find cheap supplies of pot. Its easy availability did not worry us. Smoking marijuana was no worse than smoking tobacco or drinking alcohol, both of which we did in full measure. Denholm himself kept a little store of pot hidden away. Not long ago, an actor friend told me that whenever Denholm was on location in a country where the law enforcement was more rigid, he took the precaution of hiding a bag of grass in his hotel bedroom, pinned to a curtain fold.

So we did not see mild drugs as a threat and, rightly or wrongly, we were not concerned for the children. We only became concerned when they were in their mid-teens, and, in particular, about Jennifer, who later came into contact with hard drugs. Experimentation turned into addiction with terrible consequences for her and for the rest of the family. But, as I say, in the mid-seventies, when we were trying to settle on who was going to school where, the fear of drugs was not on our minds.

Looking back, where Denholm and I made our biggest mistake was in not taking a firmer line on the choice of schools. Knowing little of the English education system and nothing of boarding schools, I looked to Denholm to take the lead. His childhood had been made miserable by a school forced on him by the family. He did not intend putting his own children through the same agonies. It was up to them to choose where they wanted to go. The logic of his good intentions failed for want of reliable information.

We listened to what other families with young children had to say but with conflicting advice on offer, decisions were invariably made on the pot-luck principle. Mark went to Falcon Manor in Northampton, along with Terry-Thomas's son Cushan. The two were close friends, so close that Cushan virtually moved in with us. We heard about Falcon Manor from another family on the island who gave the school a high rating. It became first choice for Mark and Cushan for want of any other serious recommendations.

By the time they set off for what turned out to be a modest advance in learning, Jennifer was already installed at Rosemead in Littlehampton, where she had followed closely on the heels of a best friend. But it was not long before Jennifer felt lonely and miserable in a school which seemed unable to accept that youngsters resent being treated as identikits. She lasted for two unhappy years in which she made next to no academic progress. Urging perseverance, and for want of an acceptable alternative to Rosemead, we tried to make Jennifer's life bearable with frequent visits. Whenever Denholm was in England for any time, he would take a motorcycle ride down to Southampton. His choice of vehicle immediately put him into the category of highly eccentric parents. It was a reputation much enhanced by a collision with a roundabout outside the school. He ended up in the infirmary with Matron and Jennifer in attendance. I only recently found out from Jennifer that on Denholm's visits to school or when she was leaving home after half-term he would now and again give her a tiny stash of grass. It doesn't surprise me that they kept it to themselves – Denholm didn't see anything wrong with grass, but I would have gone spare had I known.

From locations, Denholm peppered the children with letters of a hundred words or less:

Darling Jennifer,
Well, here I am in Toronto, Canada making a movie called *Partners*. Yesterday I had to fall in the river with all my clothes on, it was VERY COLD! POOR OLD DAD!!
We have some beautiful horses and dogs on the film, you would love them. I enclose a picture of my hotel. Lots of love and xxx see you soon. I miss you.
Love Dad.
I hope you can read my writing.

At fifteen, Jennifer came to London to spend a year at a crammer. It got her a respectable basic education but also reinforced the drug habit she had picked up at Southampton. With a real talent for the visual arts, Mark seemed to have the edge. He was accepted for St Martin's School of Art in London and subsequently for the School of Visual Arts in New York; where he spent a productive and pleasurable year living in the YMCA. But then he moved into lodgings and from there to a squat which he liked to present as a demonstration of communal idealism but was more an excuse for opting out. While Jennifer went for the drugs, Mark took to drink. As they went into their twenties, they were both in bad shape. Their parents were not too well, either. But that lay ahead of us and is another part of the story; now we were embarking on the 1970s and our second decade together.

214

9

Close Encounters

This is how the gossip writer on *The Sunday Express* saw us:

Denholm Elliott, the actor who is currently starring with Claire Bloom in the film The Doll's House, *was reunited with his wife Susan last week in London.*

Says Mrs Elliott, thirty-one, who now lives in Ibiza with her two children, Jennifer, eight, and Mark, six: 'I started living there in November when we decided we had to put the kids in a permanent school. They're at the Ibiza International School, which is English but has a mixture of English, French, German and Swiss children – about seventy of them. We weren't sure Denholm's work would come from London this year.

'In fact, we thought it would be America, and I didn't particularly want to go there. We had our house in Ibiza for holidays and lots of mates – Terry-Thomas and others – to go out to dinner with. So we moved there to live.

'Denholm has been doing a lot of television in London

but he regularly nips out to Ibiza for a couple of weeks. I suppose we spend about ten days in every five weeks together.

'I couldn't count the number of times he has been out to Ibiza, or me to London, but we are thinking of trying to make a deal with the airline. It costs a fortune in air fares.

'This month is pretty hectic. It was Denholm's birthday on Thursday. So I came to London for that. Jennifer is having her ninth birthday on Friday. So I have to be back for that.

'On 15 June it is our eleventh wedding anniversary and perhaps we'll be somewhere in mid-air then.'

Says Mr Elliott, fifty-one, who was once married to Virginia McKenna: 'I hadn't seen Susan for some time because she is looking after the kids.'

This was how the press saw us as our marriage entered its second decade. The one significant missing detail was that I now knew that Denholm was actively bisexual.

I was introduced to the turbulence in Denholm's sex life when he came off location for *Too Late the Hero*, a movie for which he, Michael Caine and Cliff Robertson went to the Philippines. When rehearsals started in Hollywood we worked out a family schedule basing me and the children in Hong Kong. With Mark's health in a fragile state, it was unrealistic to believe that we would be able to follow closely in Denholm's steps. But in Hong Kong we were at least within visiting distance over what was clearly going to be a long haul.

Not ever having been to Hong Kong and knowing little about the place except that it was among the more overcrowded of British colonies, I allowed the studio to make all the travel arrangements. So it was that I turned up at the Mandarin Hotel with two small children in tow – and a nanny, which was the closest I ever got to taking coals to Newcastle. Nor did I need any prompting to realise that the Mandarin was more suited to high-earning business travellers than to Mum and the kids.

Setting off in search of less formal lodgings in what I hoped was the real Hong Kong, I found a cosy-looking hotel called the Luk Kwok where the rooms were priced at a fraction of the rate I was paying at the Mandarin. The narrow streets were crowded day and night but this was a slice of China other visitors rarely encountered. How right I was. A few days after I had circulated my new address, Denholm cabled me with the revelation. 'You are living in the world of Suzie Wong.'

Living in a brothel did not greatly concern me. The girls were kind to the children and polite to me. The only awkwardness I had was with an Indian gentleman who assumed that, as I was white, I was the Australian speciality of the house. It took the concerted efforts of two guards on our floor to persuade him otherwise. Tommy Cooper, the comedian, who had played Hong Kong often, put me under the protection of a club-owner who operated just round the corner. This man was attentive to a fault and sent round a car and driver whenever I felt like an excursion, but I couldn't help pointing out to my chaperon that the Luk Kwok Hotel was right next-door to the club. The club was popular with off-duty policemen and prostitutes. They enjoyed games of skittles together before going back on the beat or to the hotel.

Denholm next wanted me to move into a flat. The motive

here was less to do with protecting my innocence than with saving on the budget, and quite honestly not having a kitchen with two young children was a bit of a hassle for such a long time.

Communications between Hong Kong and the remote village in the Philippines left much to be desired. Often our letters crossed, which led to some confusion with practical arrangements and some didn't arrive at all.

> 11 February 1969
> Hello Pot,
> Not a word from ya? The cable service here is just awful. I've sent 4 (count them) cables to ya & they just go out over the Aether (air) & disappear forever. I don't even know if this letter will arrive. It's very hot here & it will get worse when I've got into the jungle. I'll be in Hong Kong Monday 24 Feb for 6 days – that's 2 weeks from today. And then again from about 27 March for about 10 days or so.
> How are the Little Pots? 'AAH-Lo' give Jennifer a kiss & bite on your shoulders from me & Mark a up & down swinger.
> Miss you Pot & I really am getting desperate for News.
> Best of love xxx D.

From this I gathered Denholm was missing me a lot and I responded in our usual jokey romantic style, describing my relief at having heard from him and telling him how much I missed him.

The drop from this high point of mesmeric devotion to our falling-out a few weeks later was a million miles. We were all back in Los Angeles. The talk over drinks was of how everybody had had such a good time on location. To me, there did not seem to have been much choice of leisure activities: there was sex, or there was sex. That did not worry me over-much until Denholm sheepishly suggested that I should call in at what was colloquially known as the 'clap clinic' for a protective shot, 'just to be on the safe side'. The implications did not have to be spelled out for me. Maybe I should not have pressed for details. Once he started talking, he did not hold anything back. He told me that he had been to some orgies in the Philippines involving both men and women. I wouldn't have minded as much if I hadn't had to go and have the shots too.

This was too much for me. My first instinctive reaction was to declare the marriage over. We agreed on a trial separation. I left him in Los Angeles so that we could both think over what was happening to our lives together. But on the flight to London I started to think about what I was doing to Denholm and to myself. He had openly admitted his bisexuality. I did not have to force him into a confession by dissecting lies or by catching him out on clumsy prevarication. I had asked and he had told me.

Yet he had never once said that he had stopped loving me. At our lowest depths he had insisted that he still loved me, would always love me. Why, then, was I trying to break away? If, as I was now beginning to realise, I was sulking over a bruised ego, perhaps the answer was not to destroy all that we had created but to reconstruct the relationship on a different foundation. Back in London, I made up my mind to try again. Denholm was overjoyed. The trial separation had lasted less than a week.

It did not mean that our troubles were over, of course. It was one thing for me to come to terms with Denholm's sexuality; it was quite another for him to come to terms with his own true nature. For most of his life, public aversion to gay sex, enshrined in archaic law, had bred subterfuge and secrecy. The recent legislation of what the politicians described as 'homosexual acts between consenting adults in private' had released Denholm, along with so many others, from the fear of a wrecked career and tabloid pillorying. But the guilt feeling was less easily erased. There was our family to think of, and his relatives. Nina had known about Denholm's inclinations for many years before her death, but he still lived in dread of Neil finding out. There was never any question of Denholm coming out of the closet. He was happiest conducting his affairs out of the limelight, often in some distant land where he was entirely free from the prurient gaze.

Denholm's first regular boyfriend lived in Barcelona. His name was Moñolo. Twenty-five years ago, Moñolo was slim, dark-haired, not long out of his teens. He worked on a large parking lot. Denholm met him when he left his car overnight having just driven halfway across Europe. Moñolo was always a great one for receiving presents, and there was no one more adept than he at finding his way round the bar scene.

The affair with Moñolo altered Denholm's life in more ways than one. It was his first long-term male relationship – it lasted on and off for five years – and it converted him from a dominant to a passive partner. Up to then, Denholm had always been the seducer, the one who took possession. With Moñolo he embraced a lover who proved to be the stronger force.

I was never jealous of Moñolo. I was still having an active sex life with Denholm. Between us, he was always 100 per cent masculine, both in bed and in taking decisions in our home life. Even when Moñolo came over to Ibiza – my territory, as I chose to think – I was not put in second place. He checked into a hotel – all very discreet – and the three of us met together in an anonymous bar. After a decent amount of alcohol I found myself actually reassuring Moñolo that he had nothing to fear from me. I accepted that he was important to Denholm but equally he knew that he could never take Denholm away from me.

People might think that I would have been happier in a conventional marriage, but I accepted that living with an exceptional person brought far more pleasure than pain into my life. I loved Denholm very much but more than that, we enjoyed each other's company more than anyone else's, which made it easier to accept the unusual nature of our relationship.

Only once did I take serious exception to a rival lover. He was a young Moroccan Denholm picked up in a bar. He also came to Ibiza, but uninvited. He took money from Denholm – most of them did – but it was his way of doing it, by oily ingratiation that repelled me. Denholm allowed himself to be pushed around, even to be told what to wear, then worked off his humiliation by rowing. I had taken more than enough when the boy turned up at the house. Damned if I was going to spend time chatting, I went about whatever I was doing. He followed me. Suddenly, he said: 'You're not going to win, you know.'

I turned on him. 'You've got it wrong. I'm not in competition.'

The man left Ibiza for London and Denholm followed a

few days later. I saw off Denholm, and Jennifer, who was going back to school, at the airport. I kissed Denholm goodbye. I really thought that our marriage was over.

I went home and cried a lot. There was a big party that night. I went along and drank far too much. A French actor, my age, who was holidaying on the island, kept me company. When the party broke up I took him home. He was the second man I had been to bed with. It was the briefest of affairs but he reassured me about something which had been worrying me – that I was still attractive and desirable. I had no feeling of guilt.

When, a week later, Denholm rang to say that he was miserable, that he didn't want to split, that we had to find some way of living out our lives together, I was confident enough in my strength of purpose to try again. But there were to be no misunderstandings. I was not prepared for a relationship that was open on one side only, and I wanted to be taken off the pedestal on to which he had lifted me.

It was weeks before we saw each other again, interspersed with many phone calls, and when we did it was on a new footing.

I joined Denholm in London for the last days of rehearsal for *Come As You Are*. Of the many words used to describe this production 'happy' is not one of them. It was as if everybody involved was trying out a theory of perpetual friction. The focal point of disorder was Glynis Johns, who co-starred with Denholm and Joss Ackland. The kindest excuse for Glynis, who forgot her lines, missed her cues and skipped rehearsals and even performances, was that her mother was terminally ill.

Denholm was furious at such a blatant lack of professionalism and blamed the director, Allan Davis, for failing to impose discipline. It is probably true that Glynis would still have behaved erratically if her mother had been in perfect health, but Allan took the view that her neurosis could not be ordered out of existence. She had to be handled gently, with kindness and consideration. This made Denholm even more angry, to the point where he had a stand-up fight with Allan. The fracas took place in Denholm's dressing room after a performance. Joss was there, doing his best to separate the contestants. So, too, was a wide-eyed cousin of Denholm's who had come round for a quiet drink. As Joss said, it was a wonder they bothered to sell tickets at the front of the house. They would have done just as well charging admission at the stage door.

It was almost as if Glynis went out of her way to provoke Denholm, picking on insignificant grievances to stoke up his temper. There was no escape. When Denholm or Joss went out for a meal, Glynis was invariably in tow. She never carried cash but showed the patience of which she was capable of *in extremis* by waiting, interminably, for others to pay her bills. When she invaded Denholm's dressing room to complain loudly and at length at the terrible injustices heaped upon her, and Denholm responded with a weary observation – 'Darling, you're pissed' – the barb was taken as sufficient cause for a complaint to the producer.

This unfortunate man was Alex Cohen, a legendary figure on Broadway, who was now having to get used to commuting to London to sort out little local difficulties. The incident ended with a formal warning to Glynis, who managed to pull herself together for a modest run of *Come As You Are*, first at the New Theatre and then at the Strand. Even so, she had a strong back-up for emergencies, including two understudies.

I went up to Edinburgh for the opening. Our friend John Mortimer was there, sitting at a trestle table rewriting to order. He was used to the tension. One of the four plays that comprised the original *Come As You Are* was dropped entirely in rehearsal. Putting together a replacement kept everyone's adrenaline running up to and beyond the first night.

John and Denholm had a huge liking and admiration for each other and although over the years we haven't seen him as often as we would have liked we became friends for life. Throughout the entire run of *Come As You Are*, beginning with the evening I shared the express from Edinburgh to London with John, we carried on a semi-serious flirtation. We shared many drinks and laughs over his fund of stories mostly of a misspent legal career. Although he could have easily laughed me straight into bed there were two people who unwittingly put the reins on it going further. One was his daughter Caroline who was a close friend at the time. She must have watched John and I flirting when we all met at a party one evening. 'I don't really care what you decide to do as long as I don't have to call you Mother', she said. The other was Denholm. He had never really asked me not to be intimate with anyone ('. . . as long as you don't fall in love and as long as you don't have anyone else's baby') mainly because, as he said himself, it made him feel less guilty about his own indiscretions.

Denholm certainly had his own preoccupations. While he was in *Come As You Are* he met one of the loves of his life. David shared a flat with Denholm's dresser. They were playing the Theatre Royal in Brighton when Denholm, chatting over the make-up, asked his dresser if he lived with anyone. That was when David's name came up. 'Why don't you bring him in one evening?' Denholm suggested. 'Come round after the show for a drink.'

I remember the first meeting. It was, in fact, in the Theatre Royal bar. In his early forties, David was slim, slightly camp and not altogether confident in what were for him unfamiliar surroundings. He was a shop assistant, in menswear, somewhere in the West End. Denholm was clearly taken with him, enjoying the quiet diffidence of a man who was a little in awe of the famous actor. First impressions were misleading – David was more assertive than he appeared – but in these early days he went along with Denholm's gentle seduction while trying to figure out why it was that a man who put a wife and two children at the centre of his life, and made no secret of his love for them, should also want to play the gay scene.

Denholm was collecting boyfriends with an intensity that can only suggest that he was making up for lost time. It was understandable. As for so many others of his generation, the lifting of repression on gay love was like taking the bolts off a safety valve. Moreover, Denholm was nearly fifty, an age when the years start accelerating.

While he was winning over David, another long-term relationship was blossoming. Edwin also worked behind a West End counter but beyond that he had little in common with David. Edwin had come over from Barbados as a teenager. When he and Denholm met, in a bar near Marble Arch, he was in his late thirties, 'a black willow', as Denholm called him. He was easy-going, a good listener and more

225

impressed by Denholm's car than by his theatrical credentials. And there were others, many passing fancies long since lost in the pageant of gay encounters.

As the boyfriend with the deepest romantic streak, David did not take easily to Denholm's many infidelities but he was even less easily reconciled to the long periods of silence when Denholm was preoccupied with work or pleasure. A six-week gap closed by a cheery telephone call to David, inviting him to take up where they had left off, sparked a monster row and an invitation from David 'to go to hell' which was almost immediately rescinded. The pattern was often repeated.

After *Come As You Are*, Denholm tried to regain his professional equilibrium with a short engagement away from it all, playing in a revival of Noel Coward's *Design For Living* at the Los Angeles Music Center. At first, as he bemoaned in a letter to me, he felt he had made a big mistake.

12/2/71

My darling Pottles,
I am sitting here after rehearsals, thinking about you, as you-so-all, & missing you like mad & asking myself for the 1,000th time why I'm *here* – I really don't know how I am going to *stand* it. The loneliness is *mind-bending*!!! I'm seeing Howard & Lynn Sackler on Monday night & going to a movie & Chinese nosh. Please kiss the kids & yourself from me – I really can't *wait* to come home. Verdad.
　　All my love, xxx Denholm.

But within hours there was an event, a lunatic adventure of the sort that took Denholm out of himself and made life worth living again:

Next day
The sequel to this Highly Self-pitying Night which still hangs over me like a half-remembered dream, was that I roared out of my Hotel & leapt into my car & took off to Hollywood to find a Bar, any Bar – *someone to talk to*! ANNEE-WON. I was stopped by two *FU-CK-ING* great cops – *clanking* with chains & guns & Boots & Balls 'OK fella I'm not gonna send you an engraved invitation – *Pullover*.'

'Let's see ya driver's licence.'

'It's in the boot er trunk officer.'

As I opened the boot they pulled their *guns*! I suppose they thought I was going to mow them down with the spare wheel.

'How much have you had to drink?'

'Er, one vodka & tonic officer.' (I'd had half a bottle.)

'Yeh? *one* eh? Or two or 3 or 4?'

'No *honestly* officer – (hic)'

'OK – Now do *EXACTLY* as I do. Walk this line one foot touching the other & turn without lifting the back foot.'

(My mind was saying 'Cunts, I'm an *actor* do you think I can't do *that*?) So I *did* it – thank God!

'OK. Now lift the foot & close your eyes & do as I say . . . touch your nose with your left hand – right hand – right hand – left hand – put your head back – further – further *come on FURTHER*!' Finally after a long lecture they let me go – I was shaking & needed a drink BUT *BAD* REEEL *B.A.D.* I lurched into a bar & there was Hermione Baddeley! With the casting director from my show & lots of nice people so it all ended very well – with a PISS-UP!

Love xx D.

As he got older, Denholm's restlessness became almost a psychological disorder. He could be discovered totally at peace with the world – in his garden, or floating in the swimming pool, or stretched out in the sun – and anyone who came across him at that moment would assume that he was in a state of supreme contentment. And possibly he was, for a couple of months. But then he wanted to be up and off again. He once said that his favourite place in the world was the departure lounge at Heathrow.

Whenever he was in one place for very long, his mind, and his desires, soon wandered. He would knock out a quick card to Edwin or David reminding them that he was still around.

Edwin was patient and long-suffering and did not easily take offence. David was more prickly. Sharing a flat with a long-term partner (as he still does), he at least had a close friend on hand to remind him that actors were difficult to know simply because you could never be quite sure that they were not putting on an act. But David saw in Denholm his ideal and though, quite soon, he became reconciled to the idea of Denholm remaining part of a marriage, he needed reassurance that rivals were not moving into his territory. There was a big bust-up in 1976 when David worried himself into believing that Edwin was getting too close. From

Denholm had a lifelong love of powerful motorcycles but could be reckless – hence my look of apprehension.

With Denholm on location in Bilbao, Spain, for *Robin and Marian*.

At a late night private view of *Deathtrap*, the film which contained the famous kiss between Christopher Reeve (left) and Michael Caine (right).

From left to right, Pat Heywood, Geraldine McEwan, Albert Finney and Denholm in *Chez Nous*, 1975.

On a skiing trip: Mark, Jennifer and me.

Cousin Darby, Jennifer, Denholm and Mark in 1982 on Jennifer's eighteenth birthday. A days' outing from the drug clinic.

The many faces of Denholm Elliott.
Top row, left to right: *The Sound Barrier, The Cruel Sea, Station Six Sahara, Ring Round the Moon, A Touch of the Poet, Dracula.*
Middle row, left to right: *The Sea Gull, A Doll's House, Percy,* a press photo, *In Hiding,* a publicity still.

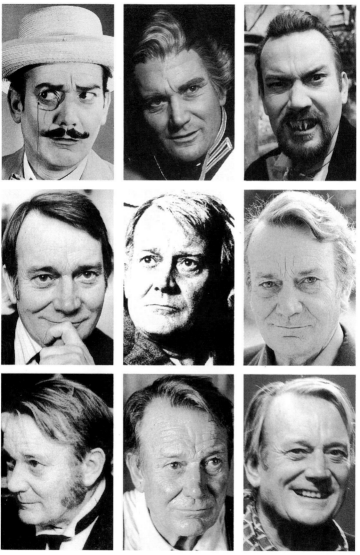

Bottom row, left to right: *Underworld*, joking between takes in *Underworld*, *Defence of the Realm*, *A Room With a View*, *Bangkok Hilton*, *Noises Off*.

Mark on the *Marco Polo* location with Dad in 1981, pretending to fight over a ham sandwich.

Jennifer and Mark with Denholm at a film premiere.

From left to right: Farley Granger, me and Bob Calhoun, on a Soho pub crawl at The Colony Room with owner, the late Ian Board.
(Photo courtesy Michael Clark.)

Brimstone and Treacle the second time around in 1982, this time with Joan Plowright and Sting.

Denholm and me with Jack Lemmon on a boat on the Hudson River during the promotional tour for *A Room With a View*.

Denholm's point of view Edwin and David were both equally important in that he wanted the reassurance of knowing that either one or the other would be there for him when the desire took him.

After the break-up with David, Denholm didn't see him for nearly six months, but in the end Denholm always had a way of diffusing anger or hurt by a cheery phone call or, more frequently, with a jokey postcard. From Spain, probably Barcelona, there was an Adonis in minute swimming trunks, flashing a wide smile as he lounges in the surf.

Come on in. Water is lovely. Weather heaven. Want to meet my friend? I expect to be back mid-April and will call.
Love Denholm

Or a Bette Davis card (Denholm appeared with her in *Madame Sin*) showing her with Joan Crawford in a still from *What Ever Happened to Baby Jane?*

Bette joins me in sending you birthday greetings from Los Angeles. She has prepared dinner for us both. She says to be sure to eat it all up – fur and all. I can't think *what* she means.

In the envelope was a second card, of a chocolate-box pussy-cat complete with pink ribbon round its neck. David was fond of cats, though not in the sense that Denholm implied.

They soon patched up their quarrel. Denholm held out little hope of changing his lifestyle, though David was encouraged to try to work the miracle. For the first time in his life, Denholm felt the confidence of total control. He knew he could do what he liked.

Though we rarely saw each other, David and I came to a sort of accommodation in which we jointly recognised any attempt to throw us off balance. Ironically, one of the more serious intrusions was made by a woman, an actress. She was star-struck; he, as ever, was struck by an unquestioning admirer. I kept as far away as I could from this little jaunt, knowing that anything I did was likely to complicate matters. David, on the other hand, played closely and cleverly, even to the extent of acting as father confessor to her as she struggled to come to terms with Denholm's idiosyncratic life. Denholm was liable to confuse telephone numbers. David was a little surprised, when answering the telephone, to be greeted with a cheery 'Hello, loveliness.'

'Who's that?' he asked before realising that it was Denholm's voice he was hearing.

'Benjamin Disraeli,' said Denholm smartly, and slapped down the receiver.

10

Location, Location, Location

Denholm had long since given up worrying about the supply of work. It came at him from all directions. Whatever is thought now of the craziness of our life in the seventies, remember that we were living at a frenetic rate. Ibiza was a whirl of eat, drink and be merry from which Denholm would spin off to play a film part here or a television role there, returning full of exuberance, eager for the next excitement.

But even with the canny Jean Diamond as his agent superior, Denholm could not guarantee an unbroken run of critical success. There was a continuing roll-call of jobs he did for the money – and the fun. One such was *Quest for Love*, a film with Joan Collins and Tom Bell that did no more for him than provide a suitable title for this book. Another was *Madame Sin*, a spoof reversal of the James Bond goodie-takes-all style of thriller. Here, the sexy hero (Robert Wagner) wound up on the mortuary slab while his sinister adversary (Bette Davis) and her oily sidekick (Denholm) emerged from the plot and counter-plot as victors of all they surveyed. The memorable episode in a none-too-subtle story of hijacking a nuclear submarine comes in the closing moments of the movie when Miss Davis, reclining in her chauffeur-driven Rolls-Royce, surveys the magnificence of Windsor Castle.

'I know what's in your mind,' says Denholm. 'But the resident family have grown attached to the place over the last couple of hundred years.'

Miss Davis makes a grand gesture of dismissal of minor details and delivers the last line of the film. 'Just find out when the lease expires.'

The location for *Madame Sin* was the island of Mull. I was eager to discover remotest Scotland but while I knew that by American standards, Britain was a small country, I did expect the basics of modern living like a half-decent restaurant, or at least a takeaway. Instead we were marooned in a cottage-style hotel in a windy landscape which tipped over into the sea. The waves were high, the rocks were jagged and every time I went out of doors I felt a gale-force wind pulling me to destruction.

Immediately I arrived I was designated general comforter, which meant acting as companion to Miss Davis. She was an early riser, 6 a.m. at the latest, and she liked someone to talk to when she went into make-up – at around 6.30. No doubt she favoured me with many caustic witticisms, but I didn't take much in. I was half asleep at the time.

Robert Wagner nicknamed Denholm Blah, Blah, which was what he said when asked for dialogue without sound. Robert was a great joker and as producer and co-star with Bette Davis, he had the power to play whatever game appealed to him – like sending me up in a helicopter and telling the pilot to run through his catalogue of stunts. When we did get back to solid ground, I tottered about like a new-born babe. Revenge was teasing him about the telephone calls he was forever expecting from Nancy Sinatra, then the love of his life. Was it her on the line or a money man in London wanting to know if we were still running to budget?

We were all in London for a year while Denholm did a series of eight plays for BBC Television. This was the renowned *Sextet* series in which six actors – Richard Vernon, Dennis Waterman, Billie Whitelaw, Michele Dotrice, Ruth Denning and Denholm – played in repertory. All the material was new, commissioned from the rising generation of television dramatists led by Dennis Potter and Peter Tinniswood. The seven months of intensive work were pure joy for Denholm who, by chance, had better opportunity than the others to show off his versatility before a mass audience. *Sextet* became known as the musical chairs of talent. Every time the music stopped, Denholm was 'it'.

'Isn't it nice,' wrote Mary Malone of the *Daily Mirror*, 'that an actor who's been around so long without much notice can suddenly emerge as the discovery of the year?' The compliment was a bit of a back-hander – Denholm could hardly be said to have been an acting recluse. But there was a general feeling that his portrayals in *Sextet* put him on to a higher level of achievement. He played a succession of nutters and losers: a cuckold husband, a pompous town councillor, a seedy layabout and, in Dennis Potter's *Follow the Yellow Brick Road*, an actor in television commercials who believes that his own life is an extension of his screen performance. When Denholm turns to the camera and sternly tells it to go away and leave him alone he is, in performance, imagining a camera that is a figment of his mental breakdown. But in reality the camera *is* there – this is, after all, a television play – a device which gives the piece a surrealistic feel, at once fascinating and disturbing.

Dennis Potter and Denholm were united in the belief that television was the true national theatre, even if Denholm's arguments for television were as much a rationalisation of the direction in which his own career had led him as an intellectual conviction of any inherent superiority of the medium. The Potter commitment to television was exclusive. He cared little for the stage or for large-screen adaptations of his work.

The association with one of the most original dramatists of the seventies did much to lift Denholm's status to the giddy heights of 'actor's actor'. Indeed, when he went on to win the 1980 Evening Standard Best Actor Award it was for Potter's *Blade on the Feather*, among other performances. Dennis Potter was unstinting in his praise. When, a few years on, Denholm played the father in his *Brimstone and Treacle*, a play banned by the BBC on the grounds that the rape of a brain-damaged girl would 'provoke outrage', he gave a vivid pen-portrait of Denholm's acting style. 'He has a manner which suggests that he is about to preside with great dignity at a court martial, yet also to be cashiered in cringing disgrace at one and the same trial, and that either pose is for him a matter both of raging disgust and total indifference.' Denholm had a second opportunity to appear in *Brimstone and Treacle*. He was the father again in the film version, made six years after the ill-fated TV original. This time he co-starred with Joan Plowright and Sting (only his second acting job, I believe).

Sextet left no time for sex. David and Edwin were temporarily abandoned though both were favoured with the occasional letter or card: 'I'm being good – just books and movies and work.'

What spare moments Denholm managed to find he spent in the BBC record library where over the course of a year a friendly custodian allowed him to record on to tape fifty-two albums of jazz and blues originals. These we proudly bore back to Ibiza where, for two years, we entertained the hillside with some of the best music known to man. Then we had a massive rainstorm and water rushed down and through the house, swamping the room in which the tapes were stored. It was the middle of the night. The children slept soundly throughout while we struggled to save what we could. I ended up standing in the garden in the pouring rain, stark naked, shaking my fist at the heavens, yelling, 'OK God, that's enough' – to Denholm's utter amazement.

For television directors, Denholm was, without question, the flavour of the year. At the BBC he was known as the 'corporation's tortured talent'. After *Sextet* he did several one-off plays, then less of a rarity in the schedules. Among the best were *Anywhere but England*, in which he played a retired RAF officer on a Mediterranean island (a thinly veiled Malta), where the natives were less than friendly, and *Song of Songs*, in which he was a cynical music critic.

He did not limit himself to the BBC. Yorkshire Television gave him a honey of a role as the alcoholic cameraman forced by necessity to shoot blue movies in *It Only Hurts for a Minute*. For Anglia he was teamed with Joyce Redman for a revival of Rattigan's *Harlequinade*, a comedy about an ageing theatrical couple struggling on with Romeo and Juliet-type roles. The beer-swilling grandma was played by Edith Evans. Once Denholm even did a week's jaunt on the children's programme *Jackanory*. It was said of him that he was one of those rare actors who developed and improved with age.

Success was a warm glow that radiated out to all those around Denholm. When he was feeling good he liked others to feel good but, as we have seen, he was inclined to distribute his favours thinly. As his friend David said, 'Denholm was prepared to love anyone who loved him.' This is what made him such good company, if you happened to be in focus.

Relaxing with Denholm was one long laugh. When we were out, he would make apt observations on life or turn a situation to hilarious account, as he did in a New York restaurant which boasted French cuisine complete with waiters with Maurice Chevalier accents. Pretending to speak only basic English, Denholm tried out his Franglais on a waiter who had clearly never been out of the Bronx but who persevered with his few words of culinary sophistication. As an exercise in non-communication it was better than a Feydeau farce and had me in hysterics. At home, it was his powers of mimicry that kept the laughter flowing. He could do a wonderful Olivier but top favourites were his impersonations of the Queen, Prince Charles, and Kenneth Williams. In more serious moments, he loved to play classical jazz on the piano.

But in the seventies our good times together were few and far between in Denholm's diary. There were long periods, up to six weeks at a time, when I was on my own in Ibiza, or would have been on my own if I had accepted the traditional role of the little woman sitting by the lighted candle in the window. Denholm was never in any doubt that I missed him. My letters were all too revealing.

Hello Pottles.
Christ, I don't know which is better – to call or not to call. I felt great for a few hours after we hung up but then depression set in. Like right now. SHIT – but it was fantastic to talk to you. I miss you so much and today's only 25 Febrero and 1 May is in fact 2 months away *not* 7 weeks.

But I had dear friends, like Sandy Pratt, who understood my predicament and in whose company I whiled away the days of Denholm's absence with fun and laughter. Sandy and I went off for a little jaunt to Barcelona, where we toured the bars and Sandy indulged himself with a mad shopping spree. As I wrote to Denholm, 'When I looked in the mirror I noticed I have crow's feet around my eyes without even moving my face at all. It must have been from laughing so much with Sandy.' There were always people calling round and there were more party invitations than I could handle. There were a few one-night stands. Then I met Marcel.

Marcel Boffin had lived on the island for a few years and had melded happily into Spanish society, but he had been born and brought up in Belgium. When he moved to Ibiza he was looking to escape the claustrophobia of semi-detached respectability. What attracted me to Marcel was his calm. He never lost his cool or his capacity for finding solutions, whether to some irritating domestic problem such as a leak in the plumbing or something far more serious like Mark's crisis with the medical establishment.

Marcel was the European champion of aikido, karate and

judo and had opened a *dojo* on the island, where I met him when Mark attended judo classes. Mark had regular treatment at Great Ormond Street for his hormone deficiency, although it didn't seem to do much good. His records were lost while being transferred on to a new computer system and during a subsequent visit he was treated for headaches, which he didn't have. At my wits' end, I took Mark home to Ibiza where everybody said not to worry. Only Marcel came up with a practical suggestion. He told me about an Eastern art with affinities to aikido which teaches self-healing and healing through controlled breathing and visualisation. Marcel was himself a practitioner but, more to the point, a Japanese master of aikido called Itzo Tsuda was visiting Ibiza to teach his own self-healing method. Marcel asked if we would like to take Mark along.

We had tried conventional medicine and found it wanting. What had we to lose? We went to see Itzo Tsuda at the *dojo*. He was a powerful man, totally self-possessed, unconcerned as to whether or not we had faith in his powers. He put his hand on Mark's back, identifying what he insisted was the growth gland. Mark responded to the gentle touch, breathing deeply in a soothing rhythm. Instant results were neither promised nor expected but over the following years, when Marcel or I practised the treatment that Itzo Tsuda had demonstrated, Mark did get stronger and took on the characteristics of a normal healthy boy. For good measure, Marcel taught him aikido.

We were lovers, on and off, for almost seven years. For the children's sake, we were always careful to hold back any display of affection. They treated Marcel as a good friend and never as a threat to Denholm who, of course, knew about and accepted the affair. Denholm rarely showed jealousy, though once or twice he was made nervous by friends who could rival him in personality. The possibility of me having an affair with John Mortimer frightened him simply because he had such a huge admiration and liking for him. In his moments of pure honesty he could not imagine why I did not take up with John.

After a while Marcel decided that he wanted to travel. I could understand his need to get away from Ibiza for a while. He decided to go to America via London. I helped organize the ticket and after talking with Denholm, decided to go with him and show him the States. The deal was that we would start and finish the trip at the same destinations in the States i.e. arrive and leave from New York. The price was incredibly cheap. The trip was superb and on our return to London we waited for Marcel to take off for Brussels. He asked if he could leave a suitcase behind. We presumed he would collect it on his way back to Ibiza via London. When he came back to London he stayed and stayed. Our home was the wrong place for him. He had no friends and no work. Trying to mark out spaces for all of us was impossible. It was driving me nuts. Even though he wasn't happy either he stayed through the selling of our Albert Street house, the move to a rented house and on to the new flat in Abbey Road.

Jennifer and Denholm both noticed that I was on the verge of a breakdown and one evening we all came to the conclusion that I should move out just for a day or two until Marcel left for Ibiza. I decided to stay at the YMCA rather than at a friend's house where I knew I could be found. The point was that we had talked this one out so many times that there was nothing more to be said. So I wrote him a letter explaining that until he left I would not return to the flat and that when he was established in his home in Ibiza we could talk again. It was all very sad. I was in hiding for five or six days at the YMCA in Tottenham Court Road. Denholm would pop around each day to bring the mail and with whatever paper work was necessary which we dealt with over lunch. Finally one morning he came by with a letter from Marcel saying he was on his way back to Ibiza and that he understood it was time for us to separate. I returned home to a very boozy family reunion.

Marcel is now in a relationship and has a small son. We remain the best of friends. We have made the transition from sexual intimacy to a warm companionship.

Riding high on his television fame, Denholm was much in demand in the West End theatre, where exposure on the box was a producer's first test of marketability. But when it came to signing on for six nights a week with two matinees thrown in, he was inclined to play hard to get. When Richard Eyre (who directed Denholm in the TV play *Past Caring*) asked him how he chose scripts, he said that he opened them midway through and if he found a few characters he would not mind having a drink with in the pub, then he went back to the beginning. This typical throwaway reply was only half the story. Yes, he dipped into scripts (sometimes after they had been lying around unopened for weeks) but when an idea or character looked at all interesting, or just different, he was absorbed. 'When I read a script I read it at once, like a child. You get the dream of it, like the feeling you have when you enter an empty house you're thinking of buying.'

He often said that he acted in the same way that a child paints. 'I asked a four-year-old boy how he painted. And he said, "I think, and then I paint my think." '

Faced with a luxury of choice, Denholm tried hard to strike a balance between what was worthwhile and what was likely to find an audience. Usually money came first but occasionally he would take on less financially rewarding roles. One of the biggest things he ever did was Strindberg's *The Father* at the tiny Open Space Theatre, which was tucked away in a side street near Euston. It was a lot of work for little financial return and by the time word of mouth brought audiences clamouring, the play and, indeed, the theatre had closed. Caught up in a property development, the Open Space was out of commission for ten years.

That production of *The Father* was staged in 1979, more than a decade after Denholm had discovered the lure of Scandinavian drama. It started when John Osborne sent him his adaptation of *Hedda Gabler*. Denholm wrote back enthusiastically. It was a lengthy version but for the good reason that John had given more depth to secondary characters like the oily Judge Brack, the role suggested for Denholm. It was not just the play that appealed to Denholm. He was excited by the prospect of working with a writer who was at the top of the premier league for new drama and, perhaps, even more taken by the idea of appearing at the Royal Court, the theatre that had rejected him, or so he chose to believe, as a young actor.

The production took some time to get going. Directed by Anthony Page, *Hedda Gabler* was eventually performed in 1972 with Jill Bennett in the title role. John saw the character as 'a bourgeois snob and a walking waste of human personality', one who 'has her fun at the expense of others'. It was a harsher interpretation than audiences were used to and may have owed less to Ibsen than to John's vitriolic relationship with Jill Bennett, who happened to be his wife.

Denholm walked away with some of the best notices. He played the 'small-minded sensualist' to perfection according to John Peter, and it was entirely complimentary when Jeremy Kingston described his Judge Brack as 'a man who can smile and smile and reveal a wilderness of nastiness with a mean laugh'. The highest praise came from John Osborne. 'He is an actor who has never given a bad performance in a long career and is now better than ever.'

There was much talk of Denholm taking on bigger roles, even of having another crack at Shakespeare. The thought of it made him shudder. 'I'd rather stay in the second line,' he told an interviewer. 'As a character actor you get interesting parts and can be in a good position to steal the film.' This is precisely what he did in Patrick Garland's film of *A Doll's House*. As the blackmailer Krogstad, he overshadowed Claire Bloom and Anthony Hopkins with his marvellous study of 'the savagery of the weakling'. The movie suffered the consequences of a low budget and fared badly against competition from a second film version, this one directed by Joseph Losey and starring Jane Fonda. It was one of the inexplicable ironies of the British film industry that having ignored Ibsen for so long it should offer *A Doll's House* twice in the same year.

It was not long before Denholm ventured deeper into Northern European drama as Vershinin in *The Three Sisters* in New York. But it was as *The Father* that he achieved greatness. This formidably difficult play was sliced back severely to run for an hour and a half without an interval. Denholm was onstage throughout to create an entirely convincing portrayal of a man driven to madness by his wife's nagging insinuations that he is not the father of his beloved daughter. Playing opposite him in perfect harmony was Diane Cilento.

Denholm knew that he had cracked it. Over a gamut of compliments the critics were unanimous in praising 'his subtle blend of bad-tempered aggressiveness and childlike vulnerability'. It was a stage representation of possessive jealousy rarely surpassed. Even if few were able to witness it, he basked in the triumph.

It was a joyous moment. It can happen some nights in the theatre when you are just right on balance, and all the rhythms are right and you are just carried by the evening. And that's the most extraordinary thing. You sink into your chair in the dressing room at the end with a large vodka or something, and you sit there for hours . . . what a woman must feel when she's just had a baby, I should think, same sort of feeling, I'm sure it is. Sense of relief. Then you hear the keys of the stage door keeper chinking away and you slowly get dressed, and you go out of the stage door, push the bar open, and the evening air hits your face, and you take a deep breath, and you say I did it! A most wonderful feeling.

But it was not like Denholm to take himself too seriously for very long. When another interviewer asked him what had inspired him in the role, he said that he had taken it because the theatre was walking distance from home.

This rather confirmed the view of John Elsom who, writing in the *Listener*, warned against overloading Denholm with star roles. He saw Denholm as 'one of nature's attendant lords'. Think of him, he urged, 'as a good-natured chap at the golf club, handicap 15 or thereabouts, too lazy to get his game together but a useful doubles partner and very good value at the nineteenth hole with his fund of risqué stories.'

There were two nasty moments in the short run of *The Father*. The first was when Michael Meyer, the ubiquitous translator of Ibsen and Strindberg and jealous guardian of his English language copyright, accused the Open Space of plagiarism. After that was smoothed over, Denholm had a fit of panic when he suddenly realised that he was about to lose his automatic right to work in America. He had been out of that country for too long. There was only one way to save his green card. That was to get on a plane, fly to New York, have his passport stamped and then fly back in time for an evening performance. It couldn't be done in a single day but taking in Sunday, the feat was possible. To be on the safe side, Denholm returned by Concorde. That took care of whatever he earned on *The Father*.

I must not give the impression that Denholm's theatre in the seventies was a consistent run of Chekhov, Ibsen and Strindberg – or, for that matter, a consistent run of successes. He took too long to decide to play Gayev in *The Cherry Orchard* at the National. Peter Hall wanted him to do it and Denholm's instinct was to accept. But memories of Stratford and his nervousness of big companies made him pause. He asked for four days to think it over. The next he heard – to his great relief, in fact – Robert Stephens had been offered the part. He became wary of overplaying his hand. As he told Dan Farson, 'I was one of the first to be offered *Sleuth* and I turned that down because I didn't think the play would work. I must have been mad.'

Conversely, he gave himself a load of trouble over an over-fast acceptance of an invitation to join the RSC. The year 1975 was memorable as the one in which Denholm reran his nightmare with the Royal Shakespeare Company. On this occasion he was not at Stratford, but in London at the Aldwych, and not in Shakespeare but in a new play from the master of literary excellence, Graham Greene.

The subject was the Victorian amateur cracksman and gentleman cricketer, A. J. Raffles, a choice not altogether unconnected with the recent success enjoyed by the RSC in bringing Sherlock Holmes to the stage. Though he did not know it at the time, Denholm helped shape the character from an early stage in the writing. He was the perfect model, said Greene, because 'there are depths of character in him, an interior behind his eyes. Like Scofield, he doesn't disclose himself at first.'

As for Denholm, when asked what had brought him back to the RSC after his previous bruising experience, he turned the compliment on Greene. It was the play that had beguiled him.

It's the first Graham Greene has written in eleven years, and if you're offered the title role in a script of his you don't think twice. I played the police officer in the film *The Heart of the Matter* and more recently I did a couple of his short stories in *Shades of Greene* on television, so I've been lucky enough to get to know him slightly – not altogether easy. He's been to a few rehearsals and there's something very awe-inspiring about him – it's like being directed by Ibsen. Like all great novelists he's constantly watching you, rather than letting you watch him.

The play *did* read well but somehow the ingenuity of the plot and the amusing surprises Greene had planted in the dialogue did not translate to live performance. Greene's artifice was in making Raffles and his sidekick, Bunny, a gay couple, a liberty that would have horrified their straitlaced originator, E. W. Hornung. Bunny has just spent two years in Reading jail with Oscar Wilde as a fellow inmate. The plot requires the chums to come to the aid of Lord Alfred Douglas by breaking into the Marquis of Queensberry's house to steal his son's rightful inheritance. Following Graham Greene's wish for an 'ill-starred loser', Denholm played Raffles as a 'once handsome youth slightly gone to seed in middle age'. His best days were behind him; his future was one of sexual seediness and disintegration. The best jokes belonged to Peter Blythe as Lord Alfred Douglas and Clive Francis as Bunny, the rival camps. The insinuation from Douglas that Raffles might be bisexual brings an angry denial from Bunny. 'Good God, no. He's never so much as looked at a woman.'

Though the critics treated Denholm kindly – Herbert Kretzmer went as far as to claim that Raffles confirmed him 'as a star in his own right' – he knew that the play was a flop. There were too many words, the action was all over the place and the whole lacked tension. The only sense of expectation was in the audience, who were waiting for something to happen. But nothing did. Denholm hated it.

After the evening performance he would take comfort in the bottle. Every night I went to collect him from the theatre and every night he walked an unsteady line to the car. In the hour between curtain call and his leaving by the stage door, he packed away more than most people drank in a week. The drive home was through Bedford Square. I was going at a steady rate, my lights were on, my indicator had winked at the appropriate moment but something – heaven knows what – attracted the law. A white car with flashing blue lights pulled in front of me.

I knew what Denholm was capable of, given the opportunity. 'Just sit there,' I told him. 'Don't move and don't say a word.' I got out of the car, stood smartly to attention and concentrated hard on the questions put to me. 'Do you know what speed you were driving at? Where are you going? Do you have your licence?'

As we were talking I was dimly aware of my passenger struggling from his seat and sliding round the side of the vehicle. As he came up beside me, Denholm held on to the car as if it were his only friend in the world. The policeman eyed him cynically. He was about to start on me again when he took another look at Denholm. 'Aren't you Denholm Elliott?'

The star of stage and screen gathered his strength for a reply. He managed two words.

'Name dropper.'

We got away with a promise from me to take Denholm straight home.

To balance against the disappointment of *Raffles* was the satisfaction of appearing with Albert Finney in *Chez Nous*, a Peter Nichols play at the Globe. The setting was a holiday home in the Dordogne presided over by Denholm as 'a child psychiatrist concerned more with children in general than with his own family'. Albert was the old friend who turns out to have fathered the child of the psychiatrist's fourteen-year-old daughter. The play was said by John Barber to be 'a penetrating insight into modern marriage and its discontents'. Harold Hobson fastened on to ten minutes 'when Denholm Elliott treads on raw nerves as if they were a carpet, a quivering portrait of a civilised, highly strung man *in extremis*'. Attempting to explain his success in the role, Denholm said, 'I'm good at playing fractured people, perhaps because I know what it's like.'

The children went to see *Chez Nous*. It was their first experience of Denholm onstage. At the interval two matinee ladies who were shocked to find that *Chez Nous* was not a traditional drawing-room comedy gave Jennifer and Mark a disapproving glare. They spoke loudly enough to be heard all round. 'I hardly think this play is suitable for children,' said one.

Jennifer wasn't putting up with that. 'Don't be so rude,' she told the woman sternly. 'Denholm Elliott is my Dad and this is his work.'

There was a visitation from Lord Olivier who confirmed that Denholm was 'living up to his promise'. In defiance of grandeur he turned up in his own black cab which he had adapted to his specifications. 'It's the best thing for getting round London,' he announced. 'They say it turns on a sixpence. Whatever that is.'

Denholm saw out the seventies with another stage appearance, in *Heaven and Hell*, two more one-act plays from John

Mortimer. The target this time was the modern church, at which John launched an attack veering from satire to farce. *Heaven and Hell* was put on at Greenwich and did not transfer to the West End.

For the rest, Denholm was globe-trotting for the movie industry or doing his bit for British television. In one year, 1978, he was working on no fewer than seven movies, including *Zulu Dawn* with Peter O'Toole and Burt Lancaster; *A Game of Vultures* with Richard Harris; *Cuba* with Sean Connery and, more memorably, *Bad Timing*, a Nicolas Roeg film with Art Garfunkel, and *Saint Jack*, directed by Peter Bogdanovich and starring Ben Gazzara. For this last movie, set in contemporary Singapore, Denholm was cast as a weak, sad character, an expat accountant who 'knows his days are numbered and life has been a waste'. One of his clients is a fast-talking, hard-drinking American (Ben Gazzara) who ostensibly works as a ship's chandler but in fact runs a classy brothel. The relationship between these two unlikely soulmates is a sub-plot which, by force of acting, rises above the major theme of American involvement in Vietnam and the softening up of young recruits in Ben Gazzara's 'rest centre'. The death of the accountant, his send-off by an offbeat company of losers who make the supreme effort to sober up for his funeral, and the final awful rejection by his wife, who does not want his ashes, are scenes which keep the image of Denholm in mind long after he has left the screen.

Saint Jack was a triumph for Peter Bogdanovich, who had followed *The Last Picture Show* with a succession of duds; for Ben Gazzara, who achieved his best role in an otherwise nondescript career, and for Denholm, who advanced far beyond his usual cameo. The achievement was greater than might appear from judging screen performances. Off the set, Denholm was not much taken with either Bogdanovich or Gazzara. We both found them bumptious and arrogant, forever trying to outdo each other in macho boorishness.

Most of the locations were within walking distance of the hotel but Bogdanovich insisted on being ferried about in a limousine so that he could recline in the rear seat, smoke a fat cigar and look like Orson Welles. This oneupmanship was lost on the actors, who knew that the limo had been hired from a local undertaker. Ben Gazzara stayed close to his director, rivalling him in cigar length and swagger. Denholm was not exactly the holy innocent but he made the effort to be pleasant and did not act as if everyone owed him a favour. Those he disliked said that he was aloof but Denholm had no interest in what they thought.

His policy of staying apart from bores and troublemakers was no guarantee of a passive life. There were times when he was dragged into battle by irresistible forces. A gigantic pain in the rear like Robert Shaw could bring out the worst in Denholm simply by refusing to leave him alone. They appeared together in *Robin and Marian*, a mediaeval romp which has the now not so merry outlaws staging a middle-age comeback. Denholm was distinctly uncomfortable as Will Scarlet, strumming his lute and singing of daring exploits long ago. The swashbucklers were more at home, though the director, Richard Lester, was asking for trouble bringing together such volatile characters as Richard Harris, Nicol Williamson and Robert Shaw. Among the principals, the only steady personalities were Sean Connery, who was Robin, and Audrey Hepburn, who came out of retirement to play Marian.

When they were shooting in Bilbao, the closest they could get to old England that was within budget, I went over from Ibiza to stay with Denholm for the shoot. In the room next to us was Nicol Williamson. I met him first on set, when he was charming and cheerful. The second time I saw him he was trying to stuff a telephone receiver down the lavatory. And he was not in a good temper. We had woken up to loud curses and a terrible crash. This had to be murder at least. We hurried to Nicol's room to find that he had ripped the telephone from the wall and was busily disposing of it in unconventional manner. When we came upon him he was complaining at the top of his voice that the loo wouldn't flush. His anger had been sparked by an operator who had cut him off in mid-call to his wife in Hollywood. Even with the inordinate time it took to put a call through to America, we ventured, wasn't he overreacting? The look he gave us was a finely judged blend of amazement and contempt. We backed away, leaving him to reflect on the iniquities of a cruel world.

If Nicol was a heavy drinker and unpredictable, Bob Shaw was a very heavy drinker and totally predictable. He could be relied upon to spoil any party. His grudge of the moment was against Sean Connery, whom he saw as his rival for superstardom. It didn't make it any easier that Sean was still trying to re-establish his market value post-James Bond, while Bob Shaw was, as he imagined, riding high towards his first million-dollar movie. He practised arrogance on whoever came into range and Denholm, apparently so easygoing, was a prime target. On my first evening, there was a great gathering with cast and crew milling about in the hotel bar. Everybody was cheerful except Bob, who was dead set on picking a quarrel. He did the rounds, niggling and provoking, without much response, until he got to me. What he wanted to talk about was Denholm, and without acknowledging that the subject was within hearing distance. 'How did you get mixed up with him? What's he got to offer? What made you want to marry him?'

When Denholm showed no reaction, Bob raised the ante. 'He fucked up on his first marriage. What makes you think he can do any better with you?'

This time Denholm did respond. He came up close to Bob and he hit him. It was all over so quickly, nobody standing near had a chance to intervene. Denholm was examining his fist with close interest, as if it had somehow acted independently, and Bob was on the floor, too surprised to retaliate. People started talking. The party resumed.

A week later I was back in Ibiza, where April Ashley, whom I had first met many years ago through Robin Maugham and who had become a good friend, had been looking after Mark and Jennifer, driving them to beaches and taking them out to lunch. If it hadn't been for her I wouldn't have been able to make the trip to Bilbao. The kids loved her and she was great fun for them. Denholm and I went to visit her in Hay-on-Wye when she was living there, but I haven't heard from her for many years. Denholm's press cuttings of the late seventies and early eighties confirmed our lunatic, nomadic life. 'The Elliotts appear to have the best of all worlds' – 'Susan is very understanding. While I go off on my toots she copes' – 'He is happily married with a son and a daughter' – 'They would like to spend more time together.'

I am still amazed that journalists did not know the truth

about Denholm's sexuality or, if they did know it, chose not to print it. I think it was because they liked him too much. There were attempts at blackmail, threats to reveal all to the tabloids if money was not handed over. We did not submit to a single demand. Since there were no repercussions I can only assume that the spicy details did not add up to a headline story. I know it is the same with some other actors who lead double lives.

That Denholm was having fun, I had no doubt. When he was in South Africa filming *Zulu Dawn*, a story went the rounds of Denholm's welcome for a fellow actor who flew in for a cameo role. Denholm suggested a drive to take in the sights. They bumped over dusty roads out into the bush. Along the way they passed mud-hut villages where, on sight of the Land Rover, young men ran alongside them, waving enthusiastically at Denholm.

'You seem to be very popular,' said the actor.

'Oh yes,' replied Denholm grandly. 'You see, I've fucked most of them.'

His passenger was shocked beyond belief. Catching his look of horror, Denholm patted him on the arm. 'Only joking.'

Alarm turned to relief. Denholm gave him a moment to compose himself.

'Some of them have fucked me.'

Meanwhile, on Ibiza, I was being pursued by a mad Spanish painter who followed me all over town, wringing his hands and declaring, with typical macho arrogance, my love for him. 'You must love me. How can you not love me?'

'Well, I don't. Sod off.'

One night he followed me home – or maybe he was there

ahead of me. Whatever, I was in bed when Romeo popped out from behind the curtains screaming that if I did not love him there had to be a rival hiding somewhere, in the cupboard or under the bed. From what I could gather from his high-pitched Spanish it was his intent to kill us both.

Maybe it was not a serious attack, though it was frightening enough at the time. Maybe I could have sorted it out myself, but luckily I did not have to put my bravery to the test. My sister Polly happened to be staying with me. Hearing the commotion upstairs she armed herself with a dinner fork and, advancing on my bedroom, voiced the immortal words, 'Unhand my sister.' Two determined women was more than the intruder could take. He backed off, shouting that my affairs – such as they were – would be made known to Denholm. He would tell all.

Revelations did not worry me but this nonsense had to stop. I knew just what to do. Two days later I went to collect Denholm from the airport. As we drove into Santa Eulalia, I told him about the threat, adding that my persecutor would almost certainly be hanging out in Sandy's Bar. We drove straight there. He was sitting alone at a table. I walked up to him with Denholm in tow. 'I believe you wanted to meet my husband.'

End of story.

There was something about Ibiza that encouraged excess while somehow making us feel that we were immune to the consequences. Regular visitors to the island had a better perspective than residents. I remember Diana Rigg describing a supper party given by Robin Maugham: a glorious sunset, champagne on the terrace; the guests, totally relaxed and uninhibited, exchanging the most bizarre stories of sexual couplings. The chatter was accompanied by yowls from the undergrowth, where two cats were mating. As Diana listened, feline passion seemed to overwhelm the party conversation until all she heard was a piercing shriek. It was, she said, a cry for all Ibiza, a perfect representation of island and people.

11

Trading Places

If movies brought in the money – £70,000 to £100,000 a movie after the release of *Saint Jack* – it was television that attracted the kudos. In 1980, Denholm won the Evening Standard Best Actor Award for four television plays, *Gentle Folk*, Dennis Potter's *Blade on the Feather, The Stinker* and the outstanding *In Hiding*. For this last play, written by Don Taylor, Denholm shared the screen with a young boy, Roger Burnett, and it says much for both actors that they struck up an entirely convincing and moving professional relationship which never once transgressed into mawkish sentimentality. The storyline is deceptively simple. The boy is staying with his aunt in the country. Bored by a spinsterish household he makes a hideaway in a derelict property. But he has to share it with a stranger who, like him, is reaching for a sort of freedom. The man is dying of cancer. With just a few weeks to live, he has broken free from a family that wants him to obey the conventions and go out with minimum fuss.

There are lines that Denholm has to speak which, heard

now, have a curiously prophetic ring.

> Suddenly my life is at an end and I don't seem to have
> lived like a man at all. Something seems to drive me to
> say, That's enough, be the man you are . . . I don't want
> to die in a hospital, to die surrounded by weeping and
> concerned people, drugged out of my senses. I've a
> horror of that. I'd much rather die alone, under the
> stars; a private agony, the way men died when they
> were animals.

In Hiding was blessed by two superb actors but the actors
were double-blessed by a superb script and sensitive direction. The ending to *In Hiding* is downbeat. The boy has been
told by everyone, including Denholm, that truth and honesty
are at the heart of all relationships. So in pursuit of what he
believes is right, he tells Denholm's family where he is, and
loses his friend.

When *In Hiding* was transmitted Denholm was working
on *Sunday Lovers*, a Bryan Forbes movie with a cast of
four: Roger Moore, Lynn Redgrave, Priscilla Barnes and
Denholm. They were filming in France just outside Bordeaux
when one evening Bryan answered the telephone to be told
that a call was coming through from St James's Palace and
would he please stand by for a few words with the Queen
Mother. The Queen Mother wanted him to congratulate
Denholm on *In Hiding*, which she had just been watching
on her television. It was, she said, one of the most touching
plays she had seen in a long time. It had brought tears to
her eyes.

Sunday Lovers ended less happily for Denholm. As Bryan

says, 'Together with Leslie Bricusse, I devised a splendid role for Denholm, which he played with his usual brilliance, but unfortunately the producer of the film subsequently emasculated his performance in the cutting room without my knowledge or agreement.'

For two television productions Denholm was once again asked to relive his schooldays. In *The Stinker*, one of the four performances which earned his BAFTA award, the bullying his character suffered at school was reprised in his adult business life. A more ambitious effort was *School Play*, written by Frederic Raphael and directed by James Cellan Jones. Both had been at Charterhouse and shared a deep and abiding hatred for their *alma mater*. Naturally, Denholm was fully in sympathy with their views. He threw himself enthusiastically into a role which required him to play a character at least forty years younger than his real age. The entire cast met the same challenge – men in boys' clothes, acting out the ridiculously beloved rituals of public school of the 1950s. A curiosity, noted by James Cellan Jones, was the tendency for the actors to start behaving, or rather misbehaving, like boys offstage as well. For much of the time he felt less like a director than a junior master trying to keep order. *School Play* has been compared to Lindsay Anderson's movie *If*. But Anderson's attack on scholastic convention climaxes, terrifyingly, in bloody revolution. For *School Play*, the ending is submission, with a new generation, once the victims, rising to the top of the pecking order and carrying on just like their predecessors. It may not be the most encouraging message but it is realistic.

By way of contrast, Denholm partnered Michael Hordern in a delightful two-hander called *You're All Right, How Am*

I? This was William Douglas Home at his comic best, with Denholm as a psychiatrist and Michael as his patient engaging in a little role-swapping. The abiding memory for Denholm was in committing a painful error that in itself deserved the attentions of an analyst. He learned the wrong part. Turning up on the first day of rehearsal confident, for once, of being word-perfect, he found that Michael was overly familiar with what he assumed to be his role. No such luck. He had to drag himself back to page one, resolving the while that never again would he go for broke without first double-checking the casting.

Of all the letters of congratulation Denholm attracted for his elevation to Best Actor, the one he tucked away in a drawer was from brother Neil.

Not *again*!! Rosemary, Susan and I were *glued* to our TV. When the results were announced such a shriek went up in Old Harry Cuckers that I thought the windowpanes would shatter.

Very impressive, me boy – and the very best of British How's yer father from us all! The upshot of all this is that 'Old-dyed-in-the-wool' at Cuckney House is receiving much more *respect* from everyone – 'There goes 'is bruvver, mate!' they all say – 'Doff the Old Topper to him' they says. 'Don't mind if I do' I says when offered a cigar and a glass of champagne . . .

And do you know what? I've just had a letter from the Chartered Surveyors inviting me to be 'president' of their Land Agency & Agricultural Division for 1982–83. And THAT – where I kum from – is *very* upper 'U' & La-di-da. Being the Prezzy is a bit of oneupmanship. *I*

think it is because *they* saw *you* on the tele . . .!!
Blessings – Neil

Denholm's jokey reply revealed his genuine conviction that his achievements – such as they were – should not be taken too seriously.

Buckinam Pallis – Toosdey.
Many thanks Dudley for yors of the 20th *INST*: (Learnt that at Secretarial Collige.) Only reason I got it – easy – everyone else is *DED* – 'Ang about long enuf & you romp 'ome – can't fail. Your presidency of the LAAD 1982–83 is *more* impressive Dud because you 'ave to use yor *Grey matter*. Now I've *never* ever done *that* Dud – not ever – don't believe in messin' wiv it!!
Love & thanks to all, Denholm

Close on the heels of the BAFTA award came an offer from Steven Spielberg, who wanted Denholm to play Harrison Ford's university superior in *Raiders of the Lost Ark*. It is easy to judge the inevitability of a success *after* a movie has broken box-office records, but when Denholm took on this cameo, at a fee that made him blanch at his power to move the hearts of accountants, *Raiders* was just another adventure story, surely a little old-fashioned in concept to make the top ten? But old-fashioned adventure turned out to be just what the punters wanted. In an undemanding role (repeated in 1989 for the third of the Indiana Jones films, *Indiana Jones and the Last Crusade*) Denholm became one of Spielberg's favourite English actors.

The most extraordinary, exciting and beautiful location I

have ever been to with Denholm was in Jordan in the city of Petra using the ancient treasury as background while filming scenes for *Indiana Jones and the Last Crusade* starring Harrison Ford and Sean Connery. The only race I have ever been in and won was a camel race. I didn't really get the credit I deserved because as the men noted rather ungallantly, 'the only reason you won is because you don't have the extra equipment between your legs'. This was said as they came limping in walking their camels behind them.

I often wonder why it was that in his later years the British public took Denholm to its heart. It is too easy to say that he was a marvellous actor. Others of his generation had great talents but did not inspire the warmth of recognition enjoyed by Denholm. Maybe in the same way as Spielberg saw Denholm as the epitome of a certain Englishness, so Denholm's admirers at home identified with his screen personality, or at least, the personality that he was usually called upon to convey. He could appear vulnerable – sometimes pathetically so – while at the same time there was within him an underlying strength of purpose. His weaknesses were forgivable because he was not ashamed of them but acknowledged them for what they were; battles to be fought. Think of him as the old soak of a reporter in *Defence of the Realm* who came through with the story of political intrigue at the cost of his own life. Or the father of a girl caught up on drugs charges in the underrated Australian TV production *Bangkok Hilton*, where he had to overcome his own terrible fears to save the girl from execution.

If I was to choose one characteristic that makes Denholm live on screen it is his ability to convey a multi-dimensional character. To every role, however small, however simple, he always added something of his own. To watch him is to see a thoughtful man, one who knows there are contradictions in his life but who does his best to reconcile the facets of a complex personality.

It was only an extension of the true Denholm. His real life was a constant struggle of competing forces. Never wanting to hurt anyone, he was forever trying to match the needs of the moment with his desire to please. Although he was not keen for me to visit him on location for *Zulu Dawn*, for example, I appreciated his efforts to think of ways of making it up to me.

15 June 1978.
Hello Pottles,
Excuse the silence, due partly to the shock of the change – it's *so* different from Singapore (*too* different for my taste) & due also to the terrible time I am having trying to decide about your trip here – I know how much you all want to come, I really do.

I'll just explain the situation to you so you can decide. Leaving aside the cost which (if we can't do a deal with an airline excursion or something will be horrendous) the *real* and only problem is this: in 2 weeks we go to a place called (sounds like) BABBANANGA in the heart of Zululand (you need a pass to enter Zululand). It is hours from the nearest village where we are & the *only* way I could see you during your trip at *all* would be to put you all in a small seaside resort called Saint Lucia – like Santa Eulalia with crocs: or in a village called Dundee 2 hours from us (it's got *one* one-star hotel!). The scenery is *beautiful* – like Scotland – and it's 5 below zero at night, it's *freezing*. The day warms up. But no jungles – no witch doctors. The whites are charming & v. helpful – the blacks you don't meet, they avoid the eye – if you talk at all it's in Pigeon English & Zulu. The point is do you want to spend a month in a small hotel or in a nice seaside resort seeing me for 2 days a week? Maybe I can get you a coach tour of the Cape or the Kruger National Park for 2 or 3 weeks & then you could join me at the end. I honestly think you would be much better off booking a hotel for 6 weeks in Venice or the Greek Islands or Marrakech from say mid-July & all August (I finish 12 August) & I could *join* you when I'm through – or even a tour of India!

Love & xxx

The loveliest letters from Denholm were funny, silly, irreverent. When work was going well he kept up a flood of them.

Hotel Gallia, Près de Ketaubia, Marrakesh, Morocco. 6/1/82

What-Ho Pottles

Here I am thinking ER (God *that's* nice) Er ... Er where was I, oh yes thinking of ya (natch, Pottles) [Ya can count on it] close brackets.

Anyway here I am, the sun is shining I'm on a grand Boulevard drinking my coffee under an orange tree with oranges on it (*hundreds*). One of those busy sidewalk cafes ... (I can recommend it).

My hotel is small, liberal, clean & very Moorish, interior courtyards (tiled) where I have my Continental B'fast. Little birds, flowers etc. Nile Bedroom (v.

moorish) bathroom en suite (sort of) B and B tax incl: £5 a day! & not lacking in charm! 'Charm' – I can 'ardly walk! (Those Moorish ladies are *so* demanding). They demand & demand like 'GET OUT OF 'ERE, you foreign infidel Pig' etc. Pause for coffee & quick look around.

Blimey!

When I arrived in Marrakesh I found – of *course* – that 'they' had lost my luggage. So I had to rush around buying socks, razor etc. The next day it turned up so I was on the main square 'Pair of sox & a razor going cheap. Don't go away sir'!

Talk about a culture shock – it takes a little time to get into it (& out of it!). Hope all is well – I check, 'Poste restante, Marrakesh, Morocco' twice a week Tu & Fri for letters etc.

Love to all D. x

There were only two possibilities for us falling out. One was an argument about relationships. I had no real problem about casual affairs – I had, after all, experienced enough of them – but as the last of the great romantics, Denholm was never entirely satisfied with brief encounters. Simon Callow got it right when he wrote about Denholm in his book *Shooting the Actor*. Without identifying Denholm, he wrote about their chance meeting in Zagreb where Denholm was appearing in *Stealing Heaven*, a movie based on the Abelard and Heloise story. As Simon explained to me: 'We had a long and cordial meal, during which we talked, as we usually did, of love, sex and art. I rarely saw Denholm but we'd got on terribly well when we first met in *A Room With a View*, and on the few subsequent occasions that we met, spoke to each other as if we were old friends. He was, as was his way, startlingly honest and vivid. We laughed a great deal, and sometimes were moved almost to tears.'

Simon had been commissioned to keep a diary. 'So that night, after supper, I faithfully recorded our conversation. When I came to write up the diary, I thought at first that I couldn't possibly use the section recording our supper. But then the writer in me rebelled at the waste of such wonderful material. I thought that if I could find a way of disguising his identity, I might yet be able to write something worth reading.'

Whether or not he succeeded in shielding Denholm from his readers I cannot say. Certainly Denholm himself never knew that his story was included. In any event, this is what appeared in the book.

The other day, however, I bumped into an old friend of mine, an actor who's appearing in another English-language film here. For him, filming abroad is perfect, a God-given opportunity to follow his romantic inclinations. He feels ill at ease and unlovely in England; abroad, he blossoms. His pursuit of sex is all-consuming, but one would hesitate to describe him as promiscuous. For him there is no such thing as casual sex. Each encounter is an overwhelming transcendence: what Holy Communion is to a Catholic, an ecstatic reunion with God. And he seems to have provoked great romantic commitment from his anonymous lovers. He may never see them again, but in the moment they give their all. It is love, of a sort. He always moves me with his stories of trysts and couplings: a time in Morocco when a young man had fallen for him on sight and stood under his window, singing for over an hour till my friend, jet-lagged and exhausted, nevertheless rose from his bed and joined the stranger for hours of love; the time in Haiti when as a challenge to him the brothel-keeper had produced a hunchbacked dwarf as a potential partner, and how the dwarf had made love more beautifully than any man he had ever known, and later, when my friend was leaving, had sought him out at the dock to bid him goodbye. Here in Zagreb he has somehow found the centre of sexual activity, a sauna, and has brought a young man back to his hotel. But the young man was cold and unloving and didn't give himself; what's worse, when he left, he had stolen a radio. And my friend's romantic heart was bruised, not for the radio, but because the god hadn't descended, and life is too short to waste a single night, a single hour of love.'

The story of the dwarf was absolutely true. It actually happened when Denholm was filming *Trading Places*.

In 1979, when Denholm was filming *Saint Jack* in Singapore, he met a boy he called Christopher. His real name was the Chinese word for lion but it was easier to give him his English name. He was working as a film extra to help finance his studies. He was slightly built, very gentle, handsome in the Chinese style. His ambition was to come to London. Denholm wanted to help him and asked me if I minded. I quickly realised that we were all three on shifting ground. Denholm was clearly besotted with the young man and was looking for something more than a flirtation. When the idea was mooted of Christopher moving to London, my only insistence was that he should have his own place and that the affair should not intrude on the children. As far as they were concerned, Christopher was a family friend whom we were helping to set up on his own. Eventually the relationship burned itself out. Denholm had too many distractions, too many other lovers, and a family he did not want to lose. Christopher went to language school and took a job in a restaurant. After a few months he met someone else.

The second and, invariably, more serious problem was money. There was no shortage of it but Denholm could never stop worrying about it. His nightmare was being dragged before the Inland Revenue and told to sell all that he had to pay his taxes. Not knowing what anything cost he happily assumed that the good things in life cost nothing – until he saw the bills. On the spur of the moment he could be incredibly generous, to family and boyfriends. A young man he fancied when he was in Australia found himself the lucky recipient of a new car. But having given freely, Denholm would wake up next day to doubts and fears. Would he ever work again? Could that be the bailiffs knocking on the door? 'There is misery in making money in this country,' he told Dan Farson. 'People lurch into my house demanding money as if I were John Wayne, adding a nought to everything.' His insecurity was the legacy of an adult life begun in a prisoner-of-war camp linked to the common actor's phobia that offers of work might dry up at any time.

We had decided to sell our house in Albert Street because the children were almost grown up and as we had been there for twenty years Denholm became afraid that he might become a 'rocking-chair type of person'. I made a deal with him. If I was able to sell the house at a good profit then I could take half the profit and invest it in any way I saw fit. This agreed, he went off to China. I sold the house well, stored the furniture and moved into a rented house. I talked to him by telephone about my plans to buy a property in Key West and then he decided to get involved with my decision. He wrote me a long letter expressing, yet again, all the possible financial problems that could arise in the coming years. I went ahead and bought the property according to our deal, plus a penthouse flat in Abbey Road that ran across the entire length of the block. And we still had change left over.

Yet Denholm could be very generous. For example, knowing how much I loved the sea, in 1965 he bought me my first boat, a rubber dinghy with an outboard motor. Three boats later, I was the proud owner of *Near Miss*, a 30 foot, 260 hp twin mercruiser Amberjack, which he bought with the proceeds of his last film, *Noises Off*.

Although Denholm remained illogical over money, he was always quick to make amends after there had been a lively discussion about it.

Pottles – *please* don't quit! A great deal of what you said is true & not too attractive. Either I badly phrased, or you misunderstood the true meaning behind my 'Earn your own living' remark. I didn't, & *don't* mean that you don't pull 10 times your own weight (the facts speak for themselves). But the 'buck' does actually stop on my desk when it comes to the raw financial facts of life. I am, in my own way, concerned for the ultimate security of my family & I am convinced that this is Nitty

Gritty time in the world & a time to contract & not to expand. It is the time to get into the castle & pull up the drawbridge. It is the time to secure the bottom line – a roof, food basics & start from there. Not only for my sake but for yours & the kids – things are *not* going to get better in my view. I think of these things a *great* deal, & not being as brave as you, my conviction builds up until I explode. I believe that you must 'trust in God, but tie your camel first'.

For the record – you are the only person I have ever really loved & still do very much. I do realise that I am a self-centred asshole – unfortunately insecurity is the ace in the hole in my game – you can't succeed without it, & you can't succeed with it. I really am so sorry I have deeply hurt you. I am very proud of what you have done in this house & in London & Ibiza & Southport (from the pictures) & I talk about you all the time with great pride to total strangers (the only people I know). I consider myself inordinately lucky to have met you, & to have been with you all these years. I truly think you are in every way truly remarkable & that remains true if we are together, or *not*.

I hope with all my heart that we *will* stay together.
With love, Denholm

Jean Diamond was against the first offer for *Trading Places*. The script was a delight. 'It has a beginning, a middle and an end,' said Denholm. 'The good guys win and the bad guys lose. What more can you ask?' But the money was not right. This was a big-budget Hollywood movie, with stars Dan Aykroyd and Eddie Murphy playing a top young commodity trader (Aykroyd) forced to change places with a black street hustler (Murphy). The identity swap is imposed by two elderly millionaires (Ralph Bellamy and Don Ameche) to settle a bet on heredity versus environment.

Denholm was to play the suave English butler, a role turned down by John Gielgud who, post-*Arthur*, had evidently had enough of portraying superior servants. That Denholm was next in line to the illustrious actor prompted Jean to raise her sights. After the first refusal, Denholm was sure he had lost out. But not a bit of it. 'Back came the offer, doubled – double everything and Concorde!'

Trading Places was a great success, and for Denholm in particular. Choosing his words with characteristic care, Alexander Walker said of Denholm's 'silent glance of disapproval' that it was like 'a twin-barrelled elephant gun levelled at the big game who employ him'. Jeeves was not in the same class. All the critics were generous to Denholm. When Jean had gathered together the cuttings she sent them off to her client with a congratulatory note: 'I think this is a case of 11 out of 10.'

But the experience of making *Trading Places* was not pleasurable. The 'big star' treatment did not appeal to Denholm, who held the view that actors who survived had to keep a sense of proportion. A little to his surprise, Denholm found himself at odds with Eddie Murphy.

I hardly talked to him and he hardly talked to me. He did praise my mobility of expression. I tried to get a much closer relationship with him, first of all because I like blacks, but he regarded that as being absolutely not on. 'I'm not an Uncle Tom. I'm an aggressive black!'

White was the worst thing you could be. I tried to play it as sensitively as I could in spite of that.

He was surrounded by lieutenants and hangers-on. I'd never seen him or heard of him when I met him. When I got into the car with his chauffeur he said, 'Since I've become a star, all these girls look at me.' At the time I thought, ooh, get you!

There was no doubt that Denholm felt out of it. In interviews he tried to laugh it off. 'On American films all the concentration is on the big boys, with all that energy flying around, and towards the end of the day when there are just ten minutes left they get round to me. Usually it goes like this: "Elliott – you don't mind if I call you by your first name – we've just got time for a couple of quick takes..." I just tend to do it off the top of my head.'

But the isolation was hard to bear. Film-making is rarely as glamorous as the showbiz pages make out and every actor must be prepared for long periods of hanging about not doing very much. Good fellowship can help to relieve the tedium but when everybody is status-conscious there is not much chance for genuine friendship. Denholm's letters from Philadelphia, written in the first days of filming, showed him at his chirpy best.

Hollo Pottlepoos,
I enclose some more bread (having done me calculations!) which you might need 'at this moment in time', 'at the end of the day' etc. etc. Hope you can cash them? Silly question. Larry O. checks in on Sunday I hope to see him – he's only here for one day.

I hope you like the photos – I'm getting some more soon. Mark called me (Big Mark) but I was out – I'm calling him tonight. I wrote to Jennifer last night – fun letter. I'll call you soon Pottlepoos. I miss you.

Lots of love D.x

After *Trading Places*, Denholm acquired respectability, which meant that writers of arts pages began to take an even greater interest in his acting technique. This presented Denholm with a slight problem. He had, in his own words, an enormous respect for his talent but he never analysed it to the point where it lost its spontaneity. In a typically back-handed way, he would say, 'Acting is a serious business, which I take seriously – in an amateurish sort of way.' To say that he approached it in an amateurish sort of way is not necessarily true. It was just his horror of sounding as though he was blowing his own trumpet which made him throw out lines like that during an interview. Throughout his career, he was never once amateurish. If ever there was a disagreement about Denholm's performance (and I cannot remember one), there was universal consent on one point: he was always the supreme professional. He was never, ever late for a performance, whether it was onstage or a shoot scheduled for 6 a.m. in the middle of the desert. I remember Denholm talking to Jennifer one evening, standing in the doorway of her bedroom, where she was preparing some lines for a piece she had to do the next day. 'The best advice I can give you is to learn your lines backwards, then get up and do them and when you do, believe every word. You cannot teach acting to another person, only technique. A person has it or doesn't,' he told her. He always said that if Jennifer decided to take up acting seriously, she would be a stunning actress.

Denholm often expressed his love of over-acting, acting like real people.

> I went on a bus in New York the other day and all the passengers were over-acting. One man dropped a dollar. He went through a huge ritual of pretences, just to pick it up. And all the time there was a woman sitting behind me barking like a dog. I like actors – such as Margaret Rutherford and Peter Lorre – who aren't afraid to over-act like real people. When I take a job I can always come up with ten different ways of doing the part. But I'll always choose the flashiest one. You've got to dress the window a bit.

His success in comedy was his ability to hold back from caricature, the very opposite of over-acting. This is why he worked so well with Michael Palin, whose comic inspiration, though gloriously wild, never quite loses touch with reality.

Their association began with an episode of *Ripping Yarns*, the series of *Boy's Own*-type adventure spoofs Michael wrote with Terry Jones. The script sent to our house was called 'Over the Andes by Frog' and was the supposed saga of the Snetterton expedition of the 1920s in which the intrepid Snetterton, played by Michael, sets out to prove a loony scientific theory by taking his collection of amphibians across the mountains. Denholm was the dilapidated British consul whose sly grin hints at depths of pleasurable depravity. He has a preoccupation with his flies. Whenever he emerges from his tumbledown shack he is buttoning them up, and whenever he retires, he unbuttons them.

Michael wrote me after Denholm's death. 'He was a "serious actor",' he wrote. 'The series had no reputation at all and yet he agreed to take part and was, as usual, inspired. His decision that the script was worth being involved with helped the confidence of Terry Jones and myself no end.'

The Missionary and *A Private Function* followed. In *The Missionary* Denholm had a choice cameo as the sports-loving bishop. I still laugh when I think of him ruminating on the perils of introducing natives to the public-school playing field. 'I was in Africa, you know. Tried to teach them the rudiments of rugby. Wasn't really their sort of thing. Tended to hold on to the ball for too long. Weeks, sometimes.' Matched with Michael Palin's writing and acting talent, Denholm gave his very best. What was the secret?

Actually, I don't believe in analysing acting very much myself. To me the essential thing is, well, it's like when a tomato is growing on a vine in the summer, and before you pick it, you touch it and a sort of dust comes off on your hand which is the *essence* of the tomato. When you read a play for the first time, you get an essential atmosphere. That's the bit to cling on to. If you pick the tomato and put it on the kitchen table, three days later it's something you buy in a shop. If you work on a thing too much you get bogged down on what sort of shoes your character should be wearing. I act like children act. It's an immediate total involvement. Cardboard sword, slippers and a wig. It's play. Once I've played them, I leave 'em on the train.

You have to have a bit of flesh, a bit of edge. I'm often given parts that aren't as big as they are colourful, but people remember them. When it's a minor or supporting role, you learn to make the most of what you're given. I can make two lines seem like Hamlet.

Here is Michael Palin again, writing from 'somewhere in Scotland' in May 1982:

Dear Denholm,

I'm sorry to have been so long in writing, but I know you were away somewhere warm & sunny and hope you had, or are having, a marvellous time. I just wanted to thank you for being so good as the bishop, and getting *The Missionary* off to a very good start. We've put together much of the material now, and your bishop comes over as a very strong, funny and believable character. It seems years since we cavorted in the gymnasium and on windswept St Pancras roofs, but it all looks very good & striking, and if we can just survive the mists & rains of Scotland we stand a good chance of bringing a very rich and complex picture in almost on time, and almost on budget! . . . As writer I was delighted with the way you brought the bishop to life, and as an actor it was good fun working together. Here's to some more!

Lots of best wishes, Michael

Denholm's explanation for his extraordinary ability to convey inner tension was: 'It's simply an actor's trick, a contraction of the muscles in the eyes. I pump blood into them from behind – I just sort of . . . push all round. It's like those people who can move their scalps, but I can't do that.

With my twin, Mark, in New York. Both of us now thoroughly grown-up.

My favourite photograph of my mother, aged eighty-one, with her caffeine and cigarettes indulging in her favourite sport of 'people-watching' in a café.

Left above: On a trip to Key West with the two Michaels behind us: Michael the manager of the Roof Top and Michael my nephew.

Left: My favourite sport: deep sea fishing off Key West.

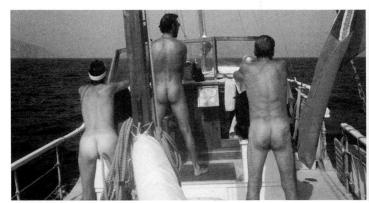

Denholm and me and the captain of the boat in our usual state of undress when out at sea off Ibiza.

Our home in Ibiza.

On my boat *Near Miss* with Nina van Pallandt. After a day out I have the usual vodka and Coke in my hand.

Denholm trying on his gear
the night before our visit to
the Palace.

16 February 1988. The official
photo at Buckingham Palace
after he was invested as a
Commander of the British
Empire by the Queen. (*Photo
courtesy The Press
Association.*)

Terry-Thomas and his sons were very good friends of ours. Here he is holding a croissant and a baby rattle. His caption was 'Sheikh, rattle and roll'.

Terry's son Cushan with our son Mark on a New York trip.

Our daughter Jennifer with Cushan.

Terry's elder son Tiger.

Denholm and Eddie Murphy in *Trading Places*. (*Photo courtesy Paramount Pictures/Kobal Collection*.)

Denholm in *Bangkok Hilton* with Nicole Kidman.

On my 'champion' camel after the race at Petra during the filming of *Indiana Jones and the Last Crusade*.

Denholm took this photo of Sean, Harrison and me after our camel race. Harrison and I had swopped hats.

Harrison Ford, Sean Connery and Denholm in *Indiana Jones and the Last Crusade*. (*Photo courtesy Lucasfilm/Kobal Collection*.)

Denholm practising deep breathing and visualisation in our London garden (another one of his creations).

Itzo Tsuda, the Japanese master who taught us all so much and who helped Mark with his growth problems.

Mark and our puppy in the part of the garden that was to become the 'Denholm Elliott Memorial Garden'.

Cock-o and Steve, who looked after Denholm's garden and the animals whenever we had to be away in the last three years of Denholm's life.

Denholm with his brother Neil at a dinner given by his niece Jane for Sir Kenneth MacMillan. Neil did not know at this time that Denholm was ill.

Jane Elliott and her father Neil. She flew from Spain to see Denholm just before we took our final trip from the hospital to Ibiza. By now she and Neil were the only ones in the family to know.

From left: Lawrence, Jennifer, Mark, me holding D.C. (Denholm's cat) and Steve with Sinbad, on the day of the Spanish funeral service. We wore black out of respect for Spanish traditions.

My sister Joyce, John Warrington of Janaway Travel, and myself (on right) taking a break from so much sadness.

Debbie Leng and Roger Taylor at the memorial service in London. (*Photo courtesy National News.*)

Denholm never missed a sunset from the day he knew that he was HIV positive.

Andrew Hammond, me, John Campbell and Claire Swingler from Red Ribbon International during one of our shows organised on Ibiza to raise money for the Denholm Elliott project: 'Ibiza Cares'.

Quite a useful thing if you're playing an emotional scene with a hangover. You think, thank God for that trick.'

An occasion when Denholm had no need to fabricate tension was on the set for *The Blue Dress*. It was one of those rare times when his private and professional life overlapped. For there, sharing the top billing, was Virginia McKenna. It was my first meeting with Ginny. As we sat down for drinks it occurred to all of us that while she was wearing a pink top with a white skirt, my colours were the same but in reverse. The match introduced an almost surrealistic feel to the occasion, much enhanced, of course, by Denholm flapping about.

But there was no cause to worry. Ginny and I behaved impeccably and enjoyed each other's company. Denholm had to agree that all went well. Which was more than could be said for *The Blue Dress*, described by the writer himself, Hugh Leonard, as a 'rotten film'. Happily, the disappointment did no damage to the mutual respect of author and actor. Meeting by chance in New York, Hugh Leonard said of the evening that he had 'never been in such excellent bad company'. Denholm introduced him to the Bloody Bullshot, a life-threatening concoction related to the Bloody Mary but with cold bouillon added.

Writing in *The Irish Times*, Hugh reminded readers that there had been 'times in the last decade when viewers might have thought that no single play or mini-series on the small screen and no new British movie was complete without a cameo performance from Denholm Elliott'. He went on to describe Denholm most memorably and accurately as an actor who 'seldom starred but always shone'.

This was true across the barometer of movie ratings from

good to fair to all-time low. There were some real bummers in the early eighties. *The Whoopee Boys*, directed by the madcap John Byrum, flopped at the box office with Denholm alone collecting points for stealing all the best scenes. The shooting was notable for an ever-shifting script. Minor corrections were liable to become major rewrites, and at a moment's notice. For Denholm the enduring memories were of Florida. We stayed in the Mutiny Hotel, where each room had a distinctive feature – and how. We slept in a four-poster bed made from papier mâché palm trees.

The Razor's Edge was Bill Murray's first serious movie, a remake of a 1946 film. It followed *Ghostbusters* and was only accepted by the money men on condition that Bill Murray signed for *Ghostbusters II*. The high-minded fable of a man obsessed with finding some meaning in life after witnessing the horrors of the First World War was slated by the critics and faded into realms of late-night television. Another remake, of *The Wicked Lady*, was knockabout fun with Michael Winner presiding. It was the film that reunited Denholm with Alan Bates (happily) and John Gielgud (less happily). A private lunch brought Denholm face to face with the great man. Neither of them could find much to say. The contrast with Denholm's close friendship with Laurence Olivier is instructive. Larry was nothing if not dominating, he made the world turn. John was in no rush to commit himself. His strength was in spotting chances, a player not a captain. He and Denholm had much in common but were more attracted to their opposites.

The Wicked Lady deserves a place in the family album for providing Jennifer with a blink-and-you'll-miss-me walk-on part. Sadly Mark, who made his debut as the young Denholm in the fantasy thriller *Underworld*, ended up on the cutting-room floor. Denholm himself was the dotty inventor of a mind-expanding drug which has the unfortunate side-effect of producing subterranean mutants. Put like that it comes over as a project that any sought-after actor could well have done without, but the storyline was from Clive Barker, a big name with horror fans; the production company was fresh off the ground (justification for Denholm accepting a modest fee) and other quality actors, like Miranda Richardson, were involved. In the event, though, it was all pretty well a disaster with the special effects winning out against corny dialogue in defiance of Alfred Hitchcock's first rule of movie-making: 'You need three things for a successful movie: a good script, a good script and a good script.'

Part Three

12

Two Score and Twenty

It was twenty years before I attempted to surprise Denholm with another birthday party and this one, his sixtieth, was much better planned. One learns. I knew he was expecting some celebration but not quite what I had arranged. I told him that the writer David Ambrose and his wife were coming over and we were going to try out a new restaurant in Camden Town. In fact it had taken me weeks to organise with the PR people for the newly opened Camden Palace to put on a buffet and drinks party for sixty people in return for allowing press and television coverage of the event.

I invited practically all the people he had worked with over the previous twenty years and all his friends, our house-keeper and family, doctors, lawyers, the lot. And, of course, Jean Diamond and her husband Martin. Our children were in on the secret from the beginning. Jennifer's boyfriend at the time was Jimmy Penfold, who had a band called Holly-wood Killers, and he and jazz singer Annie Ross, Lionel Bart and others went up on the stage and sang.

But the best bit was when we walked into Camden Palace, were led in total darkness up to a balcony, and, suddenly, the room below was flooded with light to reveal all the guests, among them John and Mary Mills, Ronald Fraser, Christopher Reeve, James Villiers, Leslie Phillips, Peter McEnery, Gary Bond, Kenny Everett, Tom Baker, Edward Fox and Albert Finney. They sang 'Happy Birthday' and hundreds of balloons were released from the ceiling.

Denholm was astonished, especially when he found out that I hadn't had to pay a penny for the party. I don't know who filmed the occasion for what channel, but I would love to have a copy of it to see again that look of total amazement on his face.

Denholm accommodated himself to the marching years by taking on the role of English eccentric. His model was Ralph Richardson ('my god' as he called him), though he held back from Richardson's hearty rumbustiousness. What he liked about the old actor – his father in two early films – was his cheerful disregard for the conventions. 'Anyone who can park his Bentley outside the Garrick, pat the bonnet and shout cheerily, "See you later, my beauty," has my money.'

He shared with Richardson the joy of motorcycling. 'My ideal is riding in the morning sunshine along a mountain road on my way to a pleasant luncheon with dear friends.'

The miracle was that he ever got there in one piece. His luck was phenomenal. He and I started on two wheels in Ibiza in the days when a mobilette was reckoned to be the easiest way of negotiating unmade roads. It was also our way of getting to know the island, experiencing the smells and the feeling of air against our faces. I came off more often than he did because for some reason on Ibiza he was more careful. We covered every nook and cranny of the island, rattling down roads that no car could ever manage.

It was in London that he seemed to lose control. It worried me sick every time he donned his helmet and took off down the road looking neither left nor right, oblivious to any other traffic.

After talking to other bike freaks, I persuaded him that if he had to ride one at all he should buy a bike with a stronger engine which would give him more control. I think the first one was a 250 Suzuki, but then he began buying stronger and more powerful machines, which was all very well except that he lived in another world and driving a hefty motorbike at the same time was not a wise thing to attempt. 'I often make up extraordinary conversations,' he said, 'particularly between pompous people whom I love to send up. It simply pops into my head and the dialogue pours out. Sometimes it's so funny that I'm riding along roaring with laughter, and people going past think I'm absolutely nuts.'

There always seemed to be someone available to give a helping hand after one of his spills. Just before we moved from Abbey Road to Kentish Town, Denholm was brought home in a very shaky state by the then Minister for Arts – I think it was Paul Channon – and his wife. I administered a very large vodka and tonic to Denholm for medicinal purposes. Denholm seemed to think that their meeting justified his accident and it took some time to persuade him that if he wanted to meet the establishment, there were better ways of doing it than falling off a motorcycle.

I finally managed to persuade him to give up the motorbikes, thank God, with a lot of help from Jean. He was also, incidentally, deaf in one ear. I used this as part of my argument that motorcycling was dangerous. Honestly, I felt as though I was performing major amputation by doing this, but I really did want him to live.

Another of his public demonstrations of eccentricity was his carrier bag.

When I go to work I always carry a plastic bag from Sainsbury's or Marks with all my things in it. I think people would recognise me from that. It doesn't weigh anything; all you're carrying is what's actually in it. It's quite logical. I lost the smart *jeune premier* image of myself and, since the press kept on telling me I was sleazy, I thought, well, why not relax and enjoy it? It's my answer to a handbag. You want your glasses if you wear them, a book, cigarettes, a few munchies, news-papers, paper, envelopes and a pen if you want to write letters. I take 'biccies', shortbread; you never know when you'll need a snack.

When Denholm turned up in Oslo, with carrier bag, for *Codename Kyril*, a four-hour mini-series, someone forgot to send a car to meet him. Eventually word got through to Beryl Vertue, the producer, that Denholm had been kept hanging around for an hour or more until the mistake had surfaced and been rectified. Distraught at such an unfriendly welcome, Beryl telephoned ahead to the Grand Hotel, Norway's finest, where the cast were staying, to ask reception to change Denholm's room. 'Give him the best you have.'

'The best?'

'The very best.'

When Denholm and his carrier bag finally arrived, he was

ushered into the lift to be taken up to the bridal suite. With
its two bathrooms, master bedroom, study and spacious living
room with a terrace and a panoramic view over the city, the
accommodation outclassed Millionaire's Row. Rushing over
to the hotel to greet her star, Beryl found him perched on
a chaise longue, still clutching his carrier bag and looking
thoroughly bewildered. 'They keep asking me about my luggage,' said Denholm. 'This *is* my luggage.'

Beryl couldn't help wondering if she had been a little hasty
with the largesse. The luxuries did not suit him. As Denholm
told a friend who expected him to have a butler and a white
limo, 'I loathe all that. I'm happy living in a box room.'

Denholm was by no means a recluse: moody – yes; intoler-
ant of the peacocks of his profession – no question.

I garden a lot. Daydream a lot. I talk hardly at all. Bits
to my wife, bits to my daughter, pass the time of day
with the neighbours. Well, generally speaking, what is
there to talk about? It's something which is incredibly
boring to me. People ask me the same bloody stupid
questions. My daughter's boyfriend came up last night
and asked me a lot of questions and round about the
seventh question I said, 'That's the last question. I'm
very tired and I'm going to bed.' I could've been there
for an hour, you know. You're in your own home, you've
got your beans on toast and your *Evening Standard*
propped up against a cup of tea, and the last thing in
the world you want to do is talk.

He was certainly impatient with anyone who took themselves
too seriously. There is a story of Denholm filming *Marco*

Polo, an interminable and costly television series of the late eighties, which is a fair reflection on his attitude.

> We were in Mongolia. One evening I wandered out thinking, whatever happens to me tonight, I'm just going to go with it. I was sitting on a stone wall and all of a sudden eight young Mongols came along on bikes, looked at me and the leader gestured to me to jump on the back of his bike. Off we went, all roaring with laughter, and we went speeding through the town, holding hands across the bikes like a Jabberwocky. Finally we sailed through the gates of the hotel and right up to where the entire cast and crew of the series were standing.
>
> I landed two inches from the faces of the director and the cameraman and do you know, they didn't even pause in their conversation about 'Well, I thought the third take was a bit better than the second' and so on. Here was this extraordinary piece of real life and they were so wrapped up in their bloody film, they didn't see it. Yet there's so much more to our game than just pumping out the product.

A favourite role for Denholm was the pretentious but rarely employed director in *The Apprenticeship of Duddy Kravitz*, the movie that launched Richard Dreyfuss on his international career. With a viewfinder in one hand and a whisky bottle in the other, Denholm transforms the filming of a bar mitzvah into a world statement on the Jewish condition. It was a barnstorming spoof of the studio prima donna. It was also the only totally nude scene of Denholm's career. A carefully placed copy of *The Financial Times*, a hat and a cigar were his props.

Denholm's rooted objection to the clutter of film-making – what some press people describe as glamour – discounted him as a Hollywood regular. We often tripped over to the States for a movie or a television special and although there were offers which included taking on a five-year contract should a series take off from a pilot, we never for one moment considered, no matter how huge the salary, taking up residence for longer than a few months. And even that had to be mulled over heavily. It was a question of getting there, doing the job, collecting the money and running.

'If I'm invited to a party given by my understudy, I go without thought. People in Hollywood wouldn't. They'd be afraid of catching a disease,' Denholm said. For neither of us was it a real world. We rarely went out to the 'in' places and if we did it would be with his Hollywood agent. Otherwise, we had people in for drinks or went to a local un-chic café. 'So many people in Hollywood end up holding a mirror to a mirror. All they want to see, to believe in, is the image they create.'

Taking Denholm and his views at face value, it was easy for interviewers and feature writers to go the extra distance with him and to record unquestioningly his delight at being alone. He was a great observer of life:

My favourite occupation is sitting at a café table, in the velvet evening air, watching people. Not just the obvious, but the tiny things. The man leaving a tip and then wondering if it is too much or too little and looking around trying to see what others are leaving. It is the little subtle bits that sometimes later come out in a performance. You don't copy the look but what it reveals underneath, the inner story of the person.

He told Mavis Nicholson, in a television interview, something he had often told me, that he could create an entire life-story from the look of the back of a person's head. Sometimes I would be sitting still at a table or in our living room and he would come up and kiss the back of my head. He said the back of my head, the way I held it when I was worried about something, or just thinking about someone, is what made him fall in love with me, and what made him love me still.

Because of our very up-front relationship, I knew that Denholm did not wander off to Barcelona or Marrakesh simply to observe the street scene. He was part of it, experiencing his freedom in the anonymity of the crowd and in the unrestrained pursuit of pleasure. I never put up any objection except to warn him to please be careful. He had been mugged several times in his life and I wanted him to return safely and unharmed.

There are in the world some very sick people who take great pleasure in causing pain to people in the public eye. It's almost as though they feel that because they have seen an actor or other public figure on the TV screen in their living room it gives them a right to interfere in his private life. It was quite a shock the first time an absolute stranger approached me and said with great glee, 'I just saw your husband with a blonde woman at the airport in Barcelona.'

The shock wasn't that he was there but the look of expectancy and then disappointment on the stranger's face when I said, 'Oh yes, that is our nanny, Lee. I put them on the plane back to London this morning.' It was the realisation that this stranger had gone out of his way to cause pain, not to me personally, but to Denholm Elliott's wife. And it was because of this that Denholm and I realised that what could happen to me would happen to our children. We discussed a hundred times during their growing years when would be the right time for each of them as individuals to be told of Denholm's bisexuality, without going into details which we felt would be totally unnecessary.

Unfortunately, one of those sick shits got to our lovely Jennifer first. I was out at the shops when she came home and told Denholm that an absolute stranger approached her in the Kings Road and said: 'Your dad is Denholm Elliott. Did you know he is gay? Well he can bugger me anytime he wants'. Denholm was terribly upset and told her that this was exactly what we had always wanted to avoid happening, but now that it had, as much as he would have done anything to prevent her being hurt, it was time to talk. And they did.

With Mark it was somewhat different. He was three years younger than Jennifer and during the discussion between the three of us, we all agreed that emotionally he wasn't ready. Also Denholm felt afraid that at that age Mark would judge him in an irreversible way. But one evening in Ibiza, when Mark was twelve, he arrived home and found Denholm sitting by the pool. Mark rubbished some queenish pretensions of a certain Ibizan gay which touched off a short fuse in Denholm. He whipped into Mark with an attack on bigotry and intolerance. He mentioned some names of close friends whom Mark had known all his life and asked, do you like so-and-so? Mark said he did. 'Well, he happens to be gay.

Does this make him a lesser person now that you know that?' Mark said that it didn't.

I was up at the house on the terrace facing the pool. I heard Denholm say, 'I've been all over the world. I've made love to men and women. I've been in orgies where everything goes on. Does this make you care about me less?' They then had quite a discussion which I couldn't hear, but after a few minutes, Mark came to me in my room.

'Are you OK?' he asked in a tone that suggested his biggest worry was how much I had overheard.

'I'm all right,' I said. 'What about you? It was a bit heavy, wasn't it?'

He nodded a few times without saying anything. Then he went out and gently closed the door.

When Denholm came upstairs he said he hadn't wanted it to be like that, but in the end, they had given each other hugs. We never, ever had a row with each other or our children without giving hugs before going to bed. It was a very important rule in our family: 'Never sleep on anger or emotional pain.'

I don't deny that Mark and Jennifer were hurt by some of the things that they now know of Denholm's past, but nothing made them love him any the less. We never wanted him to be a different person. They spent a lot of time letting him know that. He was very loving to me and to the children.

The instant judgement (as so delicately put by a Sunday tabloid after his death) that Denholm was a great actor with the morals of an alley cat would have had Denholm screaming with laughter. I know I was, just at the thought of how much he would have liked it. The cutting would definitely have had a place on our refrigerator.

Responding to Mavis Nicholson's questions for a Channel 4 profile, Denholm came closest to a public declaration of his philosophy. He talked of falling in love as 'one of the bravest things anyone can do' and went on to say that love – real love – is all about honesty. Honesty takes great courage and therefore love is brave. At this point he gave a disarming grin and a modest disclaimer: 'I really don't know what I mean.'

When he came home that night he said he was talking about the love that existed between us: without barriers, without judgement; unconditional love. A closer explanation of what he meant by courage and honesty is enshrined in the books of D. H. Lawrence. The deepest relationships are based on personal integrity that has little to do with conventional morality but everything to do with truth to self. That is what Denholm has tried to achieve in his lifetime – truth to self.

It was a philosophy that took many, many years to put into practice and one that did not guarantee happiness on the road to achieving it. In the early years he could be filled with self-loathing, convinced that he had slipped on the wrong side of the 'razor's edge between God and the Devil, between good and evil'.

Another cause for heart-searching was Jennifer's drug addiction. Meetings at the clinic and involvement with members of Narcotics Anonymous helped us both to understand that we should not take on the guilt of feeling we were responsible for Jennifer's addiction, although I do feel that we are somewhat responsible for her emotional instability. My father, apart from being emotionally unstable, was addicted to alcohol and almost every member of the family on my mother's side was an alcoholic. So if it is true that such things can be inherited, then Jennifer did not have much of a chance. But then, there are families of ten brothers and sisters and only one will have it in him to be an addict.

Denholm did his best but he simply did not know what he could say or do to help Jennifer. After she came out of the clinic, she attended NA meetings and many clean friends would come over to the house and hold meetings – you only need two people to make a meeting. Sometimes I would sit in but more often than not I would leave them to it, first because I felt that my presence would inhibit them and secondly because it was too painful for me to hear some of the things that my 'baby' had gone through during her using time.

A lot of tears were shed around that table. One night Denholm came home to find a meeting going on and Jennifer having a blub. He gave a little smile and said, 'I'll be upstairs if you need me.' Even though he didn't know what he could do, if anything, he just wanted her to know that he would be there for her.

Our family doctor, Stuart Ungar, who had also become a friend over the years, told me that the day Jennifer admitted that she had a problem and wanted help I was to call him; no matter what time or where, he would be there to help. Of course, it was a weekend when I finally got her to tell me, 'Yes, I am addicted to heroin.' I had had no idea that heroin was the problem and it was like being kicked in the stomach by a mule. But I had to keep my promise that I would help her if she came to me. What she told me later was that she was going through withdrawals and had no money and no way of getting anything without me. I took her to Stuart, who met us in his office. He gave me a prescription for methadone, a heroin substitute, and told me to guard it with my life. I was to give out only specified amounts each day. I slept with the bottle under my pillow to prevent Jennifer from getting hold of it until at last they were able to admit her into a clinic. It was the week of her eighteenth birthday.

It was during this week that I knew with all my heart, to the depths of my soul, that I was capable of murder. I tried to find the person who had given our daughter heroin. I did discover his name and I went out in search of him. I told a close friend who wanted to do a 'job' on him for me, 'No, this one is mine.' Although I found out who, I couldn't find where. My next move was to arrange through another friend an introduction to someone in the Drugs Squad who could keep a closed mouth and who owed him a favour. Two detectives came down to London from Glasgow, where they had been working on an investigation, to meet me in a pub on Abbey Road. They had no idea at that time that I was married to Denholm.

They asked me what I wanted them to do about this person. By now I had had time to pull myself together. Two weeks had passed and Jennifer was in the clinic. I really thought hard about the best way I could hurt him without causing more pain to my family. I was so filled with hatred, an emotion totally new to me and so all-consuming. I told them his name and said, 'I want him inside. I want him in jail and I want him to know that I put him there and I want him to be there for a long time.' He was subsequently arrested and spent time inside. For the last eight years, according to Jennifer, he has been out of prison and clear of drugs.

It is still a shock to me to know that I would have been

able to take another person's life without any regrets. In those moments, it didn't matter to me what would happen afterwards. As far as I was concerned, he had murdered my child. I am now glad I didn't do that because it would have caused great suffering to Mark, Denholm and Jennifer. But I do know that I was 'temporarily insane', and I still resent being made to experience the horrendous emotion of hatred.

The treatment and the follow-up with meetings seemed to be a great success and it was about two years before Jennifer slipped and used again. She had gone off to the States to stay with relatives in Texas who were members of AA, which gave me a feeling of security. But she wasn't ready to stay clean and I received a call for help from her long after she had moved out of her 'safe' house into the streets.

I told her I would only come over on a rescue mission if she was clean by the time I arrived or I would leave her standing at the airport. I arrived at the airport, picked her up at a hotel in Dallas and found that she was coming off – 'cold turkey' – methadone, a much more difficult drug to get out of your system than heroin itself. She was in a terrible state but determined. I called Denholm and told him our plan.

The two of us moved to a beach house in North Carolina, off the beaten track. I went over the entire place with microscopic attention to anything that might be taken as a drug substitute. I locked my own medicines and any alcohol in the boot of the car. She and I went to the grocery store and bought food and toothpaste and she insisted on buying the largest bottle of Scope mouthwash, which could only be found in America. We duly returned to the beach house and not more than an hour later I heard a bump from her bedroom. I found her on the floor between the bed and the wall.

296

She had consumed an entire litre of Scope, which anyone, if they read the label, could tell you is 90 per cent alcohol. She was pissed out of her tree!

It was an experience I wouldn't wish on an enemy: the sweats, the horrors, the black-outs. Denholm had arrived and was a witness to all of it too. One night she ran out into the pouring rain, stark naked, screaming at her devils – at me, at whatever else was going on in her head. We found a meeting that was held on the beach for AA. Anything would help. I drove her there. She says that she went into a total black-out from the moment she sat down until she came round during the Serenity Prayer.

That meeting introduced us to some people who offered to drive her to the next meeting – they were held several times a week but the next one was in a town forty miles away. Jennifer said that it was watching what it was doing to Denholm and me that made her keep going. She did it. She stayed clean for three years.

She met a super guy back in England whom we all loved (and still do) and they were to be married. He and Jennifer visited us in Ibiza and then went back to London. Denholm followed while I tidied things up before joining them. The day I was to catch the plane, Denholm called me. The gutter press had been on the doorstep. They were printing a story with pictures of Jennifer scoring near the needle exchange. Her dealer had set her up and made a pretty penny to boot. She was back on that stuff and the marriage was off. Eventually she cleaned up again . . . fell in love, used again and lost again. Now she is clean, I hope to God forever. We don't give up easily in this family, and I have great admiration for her strength.

13

Command Performance

From 1979, when he received a Best Supporting Actor Award from the British Academy for his performance in *Saint Jack* to 1990, when the Variety Club of Great Britain gave him the Best Actor Award for his performance in *A Life in the Theatre*, Denholm received no fewer than ten awards and nominations for his performances, and he loved getting every one. He never expected such accolades so each award came as a wonderful surprise.

Denholm's reply to a congratulatory letter from his brother Neil was typical of the way he expressed himself and his self-effacing modesty. 'Blimey, if they give me an award for taking a pee, I'll 'ave to watch my bladder. They might mow me down like 'one of them Shell barrages (and they're 'eavy yer know – 'ardly pick the bleeders up).' He also repeated a feeling he often voiced to me: 'I have the distinct feeling that I'm being "pushed" in some strange way – you see, almost everyone else is dead! i.e. Ralph Richardson, Burton, Mason, Leonard Rossiter, Kenneth More, John Gregson, etc., etc.'

Seven of those nominations and awards came from the British Academy Awards. Sometimes it became very difficult to fool him into going to the awards ceremonies because quite understandably he wasn't enthusiastic about attending formal dos with hundreds of people which lasted over six hours. But between us Jean Diamond and I managed somehow without giving away the secret. Usually it was, 'Come on Denholm, you've been on the receiving end so often now, it would be a matter of manners for you to show your face.'

On one occasion he was shooting in North Africa and the BAFTA people wanted to fly out with an award with a TV crew and film him receiving it there, live on the evening of the awards ceremony. Since everything was so hush-hush, no one called in time for me to inform them that in fact Denholm was at that very moment winging his way back to London. He had a serious abscess under one of his teeth which couldn't be treated in Africa. I picked him up at the airport and went straight to his dentist, who pulled the tooth. Meanwhile, the TV crew were wandering about the desert with only camels to interview. I did get him to the ceremony, much to the relief of the organisers, who told me of their plight when we arrived.

In 1984, Denholm teamed up once again with Michael Palin in *A Private Function*, written by Alan Bennett. It was great fun to work on and gave him the opportunity to play a villain of sorts, which he relished. 'There's nothing more enjoyable than being stared at by a million pairs of eyes that hate the sight of you,' he said in an interview. 'They think you can't do anything worse; then you do.'

However, Denholm's character provoked more laughs than hisses. The film is set in post-war black-market Britain, and he plays Dr Awaby, one of a trio of small-town bigwigs whose plot to deliver a roasted pig to the Coronation celebrations is thwarted by Michael, as the lower middle-class chiropodist, and his wife (Maggie Smith). Denholm's great line, savoured over the two weeks of filming, was in having to describe Michael as 'a silly little bunion-clipping pillock'. There were several stand-in pigs for the part and most of the members of the film would pet them in between takes as one would a dog. Denholm was the only one, to my knowledge, who contracted a terrible rash that wouldn't go away for weeks.

Michael was always generous in his praise of Denholm but I think a letter he sent me after Denholm died best expresses his admiration.

I never quite realised how much I liked him until one evening in New York when I had spent fruitless, soggy minutes trying to hail a cab on Fifth Avenue. At last one drew up and I rushed towards it. Who should get out but Denholm. Instinctively, we gave each other a great hug – and by the time I looked again, the cab had disappeared. I've rarely been so pleased to see someone. He was remarkable, as a man and an actor, and I miss him.

There were other successes to feed the ego. Best of all was Denholm's study of seedy integrity as the old soak of a journalist Vernon Bayliss in *Defence of the Realm*. The timing of this movie, brilliantly directed by David Drury, was impeccable. With Margaret Thatcher's kindergarten of pushy young Tory politicians dominating public life, the left was strong on conspiracy theories to explain why they were failing with the voters. The heavies were in power by virtue of their ruthless misuse of the system. There was some evidence to support the theory. This was the time of Ponting, Tisdall and the Whitehall moles; of the GCHQ affair and the security-connected death of anti-nuclear campaigner Hilda Murrell.

So it was not too hard to accept the storyline of the film: the cover-up of a potentially cataclysmic nuclear accident. Gabriel Byrne was the redneck reporter who lifts the lid on a sex-and-security scandal only to find that the MP he has forced into resignation is the key to a yet murkier affair involving the highest in the land. As the whistle-blower, Denholm is murdered before the film is half over. But in carrying off the best notices he moved Gabriel Byrne to rephrase a much-quoted veteran's warning: 'Never act with children, animals or Denholm Elliott.'

I was with Denholm one Sunday on location in Fleet Street. As the scene was shot he suddenly changed one of the lines to include my favourite drink, vodka and Coke, and added: 'Detente in a glass.' They let him keep the line in.

It was an irony not entirely unknown in the movie business that an apparent left-winger was, in his true life, a thorough-going conservative. Denholm was very much a Thatcher man who believed in getting a fair reward for effort.

> I resent very much having the same salary if I'm working myself into the ground as someone who is just sitting on his arse all day long. I like the gutsy, ballsy attitude to life of saying, OK, if you can make money, you can have some of it. But you've got to damn well earn it.

I've been a sort of minor actor for thirty-five or forty years, and it was only when I started making it that the inspector of taxes suddenly got on my tail and wants to meet me and have interviews. You are blamed for winning here. As long as I am an out-of-work actor and starving, they can chuck a few quid at me and that's all right, but it really gets under my skin. I don't blame people leaving the country and going to Hollywood.

I knew what inspired this declaration. The tax inspector was constantly trying to find something wrong with the way we handled our affairs.

In *Past Caring* Denholm was a feisty pensioner, the anarchic lecher of an old folks' home who gets nurse Connie Booth into bed. 'I don't get asked to play too many of these parts,' he told an interviewer. 'I was grunting and groaning like a good 'un, wasn't I? We got stuck in and after forty-five minutes we asked the director if he wanted any more variations.'

Sharing the billing was a visibly ageing Emlyn Williams in what proved to be his last role. The director, Richard Eyre, soon to be supremo of the National Theatre, was asked for thumbnail sketches of his leading actors. Of Denholm, he said: 'He is elusive; a metaphysician who is always slightly at odds with the mundane banality of everyday life and tries to dream himself out of it. And yet as an actor he's specific and meticulous and concrete.'

In other words, not easy to pin down until he was playing a part. A journalist who saw him on and off the set described him as unpredictable: 'There are sudden thunderbolts of anger and the equally alarming ricochets of laughter. His familiar, insinuating voice leads you into images which reverberate after you have parted.' Yet that too was part of the act for *Past Caring*.

In 1985 and 1986 Denholm made a distinctive contribution to several films. *Hotel du Lac*, the television adaptation of Anita Brookner's prize-winning novel, starred Anna Massey as a middle-aged novelist, alone and palely loitering beside an out-of-season Lake Geneva. Denholm was the dandified two-timer with a strong line in disconcerting double-takes. 'Oh Edith, please don't cry. I can't bear seeing women cry. It makes me want to hit them.'

While filming *Hotel du Lac*, Denholm was signed to play opposite Katharine Hepburn in a CBS television movie, *Mrs Delafield Wants to Marry*, a beautifully turned out romance which belied the popular view that love between old people is cute as long as no one takes their clothes off. The location was Vancouver in winter, an experience that led Denholm to confess his frailty in the cold and Kate Hepburn to come to his aid with a gift of a pair of long johns. They are still in the wardrobe. I use them for skiing.

Another prestige operation was *A Room With a View*. When he heard that Merchant Ivory Productions was casting the lightest and most subtle of E. M. Forster's novels, Denholm set his heart on playing Mr Emerson, the free-thinking old buffer who pushes his son (Julian Sands) into a romance with the superior Charlotte (Helena Bonham Carter). Nothing if not supremely confident in his production skills, Ismail Merchant summoned Denholm for interview. As this was the first he had had to endure for many years, Denholm decided to make the most of it. He sleeked his hair, kitted himself out in an ill-fitting tweed suit, gathered up an armful of packages and barged his way into the Merchant Ivory office just off Regent's Park. When he was through the door, he dropped all the packages. 'I was in character, bustling and larger than life. I thought, if that doesn't do it, nothing will.'

It was a hell of a role to play convincingly. Denholm had to come across as an essentially gentle character who believed that it was his strong humanist opinions that set him apart from society when, in reality, it was his awkward social manner that caused offence. His big scene was with Maggie Smith as the easily offended chaperon of the beautiful Charlotte. In a duel between logic and convention, passion welcomed and passion repressed, the comedy of manners was played out to wonderful effect. It was the anguish of seeming to try too hard that made the character so entirely believable.

Denholm saw something of himself in Emerson, the breaker of the mould who had enough self-awareness to realise that he might become an old bore. He certainly used Emerson to express some long-disguised views about his fellow countrymen. 'The conventionality of the English is something I find unattractive – the whole lack of joy in the physical. The English may love gardening and fishing but they have never struck me as being close to nature.'

A Room With a View did better in the States than it did in Britain. At the Paris Theater in New York, the movie grossed a record-breaking $1 million in fifteen weeks.

In 1986, the long-promised chance to appear in a Woody Allen film finally materialised. Many years earlier, when we were in Ibiza, a call had been put through to Sandy's Bar from Woody in New York. 'Can you do an American accent?'

Denholm said he thought he could manage a mid-Atlantic.

'Try it,' said Woody.

Denholm gave him a verse of 'Hickory, Dickory, Dock.'

'That's great,' said Woody. 'Thanks. I'll be in touch.' And he put down the receiver.

It stayed down until Woody had made *Hannah and Her Sisters*, a great hit but a film which left Denholm unimpressed and confused. Nevertheless, he had already accepted the role of Lloyd, husband of a veteran actress, in Woody's next project, *September*, and we prepared to spend the winter of 1986 at the Wyndham Hotel on Fifty-Eighth Street, where we always stayed when in New York. It was too late to turn back now and anyway the money was good.

Denholm liked directors to say 'Action' and 'Cut'. Although it pleased him to have a certain amount of freedom, he wanted a director to direct. The letter that arrived in our London home along with the script gave him an indication of what to expect by way of direction from Woody.

3 October 1986

Dear Denholm,

Enclosed is the script. Don't be intimidated by the amount of talk or quality of dialog. It's all very flexible and speeches can be put in your own comfortable words whenever you prefer to do that. There's probably occasional character inconsistencies and other foolish writing mistakes, but we'll change them all on the set or whenever they occur to you, and we'll re-shoot the ones that cause us any problems.

By page count the script appears short, but I think it actually is too long and we'll find that many points can be made quickly without some of the over-writing I've done. I've included no stage directions or business or camera shots because I'll be devising those on the set.

Finally, the overall pacing of the film will not be too fast, so these few pages will go far. You'll notice, by the way, that this is written as a play in ostensibly four acts. It is deliberately not 'opened up', and one of the interesting problems for all of us (myself, mostly) is to make it flow like a film. If anyone feels disappointed or trapped, please don't worry because no one will be held to any commitments.

Needless to say, I would like to keep everything secret – the plot, characters, anything relating to the project – because there will come a time when we can employ all that information for our own maximum advantage to the film.

We flew to New York and moved into the Wyndham Hotel. Maureen O'Sullivan, Mia Farrow's real-life mother, who was cast as her screen mother in *September*, lived on the floor above us with her husband. Right from the beginning it was a troubled production and Maureen in particular was confused as to what she was doing in it at all. Denholm could not settle on what was wanted from his performance. It was confusion all the way, with everyone clinging to the slender hope that it would all come right in the editing room.

This did not mean that we didn't have fun at the same time. Maureen and I discovered we had something in common – a love of champagne. So we became champagne partners every evening after the shoot. Shoes off, feet up and glasses filled became something she looked forward to after the confusion at the studio. We alternated suites.

The lunches were held at a restaurant near the studio in Queen's and they were, to say the least, not exactly relaxing meals. Maureen asked me to attend the lunches to lighten the atmosphere a bit and so that she had someone to laugh with, and Denholm asked me to come and sit between him and Woody to act as a translator. I thought that Woody and Denholm had a lot in common in that they were both eccentrics, but there was a definite language barrier and, being an American, I managed to understand both. Moreover, Denholm was from the old school of acting and Woody, although brilliant at what he did, was an exponent of the 'let it all hang out' style that was the hallmark of his movies.

Just before Christmas, we moved on to Toronto, where Denholm recorded *A Child's Christmas in Wales*, a television special which is now as much a part of the Canadian festive season as the holly and the ivy. Halfway through the week, there was a call from Woody. 'Are you sitting down?' he asked. 'I wanted to tell you that I have put a match to the film. I'm going to start again. Denholm will have a different role. But, don't worry, he can use the same clothes.'

He knew how much Denholm hated fittings.

From playing Maureen O'Sullivan's husband, Denholm became Mia Farrow's doting neighbour. Maureen herself was replaced by Elaine Stritch, which gives some idea of just how radical the changes were. When I broke the news to Denholm, he was philosophical. 'Same costume, same performance, more money.'

Woody asked for four weeks to rewrite the script, which gave us time to go to Ibiza for a break before returning to the Wyndham Hotel. The feeling of *déjà vu* was strong but Woody put such energy into the project, filming at breakneck speed, that we barely had time to consider what might have been had he stuck to the original concept.

In the odd spare moments, Denholm put pen to card to wing off presents to his far-flung family. Neil has kept the message that came with a handsome watch.

'I enclose somefink wot *must* 'ave fell orf the back of a truck in New York (considerin' ow much it coss me). You need a bleedin degree in *Electronics*, & by the time you've got it you won't *need* a bleedin' watch!

Enclose the destructions (in Japanese) It 'as a solar cell – lie in the sun in Key West for 6 hours & you 'ave a wound-up watch – you also 'ave 3rd degree burns. You'll love it.

All the best, yor Bro. D.

P.S. The strap is made out of old lorry tyres.

And I cannot help but follow up with the advice that went along with a copy of Stephen Hawking's *A Brief History of Time*, also to Neil.

If you 'ave *ENNY* problem with this Dudley – *Call* me. 'QUARKS'? – No prob. 'BLACK 'OLES' – 'ULLO? 'The Big Bang' – *NAUGHTY*.

D.

September was demolished and put together again in less than a month. The critics took the view that the effort was not justified.

In 1986, Denholm was nominated for an Oscar. His category, naturally enough, was Best Supporting Actor; the movie, *A Room With a View*. It was a measure of Denholm's ranking, and marketability, that he joined a line-up which included Michael Caine, Tom Berenger, Dennis Hopper, Jackie Gleason and Willem Dafoe. Furthermore, it was judged by the press to be the year's strongest category. The prize was taken by Michael Caine for *Hannah and Her Sisters*, but Denholm was left in no doubt as to his popularity among moviegoers. He was fêted everywhere he went while Jean Diamond, who joined us for the trip, was beset by producers waving six-figure contracts. Denholm turned down some of the biggest prospective money-makers as too tedious for words. It was amazing, for example, how often he was asked to reappear as the quintessential English butler from *Trading Places*. But rejecting a big deal did not imply a softening of his commercial instinct – he could make just as much from a succession of prestige, if relatively low-budget movies which needed him for a few days or weeks at most as he could from a single blockbuster which tied him up for a year.

He appeared in the television adaptation of the Evelyn Waugh classic, *Scoop*, and in *The Happy Valley*, one of two filmed versions of a high-society crime passionelle in wartime Kenya. Denholm declined to repeat the role in *White Mischief*, the second of the two movies. In this bigger-budget production with its superior storyline, the betrayed husband turned murderer was played by Joss Ackland.

In 1987 Denholm took on *Bleak House*, eight hours of BBC classical drama, which was a year in the making. 'I hoped it would lend me a bit of weight as an actor,' he said.

310

It was certainly a lavish production, with a long line-up of what an American critic dubbed as 'extraordinary though not famous English actors'. Presumably, he meant not famous in the States – Diana Rigg, Peter Vaughan, Robin Bailey, T. P. McKenna and Bernard Hepton were certainly well enough known in Britain. But even with an Arthur Hopcroft script (he also wrote *Tinker, Tailor, Soldier, Spy* and *Jewel in the Crown*), backed by production values that would not have shamed a Hollywood movie, the impact of *Bleak House* was, well, weighty, but not quite in the sense that the BBC or Denholm had in mind.

Denholm was John Jarndyce, the kindly philanthropist at the centre of this convoluted tale of lawyers' greed and mismanagement. He emerged from the swirling fog (it was pumped out of machines and gave everyone asthmatic coughs) with a determination to present a livelier image, preferably as an unmitigated and unrepentant villain.

In the 1988 Honours List, Denholm was made a CBE. The evening before the investiture, he walked about the house naked except for his top hat. It was, he said, his way of warding off delusions of grandeur. Our guest and guardian for the great occasion was Jean Diamond, who persuaded a retired banker friend of hers to chauffeur us to the Palace in his own Rolls-Royce. We made a splendid high-society party. Jean and I were matched in navy blue and white outfits while Denholm was magnificent in his morning suit, grey gloves and, of course, the top hat he had worn for his undress rehearsal the night before. After our chauffeur had managed to lose his way a couple of times, we found the Mall, and drove into the Palace courtyard at precisely 10.30 a.m.

Denholm was immediately whisked away for his briefing

on court etiquette. The chief lesson was not to overstay his welcome. After the royal handshake he was to recognise the ever so slight push of his hand as a signal to back off, taking five steps to the rear before giving the customary farewell bow. Meanwhile, we witnesses were being told not to applaud and, if we had to talk, to whisper.

It was all over in a few minutes. Denholm said later that his brief appearance before the Queen was more nerve-racking than the Oscars ceremony. But if that was so, he put on a brilliant act of repose and self-possession. In the early afternoon, Denholm had to catch the train to Manchester where he was appearing in the film *Coffin*, so before his departure we celebrated with a champagne and pheasant lunch at the Connaught. Then it was back to reality.

14

A Life in the Theatre

In the mid to late eighties, then, Denholm's career was thriving. On the surface, everything was fine; professionally, I had never known him to be more confident. He saw the film set and the television studio as his natural habitat. 'I am like a golfer who gets to know his putter. I'm much more relaxed. I can play games with the lens now. I can keep my face in my key light and my toes on the mark and show the lens my inner world. More and more often now, I can make those long putts.' Later he enthused: 'I love the idea of containing all your energy and then throwing it out a minute at a time. If you get it right, it's there forever. Lately, I've been getting it right more often.'

Whatever he had said in his early days, the magic of the theatre was fading. 'I can't bear breaking my heart every night at 8.30 and getting better at 9.10,' he complained. But it had one advantage – 'At least they don't cut you.' Yet the fascination of bringing author, actor and audience into a unity of understanding – 'You can chuck in God, too, if you're really on form' – was just too much hard work. 'I would much rather be what I am – a medium fish in the big pond of television and film – than a great British actor in the little pond of theatre.'

But if he was prepared to pace himself in public, his private life had become yet more frenetic. When other men of his age might have settled for memories, Denholm in his sixties was still driven by sex. If anything, the intensity of pursuit became greater. The risks were obvious but he did take precautions.

With his sense of economy, Denholm had to balance the thrill against the cost. Was he getting value for money? In his jottings book we have the cold reality of his late-night ruminations, written with the help of a vodka or two, but truthful for all that – and amusing to both of us. The entry is headed 'Courage is all'. It sets out his thoughts on a trip he was planning to Morocco which I'd been encouraging him to take.

12 Dec 1984
Basics. 7 Days is plenty.

Currently the pound is being bought in Marrakesh at 11.35 dirhan (in 1982 it was 10). The hotel room costs 41 per day incl. breakfast (but possibly not taxes). Dinner averages 500–600 dirhan for steak au poivre, ½ bottle vieux papes (red) and service.

Luggage incl: soap, shampoo, 600 cigs, 2 litre vodka, Poppers, cream and oil, razors (disposable)/2 vest (incl. 1 thermal), 1 packet entero vioform etc.

Final conclusion: Enormous wank being cruised, but for £400 for 10 days, better off with a good whore in London at £50 a night.

I always encouraged Denholm to spend his own money. It was his and he couldn't take it with him. But I also saw clearly that the risks were very much part of the game. Denholm believed with all his strength that facing up to risks was in itself a guarantee of immunity from danger. He was sure he would come through unscathed as he had in the past. A simple example was that no matter where we were in the world, whichever airport we were in – including New York City – he would put down his briefcase in the middle of the departure lounge and wander off in the secure knowledge that no one in his right mind would walk up and take it. Don't ask me the logic of such reasoning but he never lost that particular bet and it used to drive me crazy.

In view of his financial insecurities, I was quite surprised when in the mid-eighties Denholm jumped at my idea to buy Sandy's Bar. By now the bar had had several owners, each of them taking it further downmarket, since Sandy Pratt had retired from the scene. My idea was to put it back on its feet again, even though it would take quite a bit of restoring (the expression 'has great potential' comes to mind), run it for a few years and then sell it. So many of Sandy's former clients missed having a fun meeting place and I knew that I could make it work as long as I kept it running in the way Sandy had run it originally.

But Denholm kept saying all the wrong things. He talked as if I would be running it for the rest of my life and about how he wanted to invest in securing a financial future for me. I had never had any doubts about Denholm's earning ability and I knew I was good at judging property values from our past investments. In the mid-seventies I had even bought a tiny place with Diana Rigg in the town of San Carlos, which I turned into a gallery, and then years later I sold it quite well to Terry-Thomas. But the idea that I was going to pour drinks for a living was way out of left field. He and I had always preferred to be on the other side of the bar.

It got to the point where we had a full-powered, stand-up row in the middle of the street, which culminated in me screaming at Denholm, 'If you think I want to run a bar playing mother to a bunch of drunks for the rest of my life, you must be out of your mind!'

He pleaded with me to go through with the deal. It was obvious that he was desperately worried. But about what I could not imagine.

On the day I signed the papers that made me the owner of Sandy's Bar, I came back to the house to find Denholm pacing up and down on the terrace. He had been doing a lot of that lately, which in itself wasn't unusual, but he didn't normally do it so often. And he was not talking out loud, which was normal, but to himself.

I went to him and placed myself opposite him, forcing him to meet my eyes. 'I've signed the papers. Now tell me what is wrong. We can't go on like this. I feel as though I'm living with a stranger.'

Denholm looked at me. Then, very nervously, he said, 'You want to know? You really want to know? I'm HIV positive. I've got AIDS.'

I somehow settled on the words that were to determine the rest of our life together.

'Is that all?'

Denholm gave me a little grin. 'That's funny. The doctor told me you would say that!'

In fact, for the second time in my life I felt as though I

had been kicked in the stomach by a mule.

The lab reports returned to the office of our doctor and
friend, Stuart Ungar, on 14 October 1986 had proved
negative.

The results received by Stuart on 13 May 1987 were
positive.

16 May 1987
Dear Stuart,
I've just had the results of the test you did on me last
Wednesday. Not much fun. I can handle that (I've no
option). However, obviously if it got *out* I'd be finished.
I'm not telling anyone (even Susan) & I'm not sure I
can rely on your discretion & that of your colleagues.
Wish me luck.
D.

Another letter written the following day expressed his
worries about the press, or anyone else, for that matter,
finding out. He called it his 'cloak and dagger' letter and
asked Stuart to pay any bills in his own name. He enclosed
a cheque, asking Stuart to let him know if it was not enough;
if it was too much, 'have a drink on me, or whatever.'

Ten days later he wrote again, and by now the reality had
truly begun to sink in.

28 May 1987
Dear Stuart,
I have been doing a bit of thinking (well, you've got to
start some time). The last ten days have been pretty

grim as you can well imagine – a sort of inescapable Kafkaesque nightmare. I have *handled* it, but at a cost I wouldn't want to continue paying for the rest of my life. I know I'm imaginative but that's my nature (& my profession). However, an over-imaginative nature can cut both ways, fortunately! As the final results are not yet in, one way or the other, I think I'll leave them where *they are*, i.e. hanging in mid-air, & not inquire too deeply *just now*. This probably is very cowardly, but life has to go on, & I've got to go on *with* it, & I know what I can handle, & what I *can't*. Doubtless in due course we will get together & talk it all through (round about 2050 AD). One side-effect of all this is I've gone cold turkey on smoking. It's killing me, but I'm hanging in there! Not bad after fifty years. In the meantime, can you bury the file on all this 'Deeper than Plummet Sound'?

Yours,

Denholm

He carried all this basically alone until the moment he told me, almost four months later. In his jottings book is a note he wrote as he struggled to come to terms with the truth.

'Fear is the ultimate reality. It concentrates the mind horribly, the ultimate horror of deviation without meaning – without love. One becomes a rogue elephant.'

'I wake up every morning and it's the first thought of the day. *I've got it*!' he told me. 'Then I get on with the rest of the day.'

We agreed that this secret was to be between us. Above all else he wanted to go on working. If our news got out it would be like handing a black spot to casting directors. We didn't tell our children. We didn't even confess to Jean Diamond at that time.

Of one thing I was certain. I should not have bought Sandy's Bar. Now, even though I understood why he had encouraged me so desperately, if I was to be of emotional or physical help to Denholm, I had to be free to go wherever the work came from.

The first move towards getting me out of the hole I had unwittingly dug for myself was to gut the bar, redecorate it in the style that suggested the old Sandy's Bar, put it on its feet commercially and sell it as soon as viable. I reckoned on three years. I told Sandy that without his help and public support it wouldn't work. He made one of the most flattering comments anyone has ever made to me. 'If there is anyone who can make it work, I believe you can.' From that moment I knew I was in with a chance. I felt bad that I couldn't tell him about Denholm's illness and that I would be selling it so soon.

For months I talked with Denholm around the subject that preoccupied both of us. The newspapers were full of new reports on drugs that came and went. The experts' opinions changed by the week. They were as much in the dark as we were. Denholm went with the advice of Dr Brian Gazzard, a doctor to many people with the HIV virus, not to embark on a heavy treatment of chemicals while he was still, hopefully, a long way off being AIDS active.

Another decision hardly needed to be discussed but discuss it we did – in fact, we had often talked about it even before he contracted the virus. That was the practice of safe sex. Denholm had these discussions with Stuart Ungar as well. Now it wasn't a question of preventing him from becoming HIV positive, but of ensuring that he would not pass the virus on to anyone else.

He kept the lines open to David and Edwin, but more by letter than personal contact. He said he had trouble getting them to use condoms as they had never bothered in the years before. There was one close call Denholm told me about after he had spent a weekend in Amsterdam with David. David had expected it to be like old times but Denholm gently refused any form of intimacy. David remembers that he found some big pills in Denholm's sponge bag. When he asked what they were, he was told they were mine. David didn't believe him and Denholm didn't think he had got away with it either, so he asked me to confirm the story if David were to call and ask me.

When Denholm resumed work, we had the added problem of the insurance doctors who are chosen by whatever film company is employing you at the moment. It was a nerve-racking experience that I went through with Denholm often. As long as you can prove you are healthy enough to finish the film for which you have been employed, then all the doctors will pass you. But there was such a lack of education about the difference between HIV and active AIDS (apart from the publicity angle) that he was worried about losing a job. Not to have the option to work whenever he wanted would have killed Denholm long before the AIDS virus. He would have lost the will to live.

After filming *Killing Dad*, he signed up for *Scorchers*, a spicy relationship drama with Emily Lloyd, Faye Dunaway and James Earl Jones. He was to play Hawker, a broken English actor with a predictable love of the bottle. Filming was in Los Angeles and we were booked into the Château Marmont on Sunset with the rest of the company. I love staying in that place – it's so camp.

There was no way Denholm could carry the medication through customs – HIV positive foreigners are not allowed to enter the United States. If he were searched, he would be refused entry to the country and, worse, his secret would be exposed. On the other hand, there was no reason why I, as a US citizen, should not take the pills in for myself, as long as they didn't realise I was carrying them for anyone else. If the pills were found on me, I was within my rights to refuse an explanation.

I did get questioned once. 'Are you carrying medication for anyone else apart from yourself?' I was so surprised by the question, my face must have registered the shock I felt. 'Good God, no! Why ever should I?' was my reply.

During a break in filming on *Scorchers*, we did have one scare. It was to be the first of many to come in the years ahead. We had decided to go to a beautiful place in the desert not too far from Palm Springs and Desert Springs called Indian Wells. There we stayed in a spa where each suite had its own jacuzzi and swimming pool filled each day with fresh spring water from wells a few feet below the desert sands.

We had been there only three days when Denholm discovered a rash at waist level. By the next morning, it had circled his waist. He had a bout of shingles, which a company doctor on our return correctly diagnosed, but the treatment he prescribed fell short for a patient who was HIV positive. Having called Brian Gazzard, I was able to boost the medication to three or four times the normal level. With that and baths in a cereal or porridge-type solution (Denholm's remedy), he made a speedy recovery.

For the most part, Denholm was remarkably fit. He had been most of his life. The doctors in the past had been surprised by the strength of his heart even if his smoking habit was at least a pack a day, and for the amount of drink he put away, his liver was amazing in its powers of recovery.

As time went on we gained confidence in our medical support and took comfort from articles written about the power of mind over matter, the will to survive among HIV carriers. HIV was not necessarily a death sentence. We had to and did begin to believe that.

Denholm began to read books about meditation, visualisation and spiritual development. I left other books around, studies by doctors on patients who had been declared clinically dead and then, by the miracle of modern science, were brought back – otherwise known as near death experiences. He began to study methods of deep breathing, visualisation and self-healing with Marcel Boffin. And for the first time since I had first studied with Marcel and Itzo Tsuda in order to help Mark all those years before, Denholm allowed me to practise on him.

The reserve that outsiders saw as part of his character was now more pronounced and a few dark thoughts appeared in his press interviews. 'I think about death a lot these days and the prospect terrifies me . . . I am aware of every passing day . . . I know that time is limited.' If his peers thought Denholm a very private man, one who rarely joined in the heavy socialising that goes with film-making, they now had a near hermit. We rarely went out, even on location, except with each other, and then to places where we wouldn't run into people we knew who would encroach on our space. If I wasn't there to fend them off, he became quite adept at putting up a fifteen-foot iron wall around himself with which the intruder collided.

From around this time, Denholm began to watch the sunset every evening, unless the weather was bad. With or without me, he would set off to remote parts of Ibiza, or wherever we were, for the event. Sometimes we took out *Near Miss*, and, drink in hand, bobbing up and down, we would wait for the ever-changing spectacular shows that nature offered him. Now, sunsets make me cry.

In April 1989, a package arrived in Ibiza for Denholm. It was from Jean Diamond, who by now knew all our secrets. It was a play by David Mamet she wanted Denholm to read. It had to be important. Denholm had said no to the theatre so often in recent years that Jean was automatically disposed to give the thumbs-down to any producer with the idea of seducing him back to the stage. His latest words on the subject had sounded pretty definite. 'If you do get a play, don't even take it out of the envelope.' The remark followed a lucrative offer to take over the role of Dr Watson for a Broadway production of *Sherlock Holmes*. In the end the play did not transfer and Denholm was mightily relieved. He did not again want to be put in the way of temptation.

But there was something extra-special about *A Life in the Theatre*. To the casual eye there was little in it of much substance. David Mamet had put together a conversation piece between an old ham of the repertory circuit, playing out what he knows to be his last days, and a hungry beginner, eager for every scrap of credit to come his way. Half the

323

action takes place with the actors' backs to the auditorium as they perform their clumsy interpretation of tragedy and farce to an imaginary audience before returning to their dressing room and the real business of debating their lives.

When eventually Denholm got round to opening Jean's package and glanced at the first few pages of the script, he was hooked. He found the play 'intriguing, witty and moving' and deadly accurate on 'the tiny little jealousies of acting, the ego and the pomposity'.

On a flying visit to London he met Jean for lunch in Wheeler's, near her Soho office. His first words were: 'We have a problem.' The problem was finding a reasonable excuse for not doing *A Life in the Theatre*. It was a forlorn exercise. Eventually, Denholm said, 'Oh, Christ, I've got to do it.'

When he told me the news I was pleased and anxious – pleased that Denholm had found a challenge exciting enough to take him back to the theatre, but anxious and sad at the same time because I knew in my heart, even if his health stood up to the nightly performances for the six-month contract, that this would be his last stage play.

I knew now was the time I had to find a buyer for Sandy's Bar and I had from April until September to do so. As luck, or the Devil, would have it, a man had arrived on Ibiza who was looking for a business to take advantage of the Olympics in Barcelona in a few years' time. That was his story, and I had no reason to doubt him; nor was I really looking for anything more than first come, first served so that I could get out and be with Denholm once the play went on tour.

Remember, he was not AIDS active yet. But something inside was making me move fast. I told friends and customers that Denholm was thoroughly pissed off with me being unable to move freely with him and also that he didn't like the way some of the customers behaved towards me when they were drunk. On one occasion when I asked a customer to pay his long overdue bill and he rudely refused, Denholm stood up to hit him. So it wasn't difficult for our story to be accepted.

I spent the summer arranging payments and contracts so that the deal would be finalised in time for September. Thank God for a good lawyer! Never try to be your own. She insisted that every peseta was paid before the key was handed over. It seems I am the only person this man had not taken to the cleaners. The fact that he has since been sitting in a Spanish jail for, amongst other things, drug-trafficking, dealing and possession is, I hope, some tiny compensation to all those he abused.

Denholm joined the company of *A Life in the Theatre* for rehearsals and I joined them on tour when they opened for the first night in Brighton. If Denholm had to say an irrevocable goodbye to the stage, David Mamet's play was ideally suited to the purpose. So much of what he felt about acting – and about his life as an actor – was encapsulated in the performance he visualised for himself. As David Mamet wrote in his programme note, 'A life in the theatre is a life spent giving things away. It is a life mobile, unstable, unsure of employment, of acceptance. The future of the actor is made uncertain not only by chance, but by necessity – intentionally.'

Denholm had no trouble in identifying with those sentiments, to which he added: 'I don't think we are such a bad lot. All we ask is to earn a few bob entertaining people.

When you look at the captains of industry they are bent as a hairpin and cooking the books.'

To play the ambitious young actor, the director Bill Bryden and Denholm together chose Sam West, the son of Timothy West and Prunella Scales. It was his theatrical debut.

A Life in the Theatre did a quick tour of the provinces before coming into the West End. It was the time of year for colds and 'flu. Everyone in the company went down with a bug – except Denholm. His only mishap was at Guildford, where he experienced the horror of drying up. 'I just skipped two pages. I was still at the stage of thinking, "Where do I go next?" A two-hander is a hell of a thing and I hadn't seen an audience for ten years. Sam's eyes went to the size of Brigitte Bardot's, but luckily neither the audience nor the critics noticed a thing.'

The play opened at the Haymarket on 31 October. The night before, after the last preview, I sat with Denholm in the empty stalls chatting about the play and the audience response. Jean and Stephen Burnett, the company manager, came to join us. We went on talking and laughing for a while. Denholm was perfectly relaxed. When he got up I thought we were about to leave, but instead, he climbed up on the stage, walked to the centre and in smooth, dulcet tones recited his favourite poem – Edward Lear's 'The Owl and the Pussy-Cat.'

> The Owl and the Pussy-Cat went to sea
> In a beautiful pea-green boat,
> They took some honey, and plenty of money,
> Wrapped up in a five-pound note.
> The Owl looked up to the stars above,

And sang to a small guitar,
'O lovely Pussy! O Pussy, my love,
What a beautiful Pussy you are,
You are,
You are!
What a beautiful Pussy you are!'

Pussy said to the Owl, 'You elegant fowl!
How charmingly sweet you sing!
O let us be married! too long we have tarried:
But what shall we do for a ring?'
They sailed away for a year and a day,
To the land where the Bong-tree grows,
And there in a wood a Piggy-wig stood,
With a ring at the end of his nose,
His nose,
His nose,
With a ring at the end of his nose.

Apart from we three in the otherwise deserted auditorium, the performance was witnessed by the company fireman, who peeked through the curtains to find out what was going on. When Denholm brought the poem to an end . . .

'Dear Pig, are you willing to sell for one shilling
Your ring?' Said the Piggy, 'I will.'
So they took it away, and were married next day
By the Turkey who lives on the hill.
They dined on mince, and slices of quince,
Which they ate with a runcible spoon;
And hand in hand, on the edge of the sand,

They danced by the light of the moon,
      The moon,
      The moon,
They danced by the light of the moon.

. . . he fell to his knees and kissed the stage. 'It was a rare and deeply felt emotion, a moment to be bottled,' said Jean.

With a clutch of rave reviews to its credit, *A Life in the Theatre* was quickly established as the play to see that winter season. Unusually for the West End, Sunday matinees replaced the Monday evening performances. As Bruce Hyman remembers, these matinees 'soon became like Equity open meetings as actors who were busy throughout the week converged on the theatre to witness this great artist at the height of his powers'.

Knowing that his peers were in the audience, Denholm used the licence of playing a decrepit actor to demonstrate his power of mimicry. 'I've been a bit naughty, pinching a bit here and there from John Gielgud and Noel Coward.' A visitor backstage congratulated Denholm on his triumphant reviews. 'Yes,' he replied. 'I just wish my old Dad was here to see them. He always said I wouldn't really make it until I was sixty.'

At the turn of the year, Denholm caught 'flu, which brought on an attack of bronchitis. At the first sign of illness I took him along to a chest doctor, who pumped him with antibiotics. Despite my reservations, Denholm declared himself fit enough to go on with the play. But he had trouble with his breathing and there were nights when he could barely get his words out. The irony was that audiences did not see him as a genuinely sick actor. For them he was the consummate professional giving a moving portrayal of one man's despair of the dying light.

Heavier doses of antibiotics made little difference. One night, having watched Denholm gasp his way through a scene, Stephen Burnett said to me: 'He can't possibly carry on like this. He should be in hospital.' We debated bringing down the curtain but I knew that Denholm would be furious if we cut short his performance. When at last he came offstage I rushed him home and called Brian Gazzard. There was not much time wasted on the preliminary examination. One look was enough. I took Denholm to Westminster Hospital, where I checked him in under an assumed name.

Early the next day, they took a scraping from his lung. Denholm had pneumonia. And, yes, it was AIDS-related. In any other job, a life-threatening illness would have been enough to make the patient forget about the outside world. But Denholm worried himself into a panic about the play and what would happen if he could not get back to work quickly. I tried to reassure him although I knew that his concern was real, that without him the play would close. Within days, his understudy was having to endure the agony of knowing that customers were demanding their money back. They had come to see Denholm and without him there was no show.

By the time Denholm was discharged from hospital, *A Life in the Theatre* had closed. I now had to face up to the awful reality that whatever was in the air, Denholm was in danger of catching it, especially as it seemed his weak point would be his lungs. We both talked about this more often and more honestly than before, but without being morbid.

It was also time to let Jennifer and Mark know that he now had active AIDS. We had told Jennifer some time earlier that he was HIV positive and she had handled it very well. But because Mark had been in New York at school and would be alone with this secret, we had avoided telling him until now. He came back to London and Denholm had his time alone with him. Mark was a casualty. Emotionally vulnerable, he was not up to accepting that the father he revered was likely to die – whatever the cause. The shock was terrible and he took to drinking more than normal. He also broke up with the only girlfriend he had ever seriously considered marrying. It was incredibly painful for all of us. And Jennifer, who always acted as though she could take on the world, was dying inside. She started using drugs again around this time.

I wish I could have changed things for them but the best I could do while trying for a mood of realism was to stop short of doom and despondency. It was a hard act to pull off and I did not always succeed, but I did have some great players – Denholm, Jennifer and Mark. There were good times, too, when Denholm looked and felt fit – and those periods could stretch into months at a time when we would all be relaxed and hope that the crisis had been contained.

Denholm was well enough – and looked terrific, too – to take on the part of Smiley in *A Murder of Quality*, which brought John Le Carré's spy-master out of retirement to solve a murder in a public school. The script was a beauty and attracted a top-flight cast including Glenda Jackson as Smiley's accomplice in amateur detection and Joss Ackland as a fruity schoolmaster with nefarious interests beyond the classroom.

Denholm's efforts to express his admiration for John Le

Carré were almost wrecked when he was introduced to the writer by his real name and not as John Le Carré. He mistook him for the headmaster of Sherborne, where the film was being shot. As John remembers the conversation in a letter he wrote me after Denholm died, 'Denholm's words on realising his mistake were 'Oh, you're you – I mean him – oh, my God – yes, well, I'm so sorry – hello again.' John added: '. . . and as a man he was equally remote, equally courteous and beguiling. It was something like true fulfilment of life's ambition to have him in my film at all.'

After *A Murder of Quality* and a break in Ibiza, we went off to West Virginia, AZT and other chemical 'should it become necessary' helpers in hand, to make probably one of the most boring pictures he has ever done, *Toy Soldiers*. The location came close behind in the boring stakes – we were stuck in a motel on a highway to nowhere for four weeks. But, as Denholm said, 'the money was good' and it was not a long drive to visit his garden in North Carolina and my mother, which we did the moment filming was over.

We always rented a house on Long Beach and had family come over to us for drinks and dinner. One night, with the moon full and the tide low – which made a huge space of sand between the house and the Atlantic Ocean and meant that the waves were still and the light of the moon gently danced on the water – I looked closer and saw Denholm standing at the water's edge. Picking up a drink for him and for myself, I joined him. Alone at the edge of the sand we danced while he recited, 'The Owl and the Pussy-Cat'. When he finished we both burst into tears.

Not one of my brothers, sisters, nephews, nieces or cousins had the remotest idea what was going on – none of them even knew he was ill. But it wouldn't be long before Denholm would try to tell my sister Joyce.

We spent time with Jennifer and Mark in Ibiza and London, where Denholm had his blood levels constantly monitored by Brian Gazzard. The T-cell counts were not as good as they had been in the past and Denholm increased, by a tiny bit, the amount of AZT he was taking, and a few other drugs to give him a boost. He had a bout of thrush in the throat, which is quite common among AIDS sufferers, but we tackled it with Diflucan and it seemed to work. So we took off for Los Angeles and the last film Denholm was to make. With me in attendance carrying essential medication, the risks were containable.

The movie, Denholm's last, was *Noises Off*, an adaptation of Michael Frayn's long-running West End farce within a farce. Denholm slotted into his now familiar role of an ageing actor fond of a tipple, a part turned down by John Gielgud as 'not at all suitable'. Directed by Peter Bogdanovich, much mellowed since his days on *Saint Jack*, this latest venture was blessed by a strong cast led by Michael Caine, Carol Burnett, Christopher Reeve and Denholm. But all the stars in the Hollywood firmament could not have cracked the central problem of *Noises Off* – that being essentially a theatrical piece about a mismatched group of players trying to put on a knockabout comedy, it did not translate easily to the screen. In the end, Bogdanovich remained faithful to the stage production, which was very funny, but proved not quite what cinema-goers expected on their Saturday night out. One day it might just turn out to be a cult film.

We rented Tim Curry's house in the Hollywood Hills, just below the famous Hollywood sign. I went out to the studio almost every day to make sure Denholm took his medication, ate properly and got rest in between takes. Towards the end of filming he began to lose his appetite again and I upped the dosage of Diflucan after talking to Brian Gazzard in London. He was losing weight even though he was able to swallow the health drinks we bought in the drugstores. We would mix these with egg and all sorts of vitamins. Ice-cream and peaches went down well, too. I couldn't wait to get him back to London. His part over, we were on the first plane home and straight into his secret room at Westminster Hospital.

The doctors did more tests, one of which included giving him an injection of a drug called Hypno-val which stops the patient from suffering while a tube is put down his throat and into the lungs, where they take scrapings. When I arrived back in the room after his test, I found him struggling to push the hospital table on wheels through the door frame of the bathroom, which was too narrow to accommodate it. He was having a terrible time of it and when I asked him what exactly he was trying to accomplish, he said, 'Well, can't you see? I'm trying to get this trolley of geraniums out into our garden so that I can plant them.' Great stuff, this Hypno-val. When I told him after he came down, he was astounded.

It was then that the doctors became suspicious that he might have AIDS-related tuberculosis, though they weren't certain. Meanwhile, they were treating him for the thrush and decided that it was time to experiment with steroids in order to build him back up. In fact, in the beginning we were not sure whether he would be given a placebo or the real thing. But it wasn't long before it became obvious they were steroids and he began to regain his appetite and put on weight.

Jennifer, Mark and Jean were visiting him on a regular

basis and after a few weeks he came out of hospital looking a healthier, happier man. I was not so happy. Being unable to function unless I know exactly what's going on, I always – from the beginning – told his doctors that even though Denholm didn't want details, if I was to look after him properly I had to know everything. They told me that it would be a miracle if he saw out the year. It was early spring 1992.

Great friends of ours, the original creator and producers of *Five Guys Named Moe*, were going to New York City for the opening of the show there. Ulla Allen and Clarke Peters kept asking me to come along. All sorts of friends were going, including my great friends Schuyla Van Dyke de Curtis and Annie Ross. I couldn't tell them my worry at leaving Denholm, even for a week. I then thought about all the free mileage I had on Virgin Atlantic and asked our travel agent, John Warrington, to see what he could do about mid-class tickets for Denholm and me. John had been arranging our travelling lives for the past fifteen years and if anyone could find a way, he would.

Not only did he arrange it, but he also found some other tickets that would take me and Denholm to Key West first class on mileage that I had accumulated with another airline. Denholm was looking and feeling great but when I put it to him (especially the free mileage bit) and he agreed enthusiastically, I was still surprised. I don't know why. The real coincidence was that when Jean Diamond called and I told her we were going to New York the following week, she said, 'So am I!' I told her we were going to see *Five Guys Named Moe*, 'So am I!' she said. She had a client who was also involved in the show. That was the clincher. We were off.

The trip to New York and the show were a great success. Afterwards we left all the partying and flew to Key West, where Denholm exercised in the hotel pool and in the evenings we watched the sunsets over Mallory Docks from our balcony.

I went out on a boat with a friend of ours without Denholm because he wasn't feeling up to it that day. It's just as well, because we got stuck on a sandbar near Woman Key for hours before being rescued. I ended up with terrible burns.

With the help of Michael from the Roof Top Café we gave a farewell cocktail party for friends we had met during the years when we had a house there. No one said anything about how Denholm looked. They didn't need to. Everyone there had lost someone they loved through AIDS-related illnesses. I'm sure they knew almost as well as I did that it would be his last trip.

It was time for Denholm to tell my sister Joyce. She came over to our hotel in New York. I had already warned her that we had something to tell her, but Denholm wanted to do it himself. I kept going out of the room and coming back in again, saying, 'Have you told her yet?' and having to leave. By the time she went, he still hadn't told her in so many words but she knew anyway. The words were unimportant. It was also time for his brother Neil to be informed. This was no easier. Denholm didn't want to do it but I insisted that it would be totally unfair if his brother should find out from the newspapers before he had a chance to talk to him. Denholm called Neil and said that it was very important that he came to our house for a private talk.

Once the drinks were poured, Denholm employed one delaying tactic after another. It was the most difficult thing he had ever had to do and he could find no easy way to say what he had to say. I was forced to break in with a straight question to Denholm. 'Would you like me to tell him?'

Neil took the shock with his customary poise and I wasn't sure for a moment that he understood the full implications. 'My dear boy,' he said, 'I'm so very sorry.' He asked Denholm how he felt and was there anything he could do, and so on. I made a few more drinks. There was one thing Denholm insisted on and that was that no one else, not even Rosemary, Neil's wife, should be told. It was still 'the less they know the better' reasoning but it must have killed poor Neil to have to keep such a painful secret.

Before we went back to Ibiza the Volkswagen Polo car people requested Denholm's services to do an advertisement for a not-so-tiny sum. Although Jean and I both tried to persuade him that he did not need the money and that it was a bad idea, he still insisted on doing it. I said to him, 'I know why you are going to do this but I am going to be OK so please don't, because there are going to be repercussions.'

They came to pick him up and take him to the studio. I asked him if he wanted me to be with him but he refused help. He was so weak, yet he just had to get this one last job in the can. He was so worried about what would happen to me after he had gone. Nobody could disguise the frailty of the man and it's a wonder the producers allowed the advert to go ahead. But they did.

The next day, Jean had a phone call asking what was wrong with Denholm Elliott. 'How did you know that was going to happen?' Denholm asked me. He chalked it up to what he called my sixth sense. He had no idea how bad he looked.

We slotted in one more trip before going back to Ibiza:

we flew to Brussels for one day to see a famous homeopathic doctor called Janner. He was beautiful, and although he gave Denholm all sorts of special treatments to take back with him, I knew that it was too late. I am a firm believer in homeopathic medicine, but you must start it as soon as possible and not wait as many years as we had.

So we were off to Ibiza again but this time we relied on John at Janaway Travel and the discretion of the wonderful Isobel of DanAir to make sure that Denholm wasn't spotted by press or even curiosity-seekers. He wasn't really aware of how different he looked and he was almost oblivious, as always, of the stares of people on the street and in the airports. John would arrange that we got on the planes first and were the last off. I always found some magical explanation for why the airport cars happened to be around just when we needed them and why the first-class lounge was available to us even though we were not flying first class. He was always tired these days.

We lasted on the island until July, when Denholm started getting worse and began to lose the weight he had put on after the steroids. So once again, with the help of Isobel in Ibiza Airport and John in London and the doctors and nurses at Westminster, he entered hospital for the last time, apart from ten days at the Cromwell when I tried to give him a bit of a change before taking him back to Ibiza. He definitely had tuberculosis. He insisted on being put back on steroids but this time the pills did nothing for him apart from make him crazy. We wanted to take him off them but you can't give someone steroids then yank them away again. It could have killed him – and he wasn't ready to die. One has to be taken off gently, and in the meantime, since there was nothing left to do for him until I got him back to Ibiza, as I had promised, I had him moved to the Cromwell.

It was while Denholm was in Westminster Hospital for the last time that he gave me a present, one of Shakespeare's Sonnets.

Let me not to the marriage of true minds
Admit impediments. Love is not love
Which alters when it alteration finds,
Or bends with the remover to remove:
O, no! It is an ever fixed mark,
That looks on tempests and is never shaken;
It is the star to every wandering bark,
Whose worth's unknown, although his height be
taken.
Love's not Time's fool, though rosy lips and cheeks
Within his bending sickle's compass come;
Love alters not with his brief hours and weeks,
But bears it out even to the edge of doom.
If this be error, and upon me prov'd,
I never writ, nor no man ever lov'd.

We gave Jennifer permission to share her secret in the NA meetings. She visited Denholm in hospital every day; Mark did, too. Denholm had by then discovered mail-order companies and with the help of his credit card was buying out London. Anything he couldn't get by mail order he would send Jennifer off to buy for him. While Jennifer was out buying dozens of shirts and trousers at Kensington Market on her father's instructions, he was busy buying by telephone from Rumbelows, among other shops. I pleaded with him not to but he insisted that we needed his purchases. When I asked how it was possible for us to need three fridge-freezers, two microwaves and two ovens, his answer was simple. 'You may not need them but I want you to have them, so you must.'

I also ended up with five cars. There was another moment when, knowing how much I love birds, he decided I needed an aviary, especially constructed to hold two of each kind of bird – rather like a Noah's Ark. I bought him books on which birds got on together. When Lawrence Lovatt, Jennifer's first fiancé and still very much part of our family, came to visit he was given full instructions on how the aviary was to look along with the new total remodelling of our basement and first floor.

Dr Gazzard came to check on Denholm and found me in the hall in tears, not a thing that I had ever done in public. When I explained what was happening he jokingly, but with serious intent, teased Denholm. 'I'm going to have to remove the telephone and ask for your Gold Card if this goes on for much longer.' Denholm didn't take him seriously, not for a minute. I gave instructions to our housekeeper, Rose, not to sign for anything on our behalf. Our conservatory was already looking like a warehouse as the boxes piled up.

While Denholm was in hospital I got a whiff that the press were going to Ibiza. I quickly jumped on a plane, leaving the staff in charge, and got to my front door literally five minutes before a photographer and reporter from the *Sun* turned up. I told them we had just arrived and that Denholm would go spare if he knew they were trespassing. If they wanted a photo and an interview I would give them one in town, but they were not to come near our property again.

I met them in town with a picture from the year before which, compared with the way Denholm was now, made him look positively healthy. They asked to take photographs of my boat, and I gave them permission and the name – *Near Miss* – I even gave them the quay number. Off they went. However, I neglected to tell them that the name was not yet painted on the boat. After waiting a few days until I was sure they had left the island, I jumped on the next plane for London and Denholm.

The *Sun* published the photograph along with my story about Denholm's perforated stomach ulcer, which he had acquired by enjoying the good life, and the explanation that he was suffering the consequences of years of hard drinking. I didn't see why they shouldn't believe me. I had all the answers to their questions – I had spent some time nursing my mother back to health from exactly that problem.

Denholm's niece, Jane Elliott, called me from Spain one evening and I found myself confiding in her. I couldn't bear for her to find out the truth from the press. She flew to London and visited Denholm several times in the Cromwell.

I met Brian Gazzard in the halls of the hospital.

'Tell me now how long.'

'I would give him six weeks – but that's only a guess,' he said.

'When can I take him back to Ibiza?'

'Any time now.'

I called John. I emptied my bank account and John hired a private jet. Jean came up to see Denholm and then took me out to lunch. I told her what Gazzard had said and what my next move was. We could hardly meet each other's eyes without crying. I talked to Jennifer and she begged to be there. I said that she must arrange to have someone from the fellowship with her because I would not be able to worry about her at the same time. I needed all the help we could get.

I put the word out in the hospital that I was looking for a freelance nurse who would come with me and stay for the duration and found a marvellous New Zealander named Jo Ann. Amazingly, all this was arranged in a matter of two days. When I told Denholm we were going the next day, his face was like the sun bursting through cloud. He couldn't believe it.

Meanwhile Steve, who had been taking care of the house and animals in Ibiza for several years, prepared a full fridge and wine/vodka rack. Mark had already arrived. Steve arranged to meet us at the airport with my great friend and boating/drinking partner, Nina van Pallandt. I persuaded John to come with us to Ibiza – after all, the jet had to come back, and it was all paid for. On the Sunday morning John arrived and we took Denholm down through the lobby to a waiting Rolls-Royce which had used up the remnants of my bank account. I figured that if this was going to be his last trip, we were bloody well going to do it in style.

I don't know if he looked back at England when we left. I was too occupied hiding my own feelings by keeping busy. John had really gone the whole hog. There was champagne on board and platters of sandwiches. Denholm was as excited as a schoolboy on his way to the circus. I do know that when we flew over Ibiza, approaching it from the north – over Tagamago, where we had watched so many sunsets from the boat – Denholm found he was crying. 'I don't know why I'm crying now. It's never happened before,' he said.

Denholm and I settled down in our upstairs self-contained studio and the nurse, Jo Ann, stayed in the main house with Steve. Jennifer arrived in September with friends from NA and stayed with Mark in a converted farmhouse on our land just below the main house.

My instructions to Jo Ann were that she should only be there if things got too tough for me to do alone or if I needed a break. She found it difficult to believe that I really meant it and she had to sit on her hands to stop herself going crazy. At first we had her mixing drinks and doing the dishes out of idle frustration. But then she came into her own. It got to the point where we couldn't get Denholm up and down the stairs without a wheelchair. Even with Steve, who was doing all the hard work, the three of us found it back-breaking.

Marcel ordered a bed that could be put in the living room, one that had wheels and could be put into a sitting position so that Denholm could see his garden. We moved into the living room. Denholm loved having evening drinks on the patio and the huge sliding doors we had put in all those years ago brought the outdoors to him.

I ran into Leslie Phillips in town one day. When he suggested calling in to see Denholm I warned him to be prepared for a shock, that Denholm was quite ill. But there were no words to prepare anyone who hadn't seen him recently and had no knowledge of his illness. For Denholm himself, I had to try to minimise the awful realisation that he was wasting away by removing all mirrors and putting extra holes in his watch strap to fit his wrist.

Leslie's visit brought a lift of spirits – for a short time, because Denholm's breathing was by now shallow and he tired very easily. Leslie came bearing a gift of a rather phallic-looking flower which produced a few laughs. They had a drink together on the terrace but soon Denholm let me know that he needed rest. I was not surprised when, some time later, Leslie told me that having said goodbye to Denholm he went back to his car, leaned on the steering wheel and burst into tears.

The only other visitor I allowed up to the house was Sandy Pratt, who came twice, bearing gifts of plants, and was sensitive enough not to stay too long.

Jean arrived from London, bringing a set of Irish linen as Denholm had requested. He gave her the third degree. Where had she bought it and how was he to know it was real Irish linen? 'Well,' laughed Jean, 'I bought it in John Lewis, and if you don't believe the label which says Irish linen, then you will when I tell you the price.' He also asked her about the idea of having an aviary, like the one he had ordered in London. Jean pointed out the horrendous noise that our one cockatoo made and asked him to imagine what that would be like magnified 200 times. Denholm, who respected her advice to the last, thankfully dropped the idea.

Mark and Jennifer spent all their time with Denholm when he wasn't too tired. In the evenings they watched television with us in the living room. I was trying to create an atmosphere that suggested nothing was wrong. I went out occasionally while Jo Ann and Steve held the fort. By now we were giving Denholm liquids which he could swallow easily. We also had a mild painkiller which Jo Ann could give him if he needed it. He wasn't really in pain but he was uncomfortable.

Mark and Jennifer talked to Tiger and Cushan, Terry-

Thomas's sons, and the two boys turned up to visit Denholm. They had been part of our lives practically since their birth and were like family. Their second visit caught me unprepared. I almost lost it completely when they returned a few days later – shaved and combed, wearing suits and bearing a gift of cut flowers. I will never forget that. It was a formal goodbye.

One night I had a cry out near the cars in a field. I had reached breaking point so often. I was with Debbie and Roger and I told them what was happening to us. It was the first time I felt I had someone listening who really understood. They had gone through it with fellow Queen star Freddie Mercury a couple of years earlier and when you've been there you don't forget.

Jo Ann and I had quite a few nights we thought might be Denholm's last. Meanwhile, he was totally with us. He bitched about the fact that his voice was different and when I asked why it bothered him so much, he said, 'I'm an actor, for God's sake'.

'Well, you're not working at the moment, so it's OK.'

'Right,' he said, and we laughed. 'You're the only one who really ever understood me, aren't you? And you're the only one I have ever truly loved.'

On the night before he died, we were all in the living room. It was time to go to bed and both Jennifer and Jo Ann asked if I wanted them to stay with me. I said no, that I needed to be there with Denholm alone. Anyway, we didn't know for sure that it was going to happen tonight.

I woke up first with Steve's dog, Sinbad, jumping on the couch next to Denholm's bed, and if ever a dog could be described as throwing his arms around you, that's exactly what Sinbad did. I checked Denholm and he was sleeping. I dozed off. Then in my subconscious I heard a change in his breathing. I jumped to his side.

We had fifteen minutes before he took his last breath. It was soft, it was sweet, just like a baby's. Mark, Jennifer, Steve and Jo Ann were with us. It was 8.30 a.m. on a sunny morning, 2 October 1992.

Epilogue

We fell apart – together. After all the years of such stress our walls began to crumble. We had to go through two funerals in Ibiza. We had to have a public funeral in the church in Santa Eulalia to give the neighbours a chance to show their respects. The second ceremony took place at home, privately, with Jean Diamond, John Warrington and my sister Joyce flying in to be with us when we scattered Denholm's ashes in the D. E. Memorial Garden he had so jokingly named all those years before. We played at his request 'The Rainbow Connection' from *Kermit Goes to Hollywood*. Roger Taylor and Spike Edney sang it at the memorial service the following January in London at St James's Church, Piccadilly.

Needless to say, Jean Diamond helped me to organise the memorial service and Stephen Burnett, the company manager for *A Life in the Theatre*, and a friend who moved into my house to keep me company stage-managed the event. John Mortimer gave the address; Alan Bates read out the present Denholm had given to me while in Westminster Hospital for the last time, which was from Shakespeare's Sonnets. John Hurt recited the Jabberwocky and Leslie Phillips recited 'The Owl and the Pussy-Cat'. Mark read out a poem he had written the day after his Dad died.

Now you're gone I still feel you here in the room where
we dwell,
Surrounding countryside,
Spiritual in a whole body and mind I watched you drift
and expected the worst.
Now your cocoon is gone.
I speak to you when I'm alone, sympathetic hands
reach out.
I am speechless because I can't explain what I feel.
An upside-down world, folded inside and out.

Jennifer read the Serenity Prayer.

God grant me the serenity to accept the things I cannot change, courage to change the things I can, and the wisdom to know the difference.

One of the PoWs read out a clipping I had found from their war years.

The world's press covered the service and Michael Winner was quoted as saying: 'It deserved an Oscar for memorial services ... it made me want to come back for more ... it was pure Denholm.' The only time when I almost blew my cool (which I managed to maintain with the help of a beta-blocker dished out to me by Stuart Ungar) was when I saw

Michael Caine outside the church. We exchanged glances and both had the thought simultaneously that it was with Michael that Denholm had made his last film.

The year 1993 passed in a blur. What used to be a social drink for me became a sleeping pill. Instead of asking Stuart Ungar for something to help me sleep, I hit the vodka and Coke – every day for a year. I tried to believe that a couple of drinks after six o'clock wasn't going to do me any harm. But I knew better, and anyway, you should have seen the size of those drinks. By the time the year was over I knew I was a wreck – I was doing serious damage to my body. I made a date with myself to stop, which I did. I don't think about vodka any more but Coca-Cola just isn't the same.

I really understand how couples who have lived together for thirty, forty, fifty years give up for no apparent reason once one partner dies. I wanted to let go, to quietly slip away, to be with Denholm. It would have been so easy to close the door, to lie down and not get up again. So easy to just die. I don't know why I didn't. Probably because of Jennifer and Mark. Our time together isn't over yet.

I thought the first year was difficult – all the credit-card companies demanded their cards back and wanted fresh references now that I was a widow. All the firsts alone – Christmas, New Year's Eve, birthdays, anniversaries – as the widow. God, I hate that expression, and another is 'the late Denholm Elliott'. Late for what? Dinner? Who invented these words and please can we take them out of the English dictionary? But the second year has been worse, in some ways. Now we know that Denholm is not coming back, not going to call up. He is not on a film location and the key is not going to turn in the door.

Jennifer has been very strong and although she did slip and use drugs again she is now seeing a psychiatrist and she is clean once more. With the treatment she is getting a lot of raw nerves are being exposed and a lot of pain is being endured. She is very brave, very kind and I do love her. I don't think I could go through what she is doing now.

Mark, like me, did a high dive into a beer barrel – 'Mom, it's only beer' – and a few other substances that were not too good for him. But he, I now feel, is improving faster than either Jennifer or me. He has his painting and from his work you can see some peace coming back into his soul. He also has his band, in which he is the lead singer and lyric writer. He is very good and lucky to have an outlet to express himself. He and I have shouting matches but he is generally very kind to me and protective of both Jennifer and me. I wish he would clean his room more often.

A few hours after his death I was still sitting on the bed with Denholm while others went about the house preparing official papers. I had my back to him but my hand was on his arm. I wasn't really thinking when I felt a heat so strong, though not painful, that I had to look behind me, expecting to see the sun. Our house faces the east and my back was to the west. It was still morning. The sun was on my face, or would have been except we had the curtains drawn. The heat was so intense but so beautiful that it's hard to describe except to say that it filled my torso and stayed with me for days. Whenever I try to 'find' Denholm, I remember that feeling and it calms me.

A few months before Denholm died my surgeon, Mr Gilmore, discovered a growth in my breast and wanted to remove it immediately. For obvious reasons I didn't go back until well after the memorial service in January 1993, when I felt relaxed and well enough to face surgery. I am a firm believer in hedging your bets and so I went to see a friend who is a healer. I also went on my water diet, which basically cleans out your system, especially before an operation. I asked not to be given a pre-med because in the past I have found it stays in my system for a long time and tends to make me depressed for ages afterwards. The medical staff agreed to give me only the anaesthetic necessary to complete the operation.

The operation was performed at noon on 24 February 1993 and was a success. I came round quite quickly with no side-effects from drugs, and by evening my head was quite clear. I watched television, read the paper and went to sleep. At five o'clock in the morning a sister came in to plump up the pillows and prepare me for a visit by Mr Gilmore before six. She left a small light on by the bedside when she went out of the room.

I closed my eyes for what seemed a few minutes and when I opened them Denholm was standing at the end of my bed. He was smiling. The warmest glow filled his face and eyes. I said, 'Oh, my God, I'm so happy to see you.' He looked towards the door, then back at me, still smiling, winked and disappeared as the door to the room opened.

Mr Gilmore came in and asked what I was smiling about. I said that one day I might tell him but that he probably would not believe it anyway.

I haven't seen Denholm again. But I have felt that warm glow since and know that he is around, usually when I'm least expecting it.

Awards

1950   Best Supporting Actor, Clarence Derwent Award (Venus Observed)

Donaldson Award for Outstanding Achievement for Best Debut by an Actor 1950–1 (Ring Round the Moon)

1959   Sylvana TV Award (The Moon and Sixpence)

1979   British Academy Awards (BAFTA) Best Supporting Actor in Film (Saint Jack)

1980   Evening Standard Awards Best Actor (TV) (Blade on the Feather, Gentle Folk, In Hiding, The Stinker)

1981   BAFTA Best Supporting Actor (Film) (Raiders of the Lost Ark)

1983   BAFTA Best Supporting Actor (Film) (Trading Places)

Evening Standard Awards Best Supporting Actor (Film) (Trading Places)

1985   BAFTA Best Supporting Actor (Film) (Defence

of the Realm)

1985   American ACE Award Best Actor (TV) (Mrs Delafield Wants to Marry)

1986   BAFTA Best Actor (TV) (Hotel du Lac)

BAFTA Best Actor (Film) (A Room With a View)

American Academy Awards Oscar Nomination for Best Supporting Actor (Film) (A Room With a View)

1987   American ACE Awards Best Actor (Hotel du Lac)

1990   Hallmark TV Hall of Fame (Lifetime Achievement) (The Holy Terror, One Against the Wind, Twelfth Night, The Lark, The Invincible Mr Disraeli, Camille)

Variety Club of Gt Britain Best Stage Actor (A Life in the Theatre)

Chronology of Work

Selected Film Chronology

1949	Dear Mr Prohack (film debut)
1952	The Sound Barrier
	The Ringer
	The Holly and the Ivy
1953	The Cruel Sea
	The Heart of the Matter
1954	They Who Dare
	The Man Who Loved Redheads
1955	The Night My Number Came Up
1956	Lease of Life
	Pacific Destiny
1959	Scent of Mystery
1962	Station Six Sahara
1964	Nothing But the Best
1965	The High Bright Sun
	King Rat

	You Must Be Joking
1966	Alfie
1967	The Spy with a Cold Nose
	Here We Go Round the Mulberry Bush
	Maroc 7
1968	The Night They Raided Minsky's
	The Sea Gull
1969	Too Late the Hero
1970	The Rise and Rise of Michael Rimmer
1971	Percy
	Quest for Love
1972	The Hero
	Madame Sin
1973	A Doll's House
1974	The Apprenticeship of Duddy Kravitz
	Percy's Progress
1975	Russian Roulette
1976	Voyage of the Damned
	Partners
	Robin and Marian
	To the Devil a Daughter
1977	A Bridge Too Far
	The Hound of the Baskervilles
1978	Sweeney 2
	Watership Down (voice)
	The Boys from Brazil
1979	Saint Jack
	Zulu Dawn
	Cuba
1980	Bad Timing
	Rising Damp

1981	Raiders of the Lost Ark
	Sunday Lovers
1982	Brimstone and Treacle
1983	Trading Places
	The Missionary
1984	The Wicked Lady
	A Private Function
1985	The Razor's Edge
	Defence of the Realm
	Past Caring
	A Room With a View
1986	The Whoopee Boys
1987	Maurice
	September
1988	Return to the River Kwai
	Stealing Heaven
	The Bourne Identity
1989	Indiana Jones and the Last Crusade
	Killing Dad
1990	Scorchers
1991	Toy Soldiers
1992	Noises Off

Selected Television Chronology

1959	The Moon and Sixpence
1950–90	American Hallmark Hall of Fame (ten plays)
1979	The Stinker
1981	Marco Polo

1985	Mrs Delafield Wants to Marry
1986	Hotel du Lac
	The Happy Valley
1987	Keys to Freedom
	Bleak House
	A Child's Christmas in Wales
1988	Bangkok Hilton
	Noble House
	Codename Kyril
1990	A Murder of Quality

Selected Theatre Chronology

(*London theatres unless specified*)

1945	The Drunkard (stage debut, Amersham Playhouse)
1946	The Guinea Pig (London debut, Criterion Theatre)
1948	Frenzy
	The Green Cockatoo
	Don't Listen, Ladies!
1949	Buoyant Billions
	Horn of the Moon
	John Keats Lived Here
1950	Venus Observed (Clarence Derwent Award)
	Ring Round the Moon (Broadway debut, Martin Beck Theatre) (Donaldson Award)
1951	The Green Bay Tree (NYC)
1951–2	A Sleep of Prisoners

	Third Person
	A Fiddle at the Wedding (Brighton)
1954	The Confidential Clerk
1955	South
	The Delegate (Manchester)
1956	The Long Echo
	Who Cares?
1957	Monique (NYC)
	Camino Real
1958	King of Hearts (Liverpool)
1959	Traveller Without Luggage
	The Ark
1960	Stratford-on-Avon season: The Merchant of Venice, Troilus and Cressida, Two Gentlemen of Verona
1961	Write Me a Murder (Belasco Theater, NYC)
1963	Domino (Royal Theatre, Brighton)
1963–4	NRT tour of the States: The Crucible, Ring Round the Moon, The Seagull
1964	The Game as Played
1966–7	NRT tour of the States: A Touch of the Poet, The Imaginary Invalid, Tonight at 8.30
1970	Come As You Are
1971	Design For Living (Los Angeles Music Center)
1972	Hedda Gabler
1973	Turn On (Windsor)
1975	The Return of A. J. Raffles
	Chez Nous
1976	Heaven and Hell
1977	The New York Idea
	Three Sisters (NYC)

1979   The Father
1990   A Life in the Theatre

The Denholm Elliott Project
'Ibiza Se Preocupa'
(Ibiza Cares)

In October 1992 Denholm Elliott, one of the most prolific and respected stage and screen actors of recent years, died at the age of seventy from the complication of AIDS.

Together with his wife Susan, Denholm chose to spend the last months of his illness in the privacy and tranquillity of the Ibiza home they shared for more than thirty years. They realised first hand, however, a lack of adequate facilities on the island for those living with or affected by HIV and AIDS.

Susan recognised the need to change attitudes as well as provide real support for those who need it, and in June 1993 she set up the Denholm Elliott Project to raise funds to establish in Ibiza a respite centre for people living with HIV and AIDS, their friends, families and carers.

Ibiza Se Preocupa works in full collaboration with the Ayuntamiento de Ibiza, Ibiza's Minister of Health and the island's C'an Misses Hospital.

Recent fund-raising events have enhanced the project's profile and generated a great deal of awareness and support within the private and business community, both in Ibiza and abroad.

A donated performance of the hit West End musical, *Five Guys Named Moe* celebrated the launch of Ibiza Se Preocupa on the island last September. This was followed in Easter 1994 by two nights' donated performances at the Casino de Ibiza by the Ballet de Zaragoza, which included the world preview of *French Dinner* by the Belgian choreographer Kirsten Debrock. The ballet has since pledged continued financial support by donating the proceeds from an annual performance in Zaragoza and to return to Ibiza each year. The Nat King Cole Tribute with Clarke Peters, produced by Ulla Allen, was performed in 1994 on World AIDS Day at the Casino in Ibiza.

The Denholm Elliott Project is based at:

Southbank House
Black Prince Road
London SE1 7SJ

Telephone: 0171 582 2425
Fax: 0171 587 5127

Index